Classes in Classical Ballet

ASAF MESSERER

Classes in Classical Ballet

TRANSLATED BY OLEG BRIANSKY

1975
DOUBLEDAY & COMPANY, INC.
GARDEN CITY, NEW YORK
PREPARED BY THE NOVOSTI PRESS AGENCY,
MOSCOW

Library of Congress Cataloging in Publication Data
Messerer, Asaf Mikhaĭlovich, 1903–
Classes in classical ballet
Translation of Uroki klassicheskogo tantsa.
Includes bibliographical references.
Contents: Messerer, A. Reflections on a teaching method.
—Golubkova, YE. A system of notating the Bolshoi ballet classes.
—Golubkova, YE. Ballet classes. [etc.]
1. Ballet. I. Golubkova, E. M., joint author.
II. Bocharnikova, E., joint author. III. Title.
GV1788.M413   792.8'2
ISBN 0-385-04599-9
Library of Congress Catalog Card Number 74–33632

BOOK DESIGN BY BEVERLEY GALLEGOS

Contents

Reflections on a Teaching Method
by Asaf Messerer
13

A System of Notating the Bolshoi Ballet Classes
Elena Golubkova
29

Ballet Classes
Notation Devised by Elena Golubkova
53

CONTENTS

SIXTH CLASS

Exercises at the barre

Exercises in the center

Bolshoi Theatre Artists in Performance
411

Asaf Messerer
by Ella Bocharnikova
439

Roles and Concert Pieces Danced by Asaf Messerer
489

Ballets Choreographed by Asaf Messerer
493

Classes in Classical Ballet

Reflections on a Teaching Method

ASAF MESSERER

THE RULES of the art of ballet, the harmony of a plastic form and its beauty, and the picturesque realization of ballet productions become apparent with experience and attain their peak only after a great and systematic output of effort. Such effort chisels an image of the true professional technique of the ballet dancer, and enriches and brings to perfection the dancer's artistic skill.

The ballet artist must train daily. Otherwise, not only will he not develop his innate gifts and professional skills, he will lose inherent qualities. In essence, he will lose the ability to dance, even though he has spent several years of study in a school, learning form, technique, elasticity, and suppleness.

Dance history has preserved the names of many important teachers and famous dancers. We inherit valuable traditions from different schools of classical ballet and retain all the best that was created by our predecessors. But, though we may be able to trace back the continuous links of the classical school, we nevertheless know extremely little of the practical conduct of ballet classes. For instance, it would be marvelous to have a detailed reproduction of actual classes by Didelot, Taglioni, Bournonville, and Blasis. It would be interesting to find out in what way Gaetan Vestris, the "God of the Dance," of the eighteenth century, reached a peak of technical virtuosity and developed his legendary jump, which in turn, when taught, permitted his son Auguste Vestris to outshine his famous contemporary ballerinas. Performing mastery always calls forth admiration and raises the inevitable question: In what ways does one reach such high degrees of professionalism?

Since my earliest years, I have wished to master the "secrets" of dance knowledge. I have always been interested in the general preparatory work, by which the desired results are attained.

I also wanted to discover what it was necessary to discard from the past and what to retain as being of value. I am, in fact, interested in all the various existing concepts, laws, and principles of the classical ballet. I would like to retrace the succession of methods of teaching classical dance and the development of our own native Russian method of training. By means of what characteristics and peculiarities did the Russian method of teaching take shape? How did our remarkable masters Glouschkowsky, Kolossova, Epmonov, Sokolov, Stanislavskaya, Johansson, Gerdt, and many others teach?

Aiming at attaining knowledge in the literature of the dance, I acquainted myself with different source materials, hoping to discover in them the answers to my questions, but found only limited information.

If one wishes to speak of contemporary books in this field, then one first of all must point to such wonderful works as Agrippina Vaganova's *Fundamentals of the Classical Dance* (in the first edition of 1934); the manual of the Cecchetti method by C. Beaumont and S. Idzikowsky, *A Manual of the Theory and Practice of Classical Theatrical Dancing;* a textbook on classical dance by N. Tarassova and Tchekrigin, *Method of Classical Dance Training;* and Joan Lawson's *Classical Ballet: Its Style and Technique.* These books are invaluable textbooks on the classical dance and also take into account modern choreographic practice.

In my present book, I am not tackling the problems of classical dance as a special subject in schools. Instead, I would like to analyze the process by which dancers achieve their highest professional attainments.

The training of dancers and the acquisition of professional qualities may be divided into many different, and difficult, aspects, organically dependent upon each other. To single out any one of them seems well nigh impossible. One of the most important elements in the work of dancers is the daily class, in which one perfects one's technique, works out interpretative problems, and improves one's classical form. For the teacher conducting these classes there are many problems, since these studies ought to provide students with the fundamentals for achieving mastery.

Except for the necessity of adhering to the unity of the fundamental principles of all schools of classical ballet, the teacher is free from limitations. Any dogmatism in this field, in my opinion, narrows the development of teaching.

I have seriously studied the various teaching methods of such remarkable teachers as A. Vaganova, E. Gerdt, M. Romanova, V. Ponomarev, I. Smoltzov, A. Tchekrigin, M. Koshukova, M. Semenova, N. Dudinskaya, N. Tarasov, M. Gabovitch, S. Messerer, A. Rudenko, A. Ermolaiev, G. Petroff, V. Vasiliev, N. Baltasheev, N. Khamkov, A. Puschkin, B. Chavrov, and V. Kostrovitskaya. Despite the fact that, collectively, there is a great variety of teaching approaches, all these important pedagogues share a major trait: they are all true followers of the best tradition of the Russian school of classical ballet. Unfortunately, too little is known about the teachers who have furthered or promoted the fame of the Russian school. Until now their methods have not been explained and the creative process of teaching still remains mysterious.

I would like to urge teachers of the classical dance to establish rapport with each other, to discuss their experiences more often, to exchange opinions, and in so doing promulgate their teaching methods.

Thus, in this book, I wish to share the knowledge I have acquired through my own experience in conducting classes for the professional ballet dancer. The methods that I employ have been shaped through my own teaching and dancing years. Having begun teaching almost at the same time as I entered the Bolshoi Theatre as a dancer in my early twenties, I always and instinctively coordinated my teaching methods with my stage experience. Fulfilling various dancing roles in performances of the Bolshoi Theatre, studying under the guidance of such prominent teachers as Alexander Gorsky, Vasily Tikhomirov, and later Victor Semenov, and having begun personally to teach and stage dances, I accumulated indispensable knowledge. Now I would like to tell you about the sequence in which my professional studies developed.

I started to study classical ballet at the age of sixteen. However, I would not advise anyone to follow such an example. One has to start studying ballet at an early age, otherwise one will not only have to overcome the usual difficulties confronting the future ballet artist, but (as happened to me) to contend with tenfold more obstacles on the way to acquiring ballet technique.

However, I started at the age of sixteen, and by sheer chance. I was fascinated with sports, athletics, gymnastics, football; I knew, of course, of the existence of ballet, but it did not interest me at all. Then, one day, I went to see *Coppélia*. The leading dancers were A. Balachova and L. Joukov. To say that the performance pleased me is an understatement. I was irresistibly drawn to what I saw. It did not occur to me that it was too late to devote myself to ballet. That, however, I was told with a frank and cruel straightforwardness when I went to apply for admission to the choreographic institute of the Bolshoi Theatre, after the revelation of *Coppélia*.

I asked, "How can I start studying at the school?"

"How old are you?"

"Sixteen."

"But at sixteen we do not start, we end our studies."

"What can I do? I have decided to dance, no matter what happens."

"You should try to study in some private ballet studios."

This was the dialogue which caused my first disappointment. It indicated to me that to become a dancer it was not enough to have an all-absorbing desire and unrestrained craving for the magical world of dance.

Nevertheless, I went into ballet. I enrolled first at the studio of A. Shalomitova, whose predecessor was the famous Mikhail Mordkin. I started to study and I somehow felt lost. Not knowing anything at all, not having even an elementary understanding of the classical ballet, I stood and gazed, all eyes, during my first class. I was all wonder. The students, having had from one to seven years of study, presented themselves as a rather variegated lot of professionals and dilettantes. But all worked hard and literally sweated it out. I understood, that first day of study, that I had undertaken an unusually hard task.

The second day I was introduced to barre work. My colleagues in the studio showed me positions of the feet and the arms. Unfamiliar with ballet, I needed their help to interpret anything that the teacher instructed us to do. The class was given by Eugenia Ivanovna Pavlova, an artist of the Bolshoi Ballet. She always used to encourage me, repeating, "Try again, try again, don't be bashful." After a few classes, when I was able to grasp some "secrets" of the exercise, she asked me to do *sauts de basque* in a diagonal. I glanced at the other students and did not move. Eugenia Ivanovna merely said again, "And now your turn."

And—a miracle!—I did the *saut de basque*. I succeeded because, as it was discovered, I had a natural jump. However, my movement did not match the musical phrase. The teacher forced me to do the step again and to repeat it until I could make this complicated step fit the music.

I was promoted to a more advanced class in which my classmates, so much technically my superiors, thought very little of my ability, but my teacher, Larissa Sokolskaya, an artist of the Bolshoi Ballet, patiently gave me continuous attention. Once, Gorsky was invited to teach the class. Gorsky himself! The director of the Bolshoi, a famous choreographer and teacher . . . ! I owe him an infinite debt from those few months in the studio when I studied under him. In spite of my insufficient preparation, Gorsky gave me special attention and forced me to do the exercises.

This double burden did not seem excessive to me: youth, physical strength, and above all the desire to master the most difficult aspects of dance (which I now understood intellectually) inspired and helped me in that dreary, early period of my training while I struggled to overcome the difficulties of the classical dance technique.

My first year of study ended, the second half of which was under the tutelage of Gorsky. In particular, the classes prepared me for auditions at the choreographic institute of the Bolshoi Theatre. During some of the pre-revolutionary years, its ballet school could not supply the Bolshoi with enough dancers. There was now an acute shortage. It had become necessary to hold auditions for new students at the school, and to take new dancers into the company. That year, there was an audition for older students, the first time in the history of this venerable educational institution. Although the majority approved of the audition, some others objected to it—those who were alarmed by what they believed to be a reform in the system of ballet education.

Two students were taken into the advanced male class: F. Denisov and myself; Igor Moiseyev was taken into one of the lower grades. And so, out of about thirty or forty applicants, three happy boys were selected from the audition. The examinations were very complicated, though outwardly they looked like a normal ballet class. The exercises at the barre were taught by L. Joukov, stressing meticulously correct execution. The exercises at the center were given by I. Smoltzov, and his intricate combinations were not followed by all, but only by a few. Finally, the jumping movement were given by Vasily.Tikhomirov. He demanded precision and correctness of interpretation.

The exercises were combined in such a way that the jury, composed of the thirty best teachers of the school and the director of the theatre, E. K. Malinovsky, would not only see the natural gifts, but the degree of each student's technical training, and their preparation as dancers. In sum, those who passed the classical examination and, later, the folk dance and character dance exams could genuinely consider themselves privileged fellows.

We were deliriously happy, but our difficulties had just begun.

The topmost class of the school was given by Gorsky. I had come to understand that the ballet artist had to perceive and make fullest use of all the knowledge of his many years of preparation as the student. Therefore daily, besides attending Gorsky's class, I watched how dancers worked in other classes of my school. This way, I became acquainted with the teaching of V. Smoltzov, E. Adamovitch, G. Polivanov, L. Joukov, O. Nekrassova, and A. Djouri. In addition, during the evening hours I came to the school, found an empty studio, and, alone, standing at the barre and in the middle of the room, watching myself in the mirror, tried various movements and learned to control myself through the reflection, remembering in what ways it was easier for me to execute them in the most correct manner.

I never missed a class or a rehearsal of the company dancers. In those days, they practiced and rehearsed not in the theatre, but in two large studios of the school. This allowed the older pupils to observe the mastery of the mature danseurs and ballerinas—a great benefit for the younger generation.

In 1921 I graduated from the school and became a member of the Bolshoi Ballet. Now I was together with the other artists taking classes with Gorsky. I was in the professional class!

Here I found out how rich an imagination Gorsky possessed. He conducted the class not only as a teacher but as a gifted choreographer. He always created interesting combinations in classes, short variations which were perfect enough to have been inserted into ballets. It seemed that his choreographic imagination knew no bounds, and there was abundant proof of that even in ordinary classes. Thus, Gorsky's class was especially valuable to his pupils because of the creative way he conducted it. While Alexander Alexeevitch did not always explain the way to execute movements, he strove above all to develop artistry and artistic taste in his students. Gorsky placed great importance upon the musical accompaniment to a class and was very demanding of the pianist.

The exercises at the barre, in Gorsky's class, were simple. Barre was executed only to warm up the muscles. In the center, one immediately started the adagio: not an easy one, yet always interestingly composed and requiring the student to put to use his complete knowledge of the ballet technique.

Here are examples of some beginning enchainments in Gorsky's center work. The dancer executed a flowing *pas de bourrée suivi* to the front, which was followed by striking for a split second a position in first position, arabesque in effacé on the right foot, bringing the left leg in front, then coming down on the knee, rising in attitude croisé, tilting the head slightly downward, slowly turning in on an axis (*tour lent en attitude*), then executing a *renversé pas de bourrée en tournant en dehors,* stopping in arabesque, and stretching both arms to the front. Next, after a demi-plié in fifth position, we were made to bend the upper part of the body and, hands downward, to suddenly change to a straight forward run in a circle with raised hands to the side, a run which suggested the flight of birds. Completing the round, the students stopped in a sylphide pose, with crossed hands over the chest in fourth position croisé in demi-plié, with the back leg pointing into the floor.

Such a combination could in itself have been a fragment of a dance. In allegro, Gorsky might ask the student to execute thirty-two entrechats-six and after a short pause repeat them again. The execution of such a quantity of beats is highly demanding, even for the dancer of great endurance. But Gorsky always maintained that a ballet dancer must at any moment be in the best possible technical condition. Each movement, no matter in what combination, had to be executed with professional perfection.

Such exercises, moreover, were of enormous importance for the development of breathing. Gorsky placed great stress upon breathing, for very often on stage (as I found out on occasion for myself) a dancer will find himself in grave difficulties in the middle of a variation because he has not utilized proper breathing and has dissipated his strength in the first part of the dance. Thus, when Gorsky gave combinations, a whole variation, or a short variation, they not only exemplified his enormous choreographic creativity but were practical exercises as well, in proper breathing. They developed the dancer's knowledge and physically strengthened him. A pupil in Gorsky's class learned to conserve his strength so that it would suffice for the whole dance and not only for the beginning.

Sometimes Gorsky helped students achieve expressive execution and emotional coloration by using national folk dance themes, developing the whole class in a definite style: Russian, for instance, or Hungarian or Spanish. He often told us, "If the dancer is negligent about the artistic side of his work during class, it will be difficult for him to show artistry when he later dances."

Gorsky regularly stimulated the creative imagination and imbued me with a warm desire to become a ballet master and choreographer. After his death in 1924, I was transferred to a class taught by Vasily Tikhomirov. He directed his class in another way, which also interested me very much. It fascinated me because, when one is young, anything that is "different" has an attraction, and also because I felt that this important artist would open for me new ways in the art of dance.

The movements that Tikhomirov taught were never given at random. Logic and great harmony distinguished all his combinations. Moreover, he explained ways of executing the movements. For example, working on a jeté, he stressed an even and fixed attention on the moment of takeoff from the floor, and then the flight, the landing, and the proper completion of the pose. Often, it would turn out that a dancer who took off well and flew beautifully would not come down elastically enough, but with a thud. Tikhomirov explained that, if one linked the movement during the flight with the softness of the landing, one would get the desired results. I often asked him in what ways does one achieve plasticity in dance. He always emphasized *flowing from one movement to the next*. Tikhomirov taught me to analyze the rules and ways of execution for the classical dance. He suggested to me the idea that each class has to have its own theme.

The exercises at the barre in Tikhomirov's class, as in Gorsky's class, were not difficult. The class was quite short, usually forty-five minutes, but with almost no interruption. One movement quickly blended with another. Undoubtedly, with this method, one benefited greatly from one's compulsory daily class. But what astounded me was that not all the dancers took classes regularly. Attendance depended upon the subjective feeling of the dancer, and if he felt that he needed to work, he came to do a barre; if not, he did not appear. Tikhomirov conducted the class with the soloists, dancing himself while teaching them; furthermore, male and female dancers worked together.

In the classes of Gorsky and Tikhomirov, I mastered various "secrets" of the craft. Naturally, I was far from mastering them all, but each day brought something new. All that I learned in the morning I repeated many times in the evening, alone in the empty classroom.

What I had learned, thought over, and realized, I now wanted to discuss with others. I was lucky: in 1921 I was asked to teach in the evening choreographic classes which had been held for the past two summers at the Bolshoi Theatre. Many young students came to us from private schools; apart from the adult group, there was also a children's group. The most talented students, after terminating their evening course, were later taken into the ballet school of the Bolshoi Theatre. Everyone hoped to be accepted there, but not everyone succeeded.

To learn to teach was even more difficult than to learn to dance. In any case, although I had the experience of stage appearances (having danced a number of important parts in ballets of the current repertoire), I was only starting in the pedagogical field and was convinced that I had chosen a far from easy path.

The most difficult task was to explain movements, to analyze their execution. To be sure, I could show students steps, but to explain the reason why one has to do *this* and not *that* was quite complicated. I discussed the problem with many dancers and received contradictory responses. This piqued my interest. I asked myself why does each one explain the same thing in a different way and sometimes contradicting ideas led me to try to summarize teaching methods for my students.

After two years of working at evening courses at the Choreographic Academy of the Bolshoi Theatre, I was invited to the choreographic institute, where I started to teach the fifth class of girls. The following year, I was assigned the boys' intermediate and advanced class, which included pupils endowed with great ability, such as Alexander Rudenko, A. Sharman, A. Joukov, Alexander Rodunski, Nicolai Popko, Lev Pospekhin, and others. Some of them became first-rate dance artists; others, good ballet masters and choreographers. Taking what was best and most useful from the classes of Tikhomirov and Gorsky, watching the work of other teachers, studying myself, checking my hunches and observations on myself and on my students, I gathered, grain by grain, all that would help me in the long run to determine the best methods of teaching a class of professionals. So, in my mid-twenties, I took my first steps toward becoming a teacher.

My work as a choreographer helped that as a teacher. In 1923 I staged several concert performances, in which many of the artists of the Bolshoi Theatre danced—among them the *Czardas* by Monti. I was proud and happy, and eagerly devised new choreography; first, because I had been drawn to it since my studies with Gorsky; secondly, because I understood that the composition of dances is a splendid foundation for the development of the imagination of choreographer and teacher alike. In lively creative work, one analyzes all the better the uses of this, that, or the other movement, the possibilities of linking them, and the rationality and beauty of their combinations; and one is always searching for new combinations.

Having started to teach in the technical school of the distinguished Anatoly V. Lunacharsky, I not only perfected the classical dance, but conducted choreographic work as well. At the technical school in those days were such gifted youngsters as Vladimir Bourmeister, Nicolai Kholfin, A. Redell, M. Kroustalev, Maria Sorokina, E. May, and others. Their creative accomplishments have contributed many interesting pages to the history of Soviet choreography.

I created my first ballet, *The War of Toys,* to the music of Chopin. By opposing old and new toys, I aimed to contrast pre-revolutionary people with the present. More and more, I endeavored to find a way to reflect modern life though dance. My ballet, *The Sports Suite,* ensued: children's games, horse races, football, boxing. I was searching, not always successfully, for a way to use the classical form to express a new rhythm of life, new feelings, new aspects of contemporary heroes. I was trying to create various combinations of movements in class which would be useful in new ballets. In new ballets I verified the suitability of what I had composed in class.

I went to observe the ballet school of the Kirov. I had wanted very much to become acquainted with the classes of the famous teachers in Leningrad. My trip to the city on the banks of the Neva was very fruitful. I never tired of observing how Agrippina Vaganova conducted a class. Her eloquence in explaining movements, in telling how and why they have to be done, never ceased to delight me. She gave great significance to turning movements. She demanded that the student first of all "place the axis of the turn." It seemed like a very easy requirement. But how difficult this is, and how rarely it is accomplished! Another "easy" assignment was to keep the shoulders down when raising the hands. Yet how often—almost in every class!—did she have to remind someone about this! A remarkable interpreter of difficult classical roles, Vaganova, when she became a teacher, was able to pass on her craft to her students. Attendance at her classes provided me, a teacher in the making, with a great deal of creative enrichment.

It was also interesting to study the methods of the teacher Vladimir Ponomarev. He had a marvelous system of directing the male class, a logical and efficient development of exercises with varied jumping combinations.

Later, in Moscow, I happened to study with Victor Semenov. His classes were, for us, unusual: very difficult technically, the classes developed great endurance and strength. The exercises at the barre and in the center were built on difficult steps. The adagio in the center was always long and hard, and was always repeated twice. Semenov placed great importance upon big jumps. He created ingenious jumping combinations and always demanded a repetition of them, usually two or three times consecutively.

My teaching experience gradually enriched itself not only by observation of classes in Moscow and Leningrad, but by questioning all who knew and remembered the classes of Maria Gorschenkova, Nicolai Legat, and other famous teachers. I tried to find people who had writings or notes on the classes taught by these great teachers of the past. Tikhomirov told me how Christian Johansson and Pavel Gerdt taught. I learned that Johansson was the guardian of old academic traditions, that he held firmly to the legitimate principles and rules, and worked in great detail with complicated technical steps. Gerdt, in developing ballet technique, aimed for gracefulness, lightness, and ease of execution. His class was expressive and very "dancey." I wanted to master and select for myself and my students all the best methods that had been developed by our predecessors. I wanted to combine the dancing quality, which I got from Gorsky's classes, with the academic strictness of movements mastered under the guidance of Tikhomirov, along with the development of strength, endurance, and breadth of technique which I learned from Semenov.

Like any artist, I naturally wanted to become a good dancer. Dancing the pas de trois or the role of Siegfried in *Swan Lake,* Ocean in *The Little Humpbacked Horse,* Colas in *La Fille Mal Gardée,* the Prince in *Nutcracker,* Franz in *Coppélia,* and the title role in Stravinsky's *Petrouchka,* I was constantly searching for the best way to portray each of the parts, taking into account their special features and coloring. One had to work hard, not only in rehearsals where every detail of the dance was polished, but also in class, going over the regular technical steps to find new qualities in them, to employ them in the best taste for each choreographic composition, to find the emotional quality of a gesture which contributes to the expression of the dance, and always to make the steps light and clear.

While all that I did was not successful, I learned a great deal from experimenting. For example, in one variation I wanted to create the dynamics of flight by means of big jumps. Beforehand, I tried in class to force my strength in jumps, even reaching new heights and extension. When I brought this achievement to the stage I discovered that the big jumps adversely affected the intensity of the execution of the whole number: the quality of the dance thereby suffered rather than profited by my technical feat. I came to the conclusion that the correct execution of a dance requires economy and a proper distribution of strength.

This I started to teach to my students, for I noticed that the young artists have a peculiar desire to impress the public (and their colleagues in class) at the beginning of a dance, never giving thought to what reserves they possess, on which they can draw strength—let us say, for the final pirouette. When the dance is perfectly executed, up to a point, and the final steps deteriorate in quality of dancing, then one spoils the dance. Rightly, the audience expects the dancer to perform his dance well from start to finish.

To produce a dancing crescendo, it is necessary to learn to properly use the linking movements for repose, for recovering the breath, and then to approach the next difficult, complex, or most effective step. However, when this is done, one should by no means allow concentration, and dance intensity, to falter. The audience must observe a flawless dancing cantilena throughout all the choreographic patterns. *The dance in all its parts must seem an undivided unit.*

For the development of greater freedom and harmony in dance, I found it indispensable to learn and then to teach my students to execute all steps equally well to the right and to the left side. Another conclusion I reached during my stage career was that one must never try to put easily mastered steps in all one's variations. This is a great temptation, especially for young dancers, but such a practice impoverishes the interpretative craft and the variety of the dance. What is good for the role of Colas in *La Fille Mal Gardée* is not necessarily right for Siegfried in *Swan Lake,* and what is good for Basil in *Don Quixote* is bad for the Prince in *The Sleeping Beauty,* even though they are all related within the classical dance tradition. The classical dance is fantastically rich. Roles in ballet must always look different, so the heroes of each ballet can distinguish themselves not by their costumes, but through dance as a precise form of expression in clear, choreographic form.

Step by step, I learned the complex rules of the art of ballet. If, in the beginning of my teaching, all my attention was drawn to the clarification of methods of movement, later I started to pose much more difficult problems to myself. I tried in my classes to attain not only absolute mastery of technique, but the faultless development of expression and artistry in the execution of ballet steps. I understood that, in conducting professional ballet classes, one must have a definite system, that each class must have its special purpose, theme, problem, or leitmotif. Following the pedagogical principles of Vasily Tikhomirov, I developed individual choreographic themes during each weekly course of lessons.

This method, which I have used for many years, naturally should not be regarded as universally applicable. The variety of individual approaches to teaching produces a variety of methods of teaching. What I am absolutely sure of is the necessity of thorough preparation on the part of the teacher before each class. The teacher is obliged to come to class with a distinct knowledge of his problem for the day; he must know what he wants to achieve through the study of certain ballet exercises. The teacher of professional dancers must be equipped with special knowledge and must prepare a coherent plan for every class. Of course, one can always give a class in which there is a bit of everything, but such a class is like a lecture where one talks of "everything and nothing." In a ballet class, logic must prevail as it does in the lectures of university professors, so that the ballet student will acquire the finest dance education and the highest professional qualifications. From beginning to end, a ballet class must be conducted in correct proportions, succession, and progression of the selected exercise. Later, I shall cite concrete examples of a planned class. This discussion, by necessity, will be primarily for professionals.

A MESSERER CLASS:

During the preliminary process of working on a choreographic theme for class, I determine the construction of each combination and work out the leitmotif. I begin with exercises at the barre, to prepare the dancer's muscles to cope with any given form of the ballet exercises in their separate parts. When the muscles are sufficiently prepared, I include a whole range of leitmotifs in jumping combinations, working first with an easy form of small and average size jumps, varying them with beats, and moving on to high jumps combined with more or less complicated pirouettes.

The principle of the gradual assimilation of any ballet movement certainly does not involve placing all the strain upon a specific step for the duration of the class. Each exercise has its own value, involves one or another group of muscles, and builds upon organic combinations of different movements. But in the course of the development of some dance combinations there can be included elements of that class leitmotif.

I want again to emphasize that the choreographic theme of each class is very strictly thought out and planned by me beforehand, with due regard for all the orderly components. Using the full complexity of ballet movements, a teacher can easily vary classes by creating a wide range of combinations. In my opinion, one should take into account how busy the dancers are in rehearsals and performances when planning a class. Therefore, when I am teaching a class of dancers who are performing, I am generally inclined to ease the muscular burden and not overdo matters in class, to avoid unnecessarily tiring the dancers, thereby diminishing the value of the study period. Professional dancers know how important it is to have, at all times, an inexhaustible reserve of strength in order to keep the legs light. It is unwise for a teacher of performing dancers to build a class—especially, the exercises at the barre—solely on difficult, complicated steps. It is therefore very important for the teacher to maintain a sense of proportion. Sometimes even an easy movement may be detrimental to the dancer's legs. I am against illogical combinations of movements; that is, movements deliberately invented to make the dancer feel uncomfortable in their execution. Those who favor them probably argue that in such a manner one can develop one's knowledge and execution of complicated technical combinations. In my opinion, such a practice is unfruitful. Moreover, such a method contradicts, at the very root, the fundamental principle upon which classical ballet training is based: the natural progression in the development of muscular power and control, that prepares dancers to execute the most complicated form of movement in dance, and to interpret choreographic ideas.

I consider the musical accompaniment for a class as a most serious and important aspect of my teaching. The musical material should always assist in the education of the artist, and the development of good taste for the dancer. Music in class should be varied. It should be appropriate, clear in form, and rhythmically strict. It is advisable that the class accompanist utilize both classical music and the latest pieces of contemporary literature for the piano.

The structural basis of a ballet class is a scheme of exercises, first at the barre, then in the center of the studio. Some teachers may choose to alter the order of the exercises, at their own direction. But I hold to the following plan: first, exercise at the barre starts with deep grands pliés, grands pliés in first, second, and fifth positions, followed by battements tendus, battements tendus demi-pliés, battements tendus jetés, ronds de jambe à terre in combination with port de bras and battements relevés lents, battements fondus, battements frappés, ronds de jambe en l'air (sometimes this exercise is done in combination with the previous movement), adagio with different développés, battements doubles frappés, petits battements sur le cou-de-pied, and grands battements jetés.

Afterward I give bendings of the body (the dancer facing the barre) in combination with port de bras, then relevés on both legs in all positions or else on one leg. I finish the exercises at the barre with special movements for stretching the muscles of the legs. Such stretchings promote the development of the dancing stride. I recommend executing them in the concluding part of the exercises at the barre when the ligaments and muscles are sufficiently prepared and warmed up. The execution of stretching at the beginning of a class or at the very end, in my opinion, is inadvisable.

Following come exercises in the center of the studio. They start with a small adagio, and move into different combinations, battements tendus, battements fondus, battements frappés, ronds de jambe en l'air, grand adagio, and grands battements jetés. All these exercises can be developed in different combinations interlaced with pirouettes, finished in small and grand poses. Later there are the jumping combinations, small jumps, small jumps with beats (battus), medium jumps, big jumps, small jumps with beats in a fast tempo, complicated jumping combinations, and then, for the female dancers, exercises on pointes. The class usually ends with petits changements de pied, following port de bras with bends of the body.

Naturally, this plan can be modified in some details. For example, there is another approach to the development of movements in the grand adagio (in the center). Some teachers here include jumps. But I think at this stage of the exercises the muscles are not yet prepared for jumps. In the grand adagio I allow some forms of linking movements, such as chassé, or failli. In the combination of grands battements jetés which follows, I sometimes give a small jump, petit changement de pied, or jeté assemblé.

The proper methods of preparing and conducting male and female classes differ somewhat, but very often, in the conditions which exist in a theatre, it is necessary to teach the male and female dancers in the same class. In my teaching experience I have had to work with "classes of perfection" where both men and women customarily study together.

When one teaches mixed classes, one has to build special combinations of movements so that men and women can execute them equally well. The exercises at the barre and in the center, until the jumps, differ little in their male and female form. Therefore, they are executed simultaneously by both. Starting with the allegro, the character of the movements change. Some aspects of jumps and turns requiring great physical strength are executed only by men: for example, double sauts de basque, tours en l'air, various forms of turns such as grandes pirouettes à la seconde, complicated beats, et cetera. The combinations of allegro are usually meant for both sexes in my classes, but I change their final sections slightly. For example, if the men execute tours en l'air, then the women will do pirouettes instead. In another case, if the women execute chaînés déboulés, the men do pirouettes. It is not possible to define exactly what types of movements are suitable for each sex because everything depends upon the overall character of the combination.

When I organize my classes for the entire week, I always include a free day for the dancers, to give their muscles a rest. While one day of interruption does not seem long, nevertheless the muscles do go out of condition and one has to bring them back gradually into work. For this reason, I deliberately ease the technical difficulties in the first class of the week.

The tempo and character of movement during the whole class is quiet and moderate. This permits the teacher to check and affirm stability and balance, the exactness of the positions, and the proper placement of the body, and it also helps one to adjust all the preparatory steps. Such a thorough examination of fundamentals of a class promotes exactitude in the execution of movement and brings the dancer's muscles to a state of professional preparedness.

The combinations in my first class of the week are given in a more simple form than on other days. In the following classes that week, the combinations become more complicated, as does the character of the execution of the movements. Tempi are varied, new technical details are included, separate movements are given in different rhythms. It is extremely important to consider during each class the precise development of coordination in the dancers. Therefore I regard it as compulsory to execute the majority of combinations on the reverse side. This helps the dancer to achieve a comprehensive mastery of dance technique. Some turns—for example, pirouettes en dehors—I deliberately request on the reverse side, so that this difficult form of turns can be continually checked and strengthened. Pirouettes en dedans are given in many combinations.

In the first class of the week, the choreographic theme develops the pas assemblés; the second class is built upon sissonnes; the third class on cabrioles; the fourth on pas jetés; the fifth on pas de basques, saut de basque, and pas ciseaux, and the sixth on combinations of all the different movements stressed during the week.

In constructing such a weekly program of classes, one regulates the degree of the technical load imposed upon the dancers; of special significance, as I have remarked, in a class of performing artists. Other choreographic themes are built on combinations of movements such as pas ballotté, pas ballonné, ronds de jambe en l'air sauté, or such as pas de chat, jeté pas de chat, and gargouillade. Or one can develop the choreographic theme on jeté entrelancé, grand fouetté en tournant, sissone à la seconde en tournant, revoltades, and others.

I want to emphasize that I consider the endless repetition of exercises to be a wrong method of learning any difficult movements. This primitive method is extremely dangerous, as it may overstrain muscles and cause serious injuries in the dancer. I refer particularly to jumping movements. There are, naturally, such movements as fouetté en tournant, grande pirouette, and some others often found in variations and codas which are executed sixteen or thirty-two times. In such cases, in order to master complicated turns, it is necessary to practice them repeatedly, though here too it is important to keep a sense of proper proportion.

To achieve a high standard in dance, one must develop in harmony all the muscles of the body. Interpretative mastery involves not only brilliant execution of one or another separate virtuoso steps, but the perfection of the dance as a whole, the beauty of line, the plastic design of arms and body, the lightness of jump and flight, and the expressiveness and musicality of execution. The technique of classical ballet is varied. It consists of complicated big jumps and small quick movements, beats, turns, adagio, movements on pointes, and stability and balance. Genuinely artistic execution of the classical dance consists of the harmonious blending of technique with emotional expression, and with the uniqueness of the individual dancer's style.

In my long years of work with the Bolshoi Theatre, I have witnessed a galaxy of highly talented artists who differed in their style and in the characteristic ways they fulfilled their art. Yet all were entirely dedicated to their art. Many of them studied in my classes, and I observed with satisfaction that they unstintingly gave their total strength and concentration to their complicated and burdensome work. This passion in work was always rewarded, for it hastened the flowering of their talents. More than one generation of artists has now studied under my direction. Among them were mature masters and youngsters just graduated from the school. One generation followed another. Among the many names I can mention are Galina Ulanova, Maya Plisetskaya, Olga Lepeshinskaya, Elena Tschikvadze, Irina Tikhomirnova, Nadezhda Kapustina, V. Galenskaya, Liudmilla Bogomolova, Maya Samokhvalova, Mikhail Gabovitch, Vladimir Preobrajenski, Alexander Rudenko, Sergei Koren, A. Schoukov, Georgi Farmaniantz, Nicolai Fadeyechev, Boris Khokhlov, Yuri Zhdanov, L. Zhdanov, V. Khomiakov, Gennadi Yagudin, Vladimir Nikonov, Maris Liepa, Vladimir Vasiliev, Vladimir Tikhonov, Mikhail Lavrovsky, and others.

In 1944 Galina Ulanova came to study with me. Her astonishing ability to combine the process of study with a creative sense, her extraordinary discipline and power of concentration, can be taken as the highest standard to emulate. Ulanova knew how to take a strict combination and dance it in a ravishing form, in which the movements were graced with the purity and beauty of the classical dance.

Maya Plisetskaya studied many years with me. Her artistic nature always reveals itself in her ability to reach the peak in performing combinations in class. She tirelessly masters all problems, perfecting their minutest details. Inherent in her is a remarkable feeling for dance, a poetical, musical spirit which turns her daily hard labor in the classroom into authentic art.

A peculiarity of the interpretative art is that it can take different creative directions. Therefore it is very important for the artist to determine the best and truest path of the development of his talent, and of his artistic individuality. Here the guidance of the teacher can play a great role. I wish to urge the younger generation of ballet teachers to keep in creative contact with their older artistic colleagues, who are always ready to pass on to the young the wealth of knowledge acquired through our own teachers and of our own experiences as teachers.

Exercises at the barre

Natalia Bessmertnova, Nina Sorokina

A System of Notating the Bolshoi Ballet Classes

ELENA GOLUBKOVA

THESE NOTES of the Bolshoi Theatre ballet classes set forth the weekly cycle of instructions given by Asaf Messerer, People's Artist of the Russian Soviet Federation of the Socialist Republic and State Prize Laureate. This material makes it possible to understand the structure of classical ballet lessons.

Messerer presents the classical dance steps in a variety of simple and complicated combinations and includes in each class one or more thematic movements. This method helps to perfect all the elements in a changing pattern of steps. In a given series of lessons these themes are the pas assemblé, sissonne, cabriole, and pas jeté; then, pas de basque, saut de basque, and pas ciseaux combined in one lesson. The concluding lesson of the week varies all these steps in an intricate pattern of jump combinations.

A clear plan for each lesson, an imaginative development of choreographic themes, and an artistic direction to the lessons are all indicative of the creative methods of Asaf Messerer, one of the great choreographer-teachers of our time.

Notating the ballet classes made it necessary to define concretely certain rules established in teaching practice and to examine a number of concepts used in this system of notation.

The daily training classes of ballet dancers last one hour or somewhat longer. The first part of the lesson consists of exercises at the barre and takes approximately fifteen to twenty minutes. The remaining time is given to exercises in the middle of the classroom. In almost every instance, each combination of movements is repeated in the reverse or opposite direction, and this is always indicated. In the execution of the exercises it is necessary to take into account not only the specific particulars inherent in each movement, but also the flowing development of the whole dancing pattern. For instance, there are exercises in which the working leg (in motion) placed in front in the 5th position is moved first to the side in the 2nd position. In repeating the step in reverse with the same leg, the first movement is also made in the same direction but this time from another starting position, that is from 5th position with the leg

Exercises in the middle of the room
Class taught by Asaf Messerer

in back. In this case the concept of "in reverse" applies to a change of the starting positions in the front and back. Sometimes the execution of some combinations in the reverse direction requires a turn for certain individual movements. For instance, such an involved form as the pas de bourrée, when repeated in reverse, can be executed as pas de bourrée en tournant, etc.

The exercises in the middle of the classroom are carried out according to the teacher's instructions either by the entire class or in separate groups. Taking turns in small groups makes it possible for students to use the entire floor space more fully, which is particularly necessary in dance combinations with large movements. Also this arrangement helps to some degree to offer a rest or a short pause. An explanation is given each time as to whether there should be a rest period after a certain exercise or whether it can be repeated without one.

In the classical dance there are five leg positions. The arm positions are determined in different ways; some ballet schools accept three arm positions, others five or seven. These notations include three positions. In each of these positions the arms take a symmetrical position. At the same time, within the range of the same "sketched surface" where the arm movements occur in the positions,

POSITIONS OF THE FEET

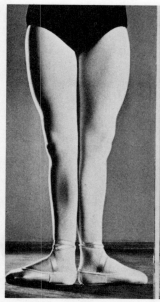 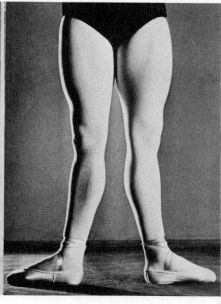 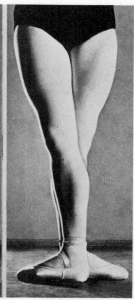

1st position   2nd position   3rd position

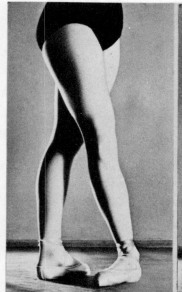 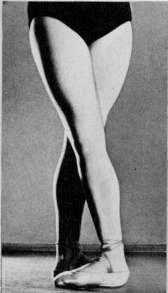 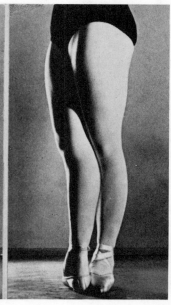

4th position   5th position   5th position

POSITIONS OF THE ARMS

Preparatory arm position A

1st position

2nd position

Tatiana Arkhangelskaya

3rd position

4th position

5th position

6th position

it is possible to fix nonsymmetrical positions of the arms. These positions derive from the 1st, 2nd, and 3rd positions and in this system of notation are designated as the arm positions, in the order of 4, 5, and 6. The preparatory position of the arms is marked as letter A. In addition to the indicated and derived positions there are other variations of the arm positions in the ballet poses and movements. These include those of the arabesque poses—1st, 2nd, 3rd, and 4th.

Sometimes the arm pattern of a certain arabesque is similar to that of a number of other poses. Thus, for instance, the arm position in preparation for pirouettes en dehors from the 4th position in croisé is similar to the 3rd in arabesque. Or in some poses of effacé back one can encounter the arm position of the 1st and 2nd arabesque. In such cases the arm positions adopted for these arabesques are conditionally indicated in the notations. It is necessary to have in mind the fact that according to the development of certain combinations, the notes for the poses of the 1st and 2nd arabesque in épaulement effacé are also conditional.

To be able to determine the direction for each movement and pose, that is to set the pattern for dance combinations, an orientation is given in the notes indicating the fixed points of the room surface (the sides and corners). The sides and corners of a square room are taken as the basis for the plan of the classroom as suggested by Professor Agrippina Vaganova in the book *The Basic Principles of the Classical Ballet*. One should add that if this plan also indicates a central point in the square of the room—"point occupied by the student in all the examples discussed in the book"—then no such indication is given in these notes since in practice the exercises are performed from various points of the room's surface. For instance, if a combination of steps does not require moving forward then it is usually performed in the center of the room. When the exercise is based on moving forward then the instructor determines the area where the student should start. A subtitle is then included in the notes, for instance: "Start from the side No. 5, or from the corner No. 6, etc." In this plan the sides of the room are indicated by the numbers 1, 3, 5, 7; and the corners 2, 4, 6, 8. To determine the direction of steps there are also indications "forward," "backward," "to the side (right and left)," "straight," "on the diagonal," "on the circle," etc.

The notations use the generally accepted French terminology. In individual cases the designation of certain elements of movement is given in Russian.

The notations of classes include exercises for the male and female dancers studying together. The exercises at the barre and in the center of the room (until the jump combinations) are usually similar for men and women. Starting from the jumps the exercises are given in separate variations, which is especially indicated in the notations: "performed by the men's class" or "performed by the women's class." Sometimes, depending on how a combination of steps is developed, the teacher gives a general assignment changing only its concluding part. Then he also gives a special explanation: "Concluding

POSITION FOR ONE ARM
(Exercises at the barre)

Preparatory arm position A

1st position

2nd position

3rd position

Ekaterina Maximova

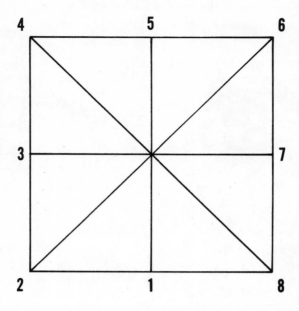

steps for the men's class," or "concluding steps for the women's class." At the conclusion of the lesson the female dancers carry out exercises on pointes.

The notation of exercises is in the form of a table divided into three parts. The left side of the table includes material related to the musical-rhythmical measure of steps. This parts determines beforehand the musical measure, the tempo, and the number of musical bars in the introduction. Further breakdown indicates the bars or the portions of the bars related on the placed line (on the central and right part of the table) to the notation of the movements. This part concludes with the total number of bars for the entire exercise.

In the table of notation each exercise is marked under a special heading indicating the basic form of steps, for example: grands pliés, battements tendus, battements tendus jetés, ronds de jambe à terre, battements fondus, etc. For the jump combination in the center, the height of the jumps is indicated for orientation—small jumps, medium jumps, and big jumps.

Next in the notation of each table follows the preparation or preparatory positions, executed before each exercise (no special explanations are given for them). Then the starting position directly preceding the exercise is indicated. The starting position is given in a separate notation, for the legs (in the middle of the table), and for the arms (at the right of the table), or for one arm when the exercise is executed at the barre. The position of the body in épaulement croisé or épaulement effacé is also defined when performed in the center of the room.

Then the teacher describes the dance combinations.

The name of each step of the classical dance in the exercise is written down in French terminology, after which explanatory indications follow: they determine either the function of the working leg, that is with which leg one should start a certain movement, in which direction it is working, etc., or the function of the supporting leg, and whether one should rise on the half toe or execute demi-pliés, etc.

It is only necessary to point out that the notation, as a rule, does not indicate demi-plié if it is an inseparable part of some form of the classical step: this can be illustrated by the jumps, their preparation and conclusion being always in the demi-plié. Only in individual cases, where it is necessary to have a full rhythmic breakdown of the jump, is the demi-plié written down in accordance with the time beat.

The varied development of combinations sometimes requires a more detailed description of their structure. It is given in the notation as the "breakdown of the movements." In the choreographic pattern the interrelation of some dance steps sometimes makes it possible to combine them. Thus, for instance, pas de basque can be concluded not in its usual form but with a petit assemblé.

The development of each dance exercise presupposes not only a flow of steps but also a rest—a pause fixing a certain position or pose. These dance pauses are indicated by the words "stay," "pause," or "balance."

In accordance with the general rule, the angle of the leg in the air is measured in various degrees—$25°$, $45°$, $90°$. In practice some digression from these levels is always possible. In regard to the $90°$ right angle, the working leg, or leg in motion, can be raised considerably higher in a well-developed dance step (such as développés and grands battements jetés), but according to the established rule not lower than $90°$.

The order of the arm movements shown in the table assumes lyric character in their plastic pattern, developing according to the established rules of the classical port de bras. The explanation of this system of notation is given only in a brief statement, defining the basic line for the development of each step form. Selection of the material and wording of the methodological principles were carried out in constant consultation with Asaf Messerer.

The class notation is illustrated with photographs of various movements and poses of the classical dance, and with the help of film sequences, the development of individual movements is shown.

The film sequences are a series of photographs showing the most typical parts of each movement. In the photographs of class exercises and in the section of Bolshoi artists in performance, the following artists of the State Academy of the Bolshoi Theatre of the USSR are included: Boris Akimov, Tatiana Archangelskaya, Natalia Bessmertnova, Tatiana Bessmertnova, Honored Artist RSFSR Liudmilla Bogomolova, People's Artist RSFSR Nicolai Fadeyechev, Nicolai Federov, Tatiana Gavrilova, Alexander Godunov, Tatiana Golikova, People's Artist RSFSR

1st arabesque

2nd arabesque

3rd arabesque

3rd arabesque

Maya Plisetskaya

4th arabesque

4th arabesque

Maya Plisetskaya

Preparatory position for pirouettes en
dehors in 4th position croisé

Position effacé back (right foot pointe
tendue) 1st arabesque arm position

Position effacé back (right foot pointe
tendue) 2nd arabesque arm position

Rimma Karelskaya

DIFFERENT "ÉPAULEMENTS"
FOR INDIVIDUAL MOVEMENTS AND POSES

Croisé front (right foot pointe tendue)
5th position arms (left arm up)

Croisé front (right foot pointe tendue)
5th position arms (right arm up)
position "under the arm"

Effacé front (right foot pointe tendue)
5th position arms (left arm up)

Croisé back (left foot pointe tendue)
5th position arms (left arm up)

Effacé back (right foot pointe tendue)
5th position arms (right arm up)

Right leg croisé front (90°)
5th position arms (left arm up)

Right leg croisé front (90°)
5th position arms (right arm up)
position "under the arm"

Right leg effacé front (90°)
5th position (left arm up)

Ekaterina Maximova

Pose with the right leg à la seconde,
in écarté front
5th position arms (right arm up)

Liudmilla Bogomolova

Pose with the right leg à la seconde,
in écarté front
2nd position arms allongée

Pose with the left leg à la seconde,
in écarté back
5th position arms (left arm up)

INITIAL POSTURES IN 5TH POSITION
(Right foot front)

Anatolai Mousatov

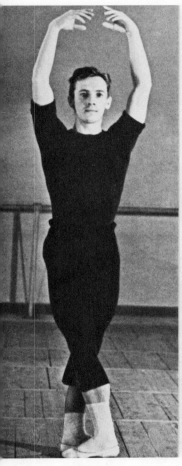  

En face Épaulement croisé Épaulement effacé

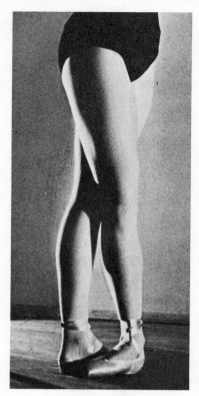

5th position croisé

5th position effacé   5th position en face

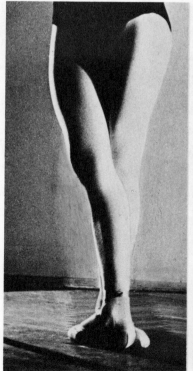 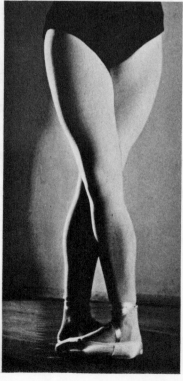

Sauté in 5th position
(left foot front)
preparatory arm
position, épaulement
croisé

Sauté in 5th position
(right foot front)
3rd position arms,
épaulement croisé

Sauté in 5th position
(right foot front)
5th position arms
allongée (left arm up)
épaulement croisé

Vladimir Nikonov

1st arabesque (in demi-plié)

2nd arabesque (in demi-plié)

3rd arabesque (in demi-plié)

4th arabesque (in demi-plié)

Isandr Shmelnitsky and Vladimir Nikonov

Pose à la seconde (45°)

Pose à la seconde (90°)

Rimma Karelskaya, People's Artist RSFSR Marina Kondratieva, Lenin Prize Laureate Mikhail Lavrovsky, Marina Leonova, People's Artist USSR and State Prize Laureate Olga Lepeshinskaya, Honored Artist RSFSR and Lenin Prize Laureate Maris Liepa, Honored Artist RSFSR Ekaterina Maximova, People's Artist RSFSR Sulamif Messerer, Anatolai Mousatov, Vladimir Nikonov, People's Artist USSR and Lenin Prize Laureate Maya Plisetskaya, Sergei Radchenko, Vladimir Romanenko, Honored Artist RSFSR Maya Samokhvalova, Ludmilla Semenyaka, Isandr Shmelnitsky, Nina Sorokina, People's Artist USSR Raissa Struchkova, Elena Tcherkaskaya, Honored Artist RSFSR and State Prize Laureate Irina Tikhomirnova, Honored Artist RSFSR and of the Moldavian Soviet Socialist Republic Vladimir Tikhonov, People's Artist RSFSR Nina Timofeyeva, People's Artist USSR and Lenin and State Prize Laureate Galina Ulanova, Honored Artist RSFSR and Lenin Prize Laureate Vladimir Vasiliev, and Yuri Vladimirov.

For the separate photographs of poses and positions of the feet, S. Adirkhaeva, People's Artist of the North Ossetian Autonomous Soviet Socialist Republic is featured.

Pose à la seconde (higher than 90°)

Ekaterina Maximova

Ballet Classes

NOTATION DEVISED BY
ELENA GOLUBKOVA

PHOTO BY JENNIE WALTON

First Class

EXERCISES AT THE BARRE

Musical-rhythmical accompaniment	DANCING EXERCISES	

Measure 3/4 *Waltz* *Tempo slow* *Introduction* *(2 bars)*	**1. GRANDS PLIÉS**	
	Preparation[1] Starting position[2] of the feet: 1st position.	Starting position of the right arm: 2nd position.
2 bars *2 bars*	GRAND PLIÉ in 1st position (moving downward, moving upward to starting position).	2nd - A A - 1st - 2nd
2 bars *1 bar*	GRAND PLIÉ in 1st position (moving downward, moving upward).	2nd - A A - 1st
1 bar	BATTEMENT TENDU with the right leg to the side (pointing the toe). Place the leg in 2nd position.	1st - 2nd 2nd

[1] Preparation (preparatory position) before the start of the exercise.
[2] Starting position, immediately following preceding exercise.

	GRAND PLIÉ in 2nd position	
2 bars	(moving down,	2nd - A
2 bars	moving up).	A - 1st - 2nd
	GRAND PLIÉ in 2nd position	
2 bars	(moving down,	2nd - A
1 bar	moving up). Then	A - 1st
1 bar	lift the right foot from heel to toe	1st - 2nd
	(position pointe tendue) and bring the foot to 5th position front.	2nd
	GRAND PLIÉ in 5th position	
2 bars	(moving down,	2nd - A
2 bars	moving up).	A - 1st -2nd
	GRAND PLIÉ in 5th position	
2 bars	(moving down,	2nd - A
1 bar	moving up).	A - 1st
1 bar	**BATTEMENT TENDU** to the side (change)[3] right foot.	1st - 2nd
	GRAND PLIÉ in 5th position	
2 bars	(moving down	2nd - A
2 bars	moving up).	A - 1st - 2nd
	GRAND PLIÉ in 5th position	
2 bars	(moving down,	2nd - A
1 bar	moving up).	A - 1st
1 bar	**BATTEMENT TENDU** to the side (change) right foot (end in 5th position front).	1st - 2nd - A

Total accompaniment
32 bars

[3] Battement tendu to the side (from the starting position of the working leg in 5th position front) should move to 5th position back.

Measure 2/4
Tempo
moderate
Introduction
(1 bar)

2. BATTEMENTS TENDUS

Preparation
Starting position of the feet:
5th position, right foot in front.

Starting position
of the right arm:
2nd position.

BATTEMENT TENDU
to the side with a pressure of the right
foot in the 2nd position.[1]
Breakdown of the movement:

Off-beat
(4th eighth)
1st eighth
2nd eighth
3rd eighth

Dégagé right foot to the side, placing
pointe tendue, bring down the foot to
2nd position, raise foot from the heel
to toe (pointe tendue), move
the foot to 5th position back.

2nd position.

4th, 1st,
2nd, 3rd
eighth

BATTEMENT TENDU
to the side, with a pressure of the right
foot in the 2nd position (ending in 5th
position front).

4th, 1st
eighth

BATTEMENT TENDU
to the front with the right foot.

2nd position.

2nd, 3rd
eighth

BATTEMENT TENDU
to the side (change) right foot.

4th, 1st
eighth
2nd, 3rd
eighth

BATTEMENT TENDU
to the back with the right foot, stand in
5th position (pause).

4 bars

Repeat the exercise in the reverse
direction.

8 bars

Repeat the whole combination once
more.

Total accompaniment
16 bars

Turn to the other side and repeat the
exercise on the other leg.

[1] The given form of battement tendu with a pressure in 2nd position is also called battement
tendu pour le pied.

Pointe tendue, in 2nd position

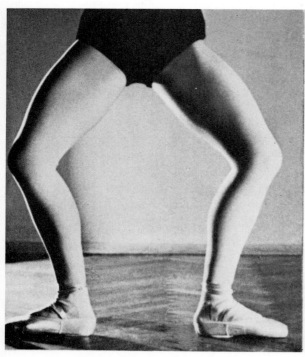

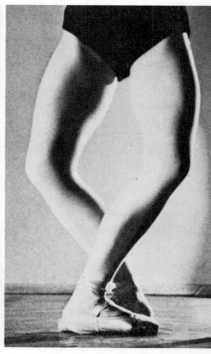

Demi-plié in 2nd position   Demi-plié in 5th position

Measure 2/4
Tempo
moderate   ## 3.   BATTEMENTS TENDUS
Introduction
(1 bar)   Preparation
                                   Starting position of the feet: Starting position of
                                   5th position, right foot front.   the right arm: 2nd
                                                                            position.

Off-beat *(4th)* *eighth* *1st, 2nd, 3rd* *eighth*	BATTEMENT TENDU front, with the right foot in demi-plié in 5th position.	2nd
	BATTEMENT TENDU to the side, with the right foot in demi- plié in 2nd position. *Breakdown of the movement:*	
4th eighth	Dégagé right foot to the side, placing pointe tendue.	2nd
1st eighth	Come down in demi-plié in 2nd position.	2nd - 1st
2nd eighth	Come up from demi-plié, simultaneously lift the right foot from the heel to the toe (pointe tendue).	1st - 2nd
3rd eighth	Move the foot to the 5th position back.	2nd
4th, 1st, *2nd, 3rd* *eighth*	BATTEMENT TENDU in the back, with the right foot in demi-plié in 5th position.	2nd
4th, 1st, *2nd, 3rd* *eighth*	BATTEMENT TENDU to the side, with demi-plié in 2nd position, right foot ending in 5th position front.	2nd - 1st - 2nd

4 bars   Repeat the combination once more.

Total Accompaniment
8 bars

                 Turn to the other side and repeat the
                 exercise on the other leg.

Measure 2/4
Tempo lively
Introduction
(1 bar)

4. BATTEMENTS TENDUS JETÉS

Preparation
Starting position of the feet:
5th position, right foot front.

Starting position of
the right arm: 2nd
position.

Off-beat	BATTEMENT TENDU JETÉ	2nd position.
(4th),	right foot, front.	
1st eighth		

2nd, 3rd	BATTEMENT TENDU JETÉ
eighth	right foot (change) to the side.

BATTEMENTS TENDUS JETÉS
BALANÇOIRE $(25°)$
right foot.
> *Breakdown of the movement:*

4th eighth	Kick back,
1st eighth	kick front,
2nd eighth	kick back,
3rd eighth	kick front.
4th eighth	Hold the leg at a 25° angle (pause).

1st eighth	Kick back,
2nd eighth	kick front.
3rd eighth	Bring down the foot in 5th position.

4th, 1st,	3 BATTEMENTS TENDUS JETÉS
2nd, 3rd	right foot (change) to the side.
eighth	

4 bars	Repeat the exercise in the reverse direction.
8 bars	Repeat the whole combination once more.

Total accompaniment
16 bars

Turn to the other side and repeat the
exercise on the other leg.

Measure 3/4
Tempo
moderate
Introduction
(2 bars)

5. RONDS DE JAMBE À TERRE

Preparation[1] Starting position of the feet[2]:	Starting position of the right arm: 2nd position.
2 bars 2 RONDS DE JAMBE À TERRE EN DEHORS[3] right leg.	2nd
1 bar 1 ROND DE JAMBE À TERRE, IN DEMI-PLIÉ.	2nd - A - 1st - 2nd
1 bar 1 ROND DE JAMBE À TERRE.	2nd
1 bar 1 GRAND ROND DE JAMBE JETÉ.	
1 bar 1 ROND DE JAMBE À TERRE.	
1 bar 1 GRAND ROND DE JAMBE JETÉ.	2nd
1 bar 1 ROND DE JAMBE À TERRE.	
8 bars Repeat the combination once more en dehors (with a change at the end of the combination: the last rond de jambe à terre is not executed, the right foot is brushed through the 1st position front, pointe tendue).	

[1] *Breakdown of the movement:*

	a. Position of the feet: 5th position right foot front.	a. right arm down, preparatory position A
1 bar	b. Dégagé right foot front (pointe tendue) simultaneously demi-plié on the left leg.	b. right arm comes up front to 1st position
1st, 2nd fourth	c. Demi-rond de jambe à terre en dehors right foot immediately stretching the left leg from demi-plié.	c. the right arm open to the side in 2nd position
3rd fourth	d. Demi-rond de jambe à terre en dehors and passé par terre (through 1st position) with right foot.	d. right arm in 2nd position

[2] Ronds de jambe à terre are executed immediately after the preparation continuing the movement of the preparatory rond.

[3] All the following combined ronds de jambe in the given combination (8 bars) are done en dehors.

8 bars	Repeat combination in the reverse direction en dedans.	
8 bars	Repeat once more the combination en dedans (change at the end of the combination: the last rond de jambe à terre is not executed, the right foot comes down into 5th position front).	

Immediately after this combination follows the following movements:

PORT DE BRAS ET BATTEMENTS
RELEVÉS LENTS (90°).

Tempo slow	*Breakdown of the movement:*	
1 bar	The body bends forward (down).	2nd - A
1 bar	The body returns to the starting position the right foot is placed forward, pointe tendue.	A - 1st - 3rd
1 bar	The body bends backward.	3rd
1 bar	The body returns to the starting position.	3rd - 2nd
2 bars	Raise the outstretched right leg slowly	2nd
2 bars	(from toe) up to 90°. Lower slowly (pointing the toe on the floor) and close in 5th position front.	2nd
1 bar	The body bends forward (down).	2nd - A
1 bar	The body returns to the starting position, slide the right leg to the side in 2nd position pointe tendue.	A - 1st - 2nd
1 bar	The body bends to the side (left).	2nd - 3rd
1 bar	The body returns to the starting position.	3rd - 2nd
2 bars	Raise the outstretched right leg slowly	2nd
2 bars	(from toe) up to 90°. Lower slowly pointing the toe on the floor and close in 5th position back.	2nd
1 bar	The body bends forward (down).	2nd - A
1 bar	The body returns to the starting position, slide the right leg back, pointe tendue.	A - 1st - 3rd

1 bar	The body bends backward.	3rd
1 bar	The body returns to the starting position.	3rd - 2nd
2 bars	Raise the outstretched right leg slowly (from toe) up to 90°.	2nd
2 bars	Slowly lower (pointing the toe on the floor) and close in 5th position back.	2nd
1 bar	The body bends forward (down).	2nd - A
1 bar	The body returns to the starting position, slide the right foot to the 2nd position, pointe tendue.	A - 1st - 2nd
1 bar	The body bends to the side (right).	The right arm comes down slightly (palm turned out).
1 bar	The body returns to the starting position.	2nd
2 bars	Raise slowly the outstretched right leg (from toe) up to 90°.	2nd
2 bars	Lower slowly (pointing the toe on the floor) and close in 5th position front.	2nd - A

Total accompaniment
64 bars

Turn to the other side and repeat the exercise on the other leg.

6.   BATTEMENTS FONDUS

Measure 2/4
Tempo slow
Introduction
(2 bars)

		Starting position of the right arm: 2nd position.
	Preparation Starting position of the feet: 2nd position, right foot pointe tendue.	
Off-beat *(4th),* *1st, 2nd, 3rd* *eighth*	BATTEMENT FONDU to the front (45°) right leg.	2nd - A - 1st - 2nd
4th, 1st, *2nd, 3rd* *eighth*	BATTEMENT FONDU to the side, right leg.	2nd - A - 1st - 2nd
4th, 1st, *2nd, 3rd* *eighth*	BATTEMENT FONDU to the back, right leg.	2nd - A - 1st - 2nd
4th, 1st *eighth*	PASS the right leg (through 1st position) to the front (45°) on demi-plié of the left leg.	2nd - A - 1st
2nd, 3rd *eighth*	PASS the right leg (through 1st position) to the back (45°) simultaneously come up from demi-plié of the left leg.	1st - 2nd
4 bars	Repeat the exercise in the reverse direction.	
8 bars	Repeat the whole combination once more, this time on half toe.	

Total accompaniment
16 bars

Turn to the other side and repeat the
exercise on the other leg.

Measure 2/4
Tempo
moderate
Introduction
(1 bar)

7.   BATTEMENTS FRAPPÉS

	Preparation Starting position of the feet: 2nd position, right foot pointe tendue.	Starting position of the right arm: 2nd position.
Off-beat *(4th),* *1st, 2nd, 3rd,* *4th eighth*	3 BATTEMENTS FRAPPÉS to the front, pointed down on the floor with the right foot, then raise the leg (25°).	2nd
1st eighth, *2nd, 3rd,* *eighth*	FLIC right foot front, bring the leg to the side, pointe tendue.	2nd - A - 1st - 2nd
4th, 1st, *2nd, 3rd,* *4th eighth*	3 BATTEMENTS FRAPPÉS to the side (change) with the right foot, then raise the leg (25°).	2nd
1st eighth *2nd, 3rd* *eighth*	FLIC right foot back, bring the leg to the back, pointe tendue.	2nd - A - 1st - 2nd
4th, 1st, *2nd, 3rd* *4th eighth*	3 BATTEMENTS FRAPPÉS to the back, pointed down on the floor with the right foot, raise the leg (25°).	2nd
1st eighth *2nd, 3rd* *eighth*	FLIC right foot back, bring the leg to the side, pointe tendue.	2nd - A - 1st - 2nd
4th, 1st, *2nd, 3rd* *4th eighth*	3 BATTEMENTS FRAPPÉS to the side (change) with the right foot then raise the leg (25°).	2nd
1st eighth *2nd, 3rd* *eighth*	FLIC right foot front, bring the leg to the front, pointe tendue.	2nd - A - 1st - 2nd
8 bars	The exercise is repeated once more on half toe.[1]	

Total accompaniment
16 bars   Turn to the other side and repeat the
                  exercise on the other leg.

[1] At the repetition of the exercise on half toe the supporting leg, in the movement FLIC
of the right foot, comes down from half toe, then rises on half toe.

Measure 2/4
Tempo
moderate
Introduction
(2 bars)

8. RONDS DE JAMBE EN L'AIR

Preparation[1]

Starting position of the feet: the right leg is off the floor to the side à la seconde (90°).	Starting position of the right arm: 2nd position.

Off-beat
(4th),
1st, 2nd,
3rd, 4th,
1st, 2nd, 3rd
eighth

4 RONDS DE JAMBE EN L'AIR (90°) EN DEHORS right leg.

2nd position.

4th, 1st,
2nd, 3rd
eighth

3 RONDS DE JAMBE EN L'AIR (45°) EN DEHORS right leg.

4th, 1st,
2nd, 3rd
eighth

3 RONDS DE JAMBE EN L'AIR (45°) EN DEHORS right leg.

4 bars

Repeat the exercise in the reverse direction.

8 bars

Repeat the whole combination once more on half toe.

Total accompaniment
16 bars

Turn to the other side and repeat the exercise on the other leg.

---

[1] *Breakdown of the preparatory movement:*

a. Position of the legs: 5th position, right foot front.

a. Right arm down, preparatory position A.

b. Petit développé with the right leg front (45°) on demi-plié of the left leg.

b. Right arm comes up front in 1st position.

c. Demi-rond de jambe en dehors (90°) right leg, simultaneously come up from demi-plié of the left leg.

c. Right arm opens to the side in 2nd position.

Measure 3/4		
(Waltz)	**9. ADAGIO**	
Tempo slow		
Introduction	Preparation	Starting position of
(2 bars)	Starting position of the feet:	the right arm: 2nd
	5th position, right foot front.	position.

3 bars	DÉVELOPPÉ[1]	A - 1st - 2nd
	right leg front.	
1 bar	PASSER LA JAMBE $(90°)$	2nd - 1st
	with the right leg.	
2 bars	DÉVELOPPÉ À LA SECONDE $(90°)$	1st - 2nd
	with the right leg.	
2 bars	DEMI-ROND DE JAMBE EN DEDANS	2nd - 1st
	right leg front $(90°)$ simultaneously	
	come down in demi-plié of left leg.	
3 bars	GRAND ROND DE JAMBE EN	1st - 2nd, then the
	DEHORS	right arm from below
	right leg, simultaneously come up	opens through front.
	from demi-plié of the left leg.	Position of arms: 2nd
		arabesque.
1 bar	PASSER LA JAMBE $(90°)$	A
	right leg.	
3 bars	DÉVELOPPÉ	A - 1st - 3rd
	right leg to the side in écarté back, the	
	body away from the barre diagonally,	
	the head position turned left.	
1 bar	Lower right leg down in 5th position	3rd - 2nd - A
	back.	

16 bars	Repeat the exercise in the reverse
	direction. (On the final développé to
	the side in écarté front, the body is
	turned to the barre diagonally, the
	head position turned to the right, the
	right arm in 2nd position allongée.)

Total accompaniment	
32 bars	Turn to the other side and repeat the
	exercise on the other leg.

[1] Développé is executed not lower than 90°.

Écarté front, right arm in 2nd position allongée

Écarté back, right arm in 3rd position

Liudmilla Bogomolova

Measure 2/4
Tempo
moderate
Introduction
(1 bar)

10. BATTEMENTS DOUBLES FRAPPÉS

Preparation
Starting position of the feet: 2nd
position, right foot pointe tendue.

Starting position of
the right arm:
2nd position.

Off-beat
(4th),
1st eighth

BATTEMENT DOUBLE FRAPPÉ
with the right foot, ending front
pointe tendue (the body leans slightly
backward, the head is turned to the
right).

2nd position.

2nd, 3rd
eighth

BATTEMENT DOUBLE FRAPPÉ
with the right foot, ending in the back
pointe tendue (the body leans slightly
to the front, the head is turned to the
right).

4th, 1st,
2nd, 3rd
eighth

2 BATTEMENTS DOUBLES FRAPPÉS
with the right foot, ending at the side
(change) pointe tendue (the body is
upright, the head position en face).

2nd position.

2 bars
Repeat the exercise in the reverse
direction.

4 bars
Repeat the whole combination once
more.

8 bars
Repeat the complete combination once
more (rising on half toe of the
supporting leg and coming down from
half toe on each battement double
frappé).

Total accompaniment
16 bars

Turn to the other side and repeat the
exercise on the other leg.

Measure 2/4
Tempo lively
Introduction
(2 bars)

11.   PETITS BATTEMENTS SUR LE COU-DE-PIED

Preparation   Starting position of
Starting position of the feet: the right arm: A.
right foot sur le cou-de-pied
front (wrapping the ankle).

Off-beat   PETIT BATTEMENT SUR LE   Position A.
(4th)   COU-DE-PIED
1st eighth   (accent on the front) right foot.

2nd, 3rd   PETIT BATTEMENT SUR LE
eighth   COU-DE-PIED
                  (accent on the front) right foot.

4th, 1st,   3 PETITS BATTEMENTS SUR LE
2nd, 3rd   COU-DE-PIED
eighth   (accent on the front) right foot.

4th, 1st   PETIT BATTEMENT SUR LE
eighth   COU-DE-PIED
                  (accent on the back) right foot.

2nd, 3rd   PETIT BATTEMENT SUR LE
eighth   COU-DE-PIED
                  (accent on the back) right foot.

Position of the foot sur le cou-de pied
front, position of the arms A

Position of the foot sur le cou-de-pied
front, arms in 3rd position

4th, 1st, *2nd, 3rd* *eighth*	3 PETITS BATTEMENTS SUR LE COU-DE-PIED (accent on the back) right foot.

4 bars	Repeat the exercise once more.	
8 bars	Repeat the complete combination once more on half toe. Then	
4 bars	BALANCE on half toe of the left foot in the varied poses: a. right foot sur le cou-de-pied front.	Lower the left arm to position A.
4 bars	b. right foot sur le cou-de-pied front.	3rd position arms.
6 bars	c. right leg raised in back (45°).	Arm position 2nd arabesque (right arm front).
2 bars	Come down from the half toe of the left foot, closing the right leg to 5th position back.	Arm position A.

Total accompaniment
32 bars

The exercise is repeated on the other
leg (turn to the other side).

2nd arabesque, the leg raised in the back at 45°

Ekaterina Maximova

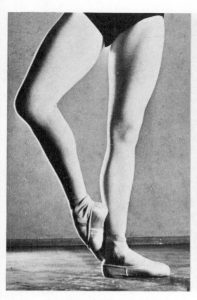

Position of the foot
sur le cou-de-pied front,
wrapping the ankle

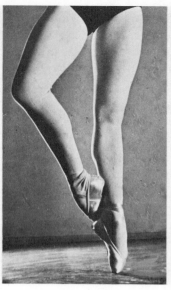

Position of the foot
sur le cou-de-pied front,
wrapping the ankle

Position of the foot
sur le cou-de-pied front

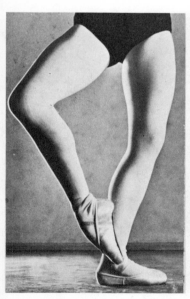

Position of the foot
sur le cou-de-pied front
(the supporting leg in
plié à quart)

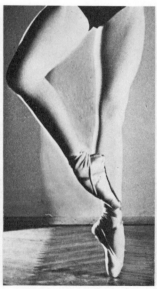

Position of the foot
sur le cou-de-pied front

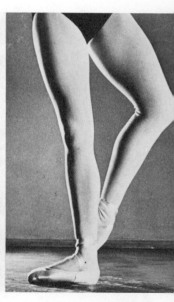

Position of the foot
sur le cou-de-pied back

Position of the foot
sur le cou-de-pied back

Position of the foot
in retiré front
(foot raised above the ankle
of the supporting leg)

Position of the foot
in retiré front

Position of the foot
in retiré back

Position of the foot
in retiré back

Position of the foot
in retiré to the side
(the leg is raised to 90°)

Measure 2/4
(March)
Tempo
moderate   **12. GRANDS BATTEMENTS JETÉS**
Introduction   Preparation   Starting position of
(1 bar)   Starting position of the feet: 5th   the right arm: 2nd
                              position, right foot front.   position.

                              GRAND BATTEMENT JETÉ PIQUÉ
                              to the front, right leg.
Off-beat   *Breakdown of the movement:*
(4th) eighth   Kick leg up.   2nd position.
1st eighth   Lower leg to pointe tendue.
2nd eighth   Kick leg up.
3rd eighth   Lower leg in 5th position front.

                              GRAND BATTEMENT JETÉ PIQUÉ
                              to the side, right leg.
                                  Breakdown of the movement:
4th eighth   Kick leg up.
1st eighth   Lower leg to pointe tendue.
2nd eighth   Kick leg up.
3rd eighth   Lower leg in 5th position back.

                              GRAND BATTEMENT JETÉ PIQUÉ
                              to the back, right leg.
                                  Breakdown of the movement:
4th eighth   Kick leg up.   2nd position.
1st eighth   Lower leg to pointe tendue.
2nd eighth   Kick leg up, then

                              GRAND BATTEMENTS JETÉS
                              BALANÇOIRE
                              right leg.
3rd, 4th   *Breakdown of the movement:*
eighth   Kick leg (through 1st position) front.

1st, 2nd   Kick leg (through 1st position) back.
eighth

3rd eighth   Lower leg in 5th position back.

4 bars   Repeat the exercise in the reverse
                              direction.

Total accompaniment
8 bars

                              Turn to the other side and repeat the
                              exercise on the other leg.

Measure 3/4
(Waltz)
Tempo slow
Introduction
(2 bars)

13. PORT DE BRAS AND BENDING OF THE BODY

	Preparation Starting position of the feet: 1st position, facing the barre.	Starting position of the arms: both hands on the barre.
2 bars	Body bends backward.	Hands on the barre.
2 bars	Body returns to the starting position, then DÉGAGÉ right foot to the side, pointe tendue.	Right arm in 2nd position.
2 bars	Body bends to the left side.	Right arm goes up into 3rd position.
2 bars	Body returns to the starting position. Place right foot in 1st position.	Right arm lowers into the 2nd position. Place right hand on the barre.
8 bars	The combination is repeated on the other leg.	
2 bars	Body bends backward.	Hands on the barre.
2 bars	Body returns to the starting position. DÉGAGÉ right foot to the side, pointe tendue.	Left arm in 2nd position.
2 bars	Body bends to the right side.	Left arm goes up into 3rd position.
2 bars	Body returns to the starting position. Place right foot in 1st position.	Left arm lowers into the 2nd position. Place left hand on the barre.
8 bars	The combination is repeated on the other leg.	

Total accompaniment
32 bars

Initial position for the stretching of the legs
(leg placed on the barre)

Stretching to the side

Measure 3/4
(Waltz)
Tempo slow
Introduction
(2 bars)

13a. STRETCHING OF THE LEGS AND BENDING OF THE BODY

Preparation

Starting position of the feet: right leg
is held to the side (placed on the barre,
turned out sideways from the heel)
facing the barre.

Starting position of
arms: both hands on
the barre.

STRETCHING TO THE SIDE
Breakdown of the movement:

2 bars

The right leg slides (turned out
sideways from the heel) on the barre
to the right, simultaneously the body
leans toward the right leg.

2 bars

The body returns to the starting
position, simultaneously the right leg
slides back into the starting position.

The left arm opens
to the side, goes up
and (jointly with the
leaning of the body)
continues the
movement to the
right. The left arm
comes down to the
side returns to the
starting position (on
the barre).

Stretching to the side

Elena Tcherkaskaya

STRETCHING TO THE SIDE
Breakdown of the movement:

2 bars	Without taking the right leg off the barre, bend the body to the left; simultaneously the right leg slides along the barre to the right.	The right arm opens to the side, goes up and (jointly with the leaning of the body) continues the movement to the left.
2 bars	Then the right leg slides back into the starting position; simultaneously the body returns to the starting position.	The right arm comes down to the side, returns to the starting position (at the barre).
8 bars	Repeat the exercise once more on half toe. End the stretching on half toe, lift the right leg (above the barre) and hold up a short time; then lower the leg into 1st position.	Hands on the barre.

Total accompaniment
16 bars

(*Pause*)
Repeat the exercise on the other leg.

Measure 2/4
Tempo lively
Introduction
(1 bar)

14.   RELEVÉS

Preparation	Starting position of
Starting position of the feet: 1st	arms: both hands on
position, facing the barre.	the barre.

8 RELEVÉS
in 1st position.
Breakdown of the movement:

Off-beat
(4th) eighth,
7 bars,
1st, 2nd, 3rd
eighth

Demi-plié in 1st position, rise on half   Hands on the barre.
toe, come down from half toe in
demi-plié and so forth.

4th eighth,
7 bars,
1st, 2nd, 3rd
eighth

16 RELEVÉS   Hands on the barre.
in 1st position (without demi-plié).

Total accompaniment
16 bars

Relevé in 1st position

EXERCISES IN THE CENTER

Measure 3/4
(Waltz)
Tempo slow
Introduction
(2 bars)

1. SMALL ADAGIO

Preparation
Starting position of the feet:
1st position.

Starting position of
arms: 2nd position.

	GRAND PLIÉ in 1st position	
2 bars	(moving downward,	2nd - A
1 bar	moving upward).	A - 1st
1 bar	Rise on half toe (then down from half toe).	1st - 2nd 2nd - A
1 bar, *1st, 2nd* *fourth,* *5th eighth*	DÉVELOPPÉ with the right leg front, en face.	A - 1st
6th eighth *2 bars*	DEMI-PLIÉ on the left leg.	1st - 2nd
	STEP ON the right leg front.	
	RAISE the left leg back (90°).	
1 bar, *1st, 2nd* *fourth,* *5th eighth*	BRING[1] the left leg to the side à la seconde (90°).	2nd
6th eighth *2 bars*	DEMI-PLIÉ on the right leg.	2nd
	STEP ON the left leg to the side.	
	RAISE the right leg à la seconde (90°).	
3 bars	BALANCE in second position (90°) rising slowly on the half toe of the left foot.	2nd - 3rd

[1] Demi-rond de jambe en dedans (at 90°).

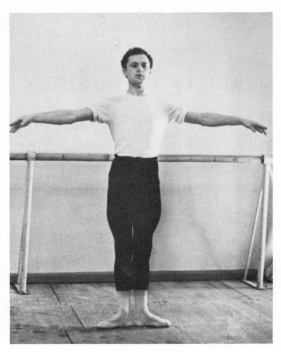

Initial position: 1st position of the feet,
2nd position arms

Grand plié in 1st position

Vladimir Nikonov

1 bar	Come down from half toe of the left foot, and bring the right leg in 1st position.	3rd - 2nd

16 bars	Repeat the exercise on the other leg.
32 bars	Repeat the whole combination in the reverse direction.

Total accompaniment
64 bars

Measure 2/4
Tempo
moderate

2. BATTEMENTS TENDUS

Introduction *(1 bar)*	Preparation Starting position of the feet: 5th position, the right foot in front, en face.	Starting position of arms: 2nd position.
Off-beat *(4th)* *1st eighth*	BATTEMENT TENDU to the front, with the right foot.	2nd position.
2nd, 3rd *eighth*	BATTEMENT TENDU to the side (changing) with the right foot.	
4th, 1st, *2nd, 3rd* *eighth*	BATTEMENT TENDU to the back, with demi-plié in 5th position with the right foot.	
4th, 1st, *eighth*	BATTEMENT TENDU to the front, with the left foot.	
2nd, 3rd *eighth*	BATTEMENT TENDU to the side (changing) with the left foot.	
4th, 1st, *2nd, 3rd* *eighth*	BATTEMENT TENDU to the back, with demi-plié, in 5th position with the left foot.	
4th, 1st, *2nd, 3rd* *eighth*	3 BATTEMENTS TENDUS JETÉS to the side (changing) with the right foot.	2nd position.
4th, 1st, *2nd, 3rd* *eighth*	3 BATTEMENTS TENDUS JETÉS to the side (changing) with the left foot.	

CONCLUDING MOVEMENT FOR THE MEN'S CLASS:

4th eighth	PRÉPARATION POUR PIROUETTES EN DEHORS. (Dégagé with the right foot to the side, lower to the second position in demi-plié.)	2nd 6th (right arm is bent).
1 bar *1st, 2nd, 3rd* *eighth*	PIROUETTES EN DEHORS. (End in 5th position, with the right foot back.)	The right arm opens during the movement, then the arms meet between A and 1st (end in 2nd position).

CONCLUDING EXERCISE FOR THE WOMEN'S CLASS:

4th eighth *1st, 2nd* *eighth* *3rd, 4th* *eighth*	PREPARATION POUR PIROUETTES EN DEHORS. (Demi-plié in 5th position, rise on half toe of the left foot, simultaneously bring the right foot sur le cou-de-pied front, then bring the right foot back in 4th position croisé and lower in demi-plié.)	A A - 1st Position 3rd arabesque (right arm forward).
1st, 2nd, 3rd *eighth*	PIROUETTES EN DEHORS. (End in 5th position, right foot back.)	The right arm opens during the course of the movement, then the arms meet between A and 1st position (end in 2nd position).

8 bars	The exercise is repeated on the other leg.

Total accompaniment
16 bars

(*Pause*)
The exercise is repeated in the reverse direction (pirouettes remain en dehors).

Measure 3/4
Tempo slow
Introduction
(2 bars)

3. BATTEMENTS FONDUS

Preparation
Starting position of feet: 5th position   Starting position of
croisé, right foot front.   arms: 2nd position.

BATTEMENT FONDU
to the front, croisé (45°) with the
right foot, up on half toe of the left
foot.
    Breakdown of the movement:

Off-beat   Raise on half toe in 5th position.   2nd - A
(2nd, 3rd)
fourth

1st fourth   Lower the left leg in demi-plié,
                   simultaneously bring the right foot sur
                   le cou-de-pied front.

2nd, 3rd   Stretch the right foot front (45°)   1st - 6th (the right
fourth   croisé, simultaneously rise on half toe   arm is bent).
                   of the left foot.

1st fourth   DEMI-PLIÉ   6th (the right arm is
                   on the left leg.   bent).

2nd fourth   RELEVÉ
                   on half toe on the left foot.

3rd fourth   Stay on half toe.

BATTEMENT FONDU TOMBÉ
back, croisé, with the left leg.
    Breakdown of the movement:

1st fourth   Tombé with the right leg front, to   A
                   croisé, simultaneously bring the left
                   foot sur le cou-de-pied back.

2nd, 3rd   Stretch the left leg back (45°) to   Through the 1st
fourth   croisé, simultaneously rise on half toe   position of arms the
                   of the right foot.   3rd arabesque (left
                                                               arm front).

1st fourth   DEMI-PLIÉ   3rd arabesque (left
                   on the right leg.   arm front).

2nd fourth   RELEVÉ
                   on half toe of the right foot.

3rd fourth   Stay on half toe.

	BATTEMENT FONDU TOMBÉ to the side, with the right leg. *Breakdown of the movement:*	
1st fourth	Tombé with the left leg back, simultaneously bring the right foot sur le cou-de-pied front.	A
2nd, 3rd fourth	Stretch the right foot to the side à la seconde (45°), simultaneously rise on half toe of the left foot.	1st - 2nd
1st fourth	DEMI-PLIÉ on the left leg.	2nd
2nd fourth	RELEVÉ on half toe of the left foot.	
3rd fourth	Stay on half toe.	
1st fourth	TOMBÉ right foot to the side.	2nd (turning palms out).
2nd, 3rd fourth	PAS DE BOURRÉE EN DEHORS (changing feet) stepping to the side twice.	2nd
1st fourth	End in 4th position (wide), in croisé the left leg in front in plié à quart.	6th (the left arm is bent).
2nd fourth	Stay in this position preparing for tour en dedans.	
3rd fourth	DEMI-PLIÉ in 4th position.	
2 bars	TOURS EN DEDANS in attitude effacée on the right leg.	5th (right arm up).
	ALLONGÉE with the right leg to the back, in effacé simultaneously demi-plié on the left leg (the body leans slightly forward).	5th allongée (right arm up).
1st, 2nd fourth	PAS DE BOURRÉE EN DEHORS (changing feet to the side twice).	2nd - A
3rd fourth	End in 4th position (wide), in croisé the right leg in front in plié à quart.	6th (right arm is bent).
1st, 2nd fourth	Stay in this position preparing for tour en dedans.	
3rd fourth	DEMI-PLIÉ in 4th position.	

Pas de bourrée en dehors, ending in 5th position croisé

Ekaterina Maximova

2 bars	TOURS EN DEDANS in attitude effacée on the left leg	5th (left arm up).
	ALLONGÉE with the left leg to the back, in effacé, simultaneously demi-plié on the right leg (the body leans slightly forward).	5th allongée (left arm up).
1st, 2nd *fourth*	PAS DE BOURRÉE EN DEHORS (changing feet) to the side twice.	2nd
3rd fourth	End in 5th position, in croisé, the left foot in front.	A

Tour en dedans in attitude, ending in attitude effacée allongée

| *1st fourth* | Stay in 5th position (pause). |

| *16 bars* | Repeat the exercise on the other leg. |

Total accompaniment
32 bars   (*Pause*)

Repeat the combination in the reverse direction. (After tours en dehors in attitude, croisée-allongée, follow with pas de bourrée en tournant en dehors, etc.)

Tour en dehors in attitude, ending in attitude croisée, allongée

Rimma Karelskaya

Measure 2/4
Tempo
moderate
Introduction
(1 bar)

4. BATTEMENTS FRAPPÉS

Preparation
Starting position of the feet: 2nd
position, right foot in pointe tendue.

Starting position of
arms: 2nd position.

Off-beat
(4th) eighth,
1st, 2nd, 3rd
eighth

3 BATTEMENTS FRAPPÉS
to the side (change) pointing the toe
on the floor with the right foot.

2nd position.

4th, 1st,
2nd, 3rd
eighth

2 BATTEMENTS DOUBLE FRAPPÉS
to the side (change) pointing the toe
on the floor with the right foot.

4th eighth,
1st, 2nd, 3rd
eighth

RAISE
the outstretched right leg to 45° à la
seconde and follow with

3 RONDS DE JAMBE EN L'AIR
(45°) EN DEHORS
with the right leg.

4th, 1st,
2nd, 3rd
eighth
4th eighth

3 RONDS DE JAMBE EN L'AIR
(45°) EN DEDANS
with the right leg, follow with a small
stroke upward into

The palms turn
inward (slight stroke
upward).

1st, 2nd
eighth

FLIC-FLAC EN TOURNANT
EN DEDANS
with the right foot.

A

3rd, 4th
eighth

DEMI-PLIÉ
on the right leg, simultaneously bend
the left foot sur le cou-de-pied front.

PRÉPARATION POUR PIROUETTES
EN DEDANS
in 4th position.
    Breakdown of the movement:

1st, 2nd, 3rd
eighth

Rise on half toe of the right foot,
simultaneously bring the left foot back
and stand in 4th position croisé, the
right leg in plié à quart.

A - 1st
6th (right arm is
bent).

4th eighth	DÉGAGÉ with the left foot to the side (45°) on demi-plié of the right leg.	The right arm opens during the movement, then the hands meet between A and 1st, ending in the 1st position (wide).
1 bar *1st, 2nd, 3rd* *eighth*	PIROUETTES EN DEHORS. (End in 5th position, left foot front.)	

8 bars	The exercise is repeated on the other leg.

Total accompaniment
16 bars

(*Pause*)
Repeat the combination once more.

Measure 3/4
(Waltz)
Slow tempo
Introduction
(2 bars)

5. GRAND ADAGIO

	Preparation Starting position of the feet: 5th position, croisé, right foot front.	Starting position arms: A.
Off-beat *(6th) eighth* *1st fourth*	GLISSADE (do not change) with the right foot front diagonally to corner No. 2 (end 5th position demi-plié).	A, follow by opening slightly the hands to the side and closing again.
2nd, 3rd *fourth*	PETIT DÉVELOPPÉ (45°) with the right foot front, effacé, remaining on the left leg in demi-plié.	A - 1st
3 bars	STEP on the right leg. RAISE the left leg back to 90°, in effacé (position 1st arabesque).	1st Arabesque (right arm in front).
3 bars	Stand in this position, rising on half toe of the right foot.	

Attitude croisée

Maya Plisetskaya

1 bar	PASSER LA JAMBE $(90°)$ with the left leg (lower from half toe to flat foot).	A
2 bars	DÉVELOPPÉ with the left leg in front, croisé (lean the head slightly to the front, look to the left under the arm).	A - 1st, 5th (left arm up).
2 bars	DEMI-PLIÉ on the right leg. STEP OVER on the left leg front.	5th (right arm up).
4 bars	RAISE the half-bent right leg back $(90°)$ in attitude croisée, stand in this position, rising on half toe.	

GRAND PORT DE BRAS

Breakdown of the movement:

2 bars	Come down from the half toe of the left foot into a deep demi-plié, simultaneously lean the body forward down, bring the right leg in the floor pointe tendue back, in croisé.	The right arm (simultaneously with the body bending forward) stretches front, lowers down, when both hands meet in 1st position.
1 bar *1st, 2nd* *fourth*	Straighten the body and move onto the right leg (step on the full surface of the foot), stretching the left leg front, pointe tendue, croisé.	The right arm moves upward, the right arm opens to the side: 5th position arms.
	Bend backward, then straighten the body and move to the left leg, which is slightly bent at the knee—plié à quart, step into the preparatory position for tours en dedans in 4th position (wide) croisé.	5th position arms, then the left arm lowers in a circular movement to the side, and continues forward, bending at the elbow: 6th position arms.

Maya Samokhvalova (Volodina)

Grand port de bras (the body leaning forward and down, supporting leg in demi-plié)

3rd fourth	DEMI-PLIÉ	6th (left arm is bent).
2 bars *1st fourth*	TOURS EN DEDANS À LA SECONDE (90°) with the right leg, bring the leg back at the end of the turn, in effacé (coming down from half toe of the left foot) end in 2nd position arabesque, in effacé (facing the direction of corner No. 8).	The left arm opens in the course of the movement, comes through 3rd position, ending in 2nd arabesque position (right arm front).
2nd, 3rd, 1st, *2nd fourth*	Stand in 2nd arabesque.	
3rd fourth	DEMI-PLIÉ on the left leg.	The right arm opens to the side, moves up.
1st fourth	RENVERSÉ EN DEHORS on half toe of the left foot, the right leg bent backward 90° in attitude.	

Attitude croisée

Maya Plisetskaya

2nd, 3rd *fourth*	PAS DE BOURRÉE EN TOURNANT EN DEHORS (stepping to the back twice) then	The arms meet in 1st position.
1 bar	TOMBÉ with the right foot to the side in second position. Simultaneously DÉGAGÉ left leg à la seconde (45°).	A - 2nd allongée (the wrists are turned palms down).
	SOUTENU EN TOURNANT EN DEDANS *Breakdown of the movement:*	
1st, 2nd	Bring up the left leg in front to the right leg and make a full turn of both feet on the half toes. End épaulement croisé (right foot front), then, without coming down from half toe,	A - 1st - 3rd
3rd fourth	DÉGAGÉ with the right foot front (slightly above the floor) in croisé.	
1st fourth	Step in 4th position (wide), croisé, the right leg in plié à quart.	The right arm comes forward, bending at the elbow. The left remains open to the side: 6th position arms.
2nd fourth	Stand in the preparatory position for tours en dedans.	6th arm position (the right arm is bent).
3rd fourth	DEMI-PLIÉ	
3 bars	TOUR EN DEDANS in 1st arabesque (end turn in 1st arabesque facing in direction of side No. 3).	1st arabesque (right arm in front).
1st, 2nd *fourth* *5th eighth*	Lower the left leg in 5th position front, épaulement croisé.	A

Total accompaniment *32 bars*

(*Pause*)
Repeat the combination on the other side.

Renversé en dehors, pas de bourrée en tournant en dehors

Nina Sorokina

Measure 2/4
(March)
Moderate
tempo
Introduction
(1 bar)

6. GRANDS BATTEMENTS JETÉS

Preparation

Starting position of the feet: 5th position, en face, right foot front.	Starting position arms: 2nd position.

Off-beat
(4th)
1st eighth

GRAND BATTEMENT JETÉ
front, with the right leg.

2nd position.

2nd, 3rd
eighth

GRAND BATTEMENT JETÉ
to the side (change), right leg.

4th, 1st
eighth

GRAND BATTEMENT JETÉ
back, right leg.

2nd, 3rd
eighth

Stand in 5th position (pause).

4th eighth
1 bar
1st, 2nd, 3rd
eighth

Repeat the movements on the other
leg.

CONCLUDING EXERCISE FOR THE MEN'S CLASS:

PRÉPARATION POUR PIROUETTES
EN DEHORS
with the right foot.

Breakdown of the movement:

4th, 1st, 2nd
3rd, 4th, 1st
eighth

Demi-plié in 5th position, rise on half   A
toe of the left foot, the right foot sur le
cou-de-pied front. Stay on half toe.
toe.[1] Then

2nd eighth
3rd, 4th
eighth

dégagé the right foot to the side (25°).   1st - 2nd
Come down in 2nd position in   6th (the right arm is
demi-plié.   bent).

1 bar
1st, 2nd, 3rd
eighth

PIROUETTES EN DEHORS.
(End in 4th position, croisé, right foot
back, left leg front in plié à quart.)

The right arm opens
during the course of
the movement, then
both hands meet
between A and 1st
(wide) position
(palms forward).

[1] The instruction "stand on half toe" is given specifically (in this instance) to promote
balance.

CONCLUDING EXERCISE FOR THE WOMEN'S CLASS:

PRÉPARATION POUR PIROUETTES
EN DEHORS
right foot.

Breakdown of the movement:

4th, 1st, 2nd, 3rd, 4th, 1st eighth	Demi-plié in 5th position, rise on half toe of the left foot, right foot sur le cou-de-pied front. Stay on half toe.	A
2nd eighth 3rd, 4th eighth	Bring the right foot back in croisé and come down in demi-plié in 4th position.	1st 3rd arabesque right arm front.
1 bar 1st, 2nd, 3rd eighth	PIROUETTES EN DEHORS. (End in 4th position, croisé, right foot back, left leg front in plié à quart.)	The right arm opens during the course of the movement, then the arms meet between A and 1st, ending in 1st position (wide) (palms slightly turned out).

8 bars	Repeat the combination on the other leg.

Total accompaniment
16 bars

(Pause)
The exercise is repeated in the reverse direction (pirouettes remain en dehors).

Measure 2/4
Tempo
moderate
Introduction
(1 bar)

7. SMALL JUMPS

Preparation
Starting position of the feet: 5th   Starting position of
position, croisé, left foot front.   arms: A.

Off-beat *(4th)* *1st eighth*	ASSEMBLÉ to the side (changing)[1] with the right leg, change épaulement croisé.	A
2nd, 3rd *eighth*	ASSEMBLÉ to the side (changing) with the left leg, change épaulement croisé.	
4th, 1st *eighth*	SISSONNE TOMBÉE to the front, in effacé, with the left leg.	The left arm carries front through the 1st position, simultaneously the right arm moves to the side (palms slightly turned out).
2nd, 3rd *eighth*	ASSEMBLÉ with the right leg (through 1st position) front, in croisé.	The palms turn in, the right arm lowers slightly, then both arms rise fluidly forward up (the left higher than the right) and lower down.

2 bars	Repeat the exercise on the other leg.
4 bars	Repeat the whole combination once more.

Total accompaniment
8 bars

(*Pause*)
The exercise is repeated in the reverse
direction.

[1] The movement assemblé to the side (from the starting position of the working leg in 5th position back) ends in 5th position front.

Measure 2/4
Tempo
moderate
Introduction
(2 bars)

8. SMALL JUMPS WITH BEATS

Preparation
Starting position of the feet: 5th position croisé, right foot front.

Starting position of arms: A.

ÉCHAPPÉ-SAUTÉ À LA SECONDE
Breakdown of the movement:

Off-beat	Jump to 2nd position (en face).	A - 1st - 2nd
(4th)	Jump in 2nd position.	2nd
2nd, 3rd	Jump to 5th position (right foot back).	2nd - A
eighth		
4th, 1st		
eighth		

2nd, 3rd	ENTRECHAT ROYAL	A
eighth	(ending épaulement croisé).	
4th, 1st	ENTRECHAT-QUATRE	
eighth		

2nd, 3rd	ENTRECHAT-TROIS	The left arm bends
eighth	(the right foot ends sur le cou-de-pied	in front,
	back) changing the épaulement croisé.	simultaneously the
		right arm moves to
		the side: 6th position
		of arms.

4th, 1st	GLISSADE	The arms open to the
eighth	(do not change) with the right foot	side, then - A.
	in front diagonally to corner No. 2.	
2nd, 3rd	BRISÉ	The right arm pulls
eighth	front (diagonally to corner No. 2)	forward through the
	with the right leg, ending in 5th	1st position (in the
	position, right foot back.	course of the
		movement), the left
		to the side (the palms
		down), followed by
		position arms A.

4 bars   Repeat the exercise on the other leg.

Total accompaniment
8 bars   *(Pause)*

Repeat the combination in the reverse direction.

Measure 3/4
(Waltz)
Tempo
moderate
Introduction
(2 bars)

9. MEDIUM JUMPS

Preparation
Starting position of the feet: 5th
position, croisé, right foot front.

Starting position of
arms: A.

Off-beat *(3rd)* *fourth,* *1st, 2nd* *fourth*	SISSONNE FERMÉE with the left leg back, in effacé (jump into 1st arabesque, traveling forward diagonally to corner No. 2).	A - 1st arabesque (the right arm in front), then A.
3rd, 1st, 2nd *fourth*	SISSONNE FERMÉE with the right leg back, in croisé (jump into 4th arabesque, traveling forward diagonally to corner No. 2).	A - 4th arabesque (left arm in front), then A.
3rd, 1st, 2nd *fourth*	SISSONNE OUVERTE with the left leg to the side, en face.	1st - 2nd (hands turned out).
3rd fourth	COUPÉ-DESSOUS left foot.	2nd allongée (palms down).
1st, 2nd *fourth*	ASSEMBLÉ to the side, with the right leg, end in 5th position back.	End arm position A.

4 bars	Repeat the exercise on the other leg.
8 bars	Repeat the whole combination once more.

Total accompaniment
16 bars

(*Pause*)
Repeat the combination in the reverse
direction.

Measure 3/4
(Waltz)
Tempo lively
Introduction
(2 bars)

10. BIG JUMPS

Preparation
Starting position of the feet: 5th   Starting position
position, croisé, right foot front.   arms: A.

Off-beat
(2nd and   *Beginning from corner No. 6.*
3rd)
fourth,   FAILLI   A - 2nd allongée
1st, 2nd   with the left foot (ending front, in   (palms down), 6th
fourth   croisé).   (left arm is bent,
                                                       palms down).

3rd, 1st   SISSONNE TOMBÉE EN TOURNANT   The right arm opens
fourth   EN DEHORS   front through the
                   with the right leg forward, in effacé.   1st position,
                                                       simultaneously the
                                                       left arm moves to the
                                                       side (hands turned
                                                       out).

2nd, 3rd, 1st,   PAS DE BOURRÉE EN DEHORS   2nd (hands turned
2nd, 3rd,   (changing feet, traveling forward   in), end position
1st, 2nd   diagonally to corner No. 2).   arms A.
fourth   GRAND ASSEMBLÉ ENTRECHAT-SIX   2nd allongée
                   VOLÉ, IN ÉCARTÉ   (outstretched arms,
                   (moving to corner No. 2) with the   palms down, right
                   right leg.   arm raised higher
                                                       than the left). End
                                                       position arms A.

3rd, 1st, 2nd,   FAILLI   A - 2nd allongée - A.
3rd, 1st, 2nd   with the left foot (ending front, in
fourth   croisé).

                   GRAND ASSEMBLÉ ENTRECHAT-SIX   2nd allongée (arms
                   VOLÉ, IN ÉCARTÉ   outstretched, palms
                   (moving to corner No. 2) with the   down, the right arm
                   right leg.   higher than the left).
                                                       End position arms A.

3rd, 1st   STEP - PIQUÉ   1st arabesque going
fourth   (on half toe) right foot, to the front in   through 1st position
                   diagonal to corner No. 2.   (right arm in front).

2nd, 3rd, *1st, 2nd* *fourth*	LIFT left leg back (45°) in effacé, stand in 1st arabesque effacé.	1st arabesque.
3rd fourth, *1 bar,* *1st, 2nd* *fourth*	CHASSÉ with the left leg back, effacé (with a half turn to the left). STEP - COUPÉ with the left leg, moving to corner No. 5. GRAND ASSEMBLÉ ENTRECHAT-SIX VOLÉ EN TOURNANT EN DEDANS[1] with the right leg, end in 5th position croisé, right foot front.	2nd allongée. 3rd
3rd, 1st *fourth*	SISSONNE TOMBÉE with the left leg, effacé.	2nd (hands turned out).
2nd, 3rd *fourth,* *1st, 2nd* *fourth*	PAS DE BOURRÉE EN DEHORS (changing feet) stepping to the side twice, on the third step hold in demi-plié of the right foot, the left foot sur le cou-de-pied back.	2nd (hands turned in), end in 6th (right arm bent).

CONCLUDING EXERCISE FOR THE MEN'S CLASS:

3rd, 1st, 2nd,	COUPÉ DESSOUS left foot.	6th (right arm bent).
3rd, 1st, 2nd *fourth*	SISSONNE RENVERSÉE EN DEHORS (in attitude, with the right leg). PAS DE BOURRÉE EN TOURNANT EN DEHORS	5th position arm going through 1st (left arm up). 2nd - 6th (right arm bent).
3rd, 1st *fourth*	PETIT ASSEMBLÉ with the left leg back, croisé.	6th (right arm bent).
2nd, 3rd, *1st* *fourth*	DOUBLE TOUR EN L'AIR EN DEHORS (end in 5th position, right foot back).	The right arm opens during the movement, then both arms meet between A and 1st, ending in 1st position (wide).

[1] The movement is executed without beats by the women—grand assemblé volé en tournant en dedans.

CONCLUDING EXERCISE FOR THE WOMEN'S CLASS:

3rd fourth	COUPÉ-DESSOUS with the left foot.	5th position going through 1st (left arm
1st fourth	SISSONNE RENVERSÉE EN DEHORS in attitude, with the right leg.	up).
2nd, 3rd, *1st, 2nd* *fourth*	PAS DE BOURRÉE EN TOURNANT EN DEHORS (stepping to the back twice). End in 4th position croisé, right leg front in plié à quart.	2nd 6th (right arm bent).
3rd fourth	DÉGAGÉ left leg to the side (45°) on demi-plié of the right leg.	The right arm opens during the movement, then both arms meet
1 bar, *1st fourth*	PIROUETTES EN DEDANS (end in 5th position, croisé, left foot front).	between A and 1st, ending in 1st position (wide).

Total accompaniment
16 bars

(*Pause*)
Repeat the exercise once more.

(*Pause*)
Repeat the combined exercises on the
other leg (starting from corner No. 4).

Measure 2/4
Tempo lively
Introduction
(2 bars)

11. SMALL JUMPS WITH BEATS

Preparation
Starting position of the feet: 5th   Starting position
position croisé, left foot front.   arms: A.

Beginning from corner No. 6.

Off-beat
(4th),
1st eighth

BRISÉ
front (diagonally to corner No. 2)
with the right foot.

A, the arms gradually
come up, the right to
the front (during the
course of the
movement), the left
to the side.

2nd, 3rd
eighth

BRISÉ
front, with the right foot (continue to
travel diagonally.

4th, 1st
eighth

BRISÉ
front, with the right foot (continue to
travel diagonally).

2nd, 3rd
eighth

ENTRECHAT-QUATRE

A

4th eighth,
5 bars,
1st, 2nd, 3rd
eighth

Repeat this combination 3 times
consecutively (continuing to travel
diagonally to corner No. 2).

Total accompaniment
8 bars

(Pause)
Repeat the exercise on the other leg
(beginning from corner No. 4,
traveling forward diagonally to
corner No. 8).

Measure 3/4
(Waltz
brillante)
Tempo lively
Introduction
(2 bars)

12.   BIG JUMPS

Preparation   Starting position of
Starting position of the feet: 4th   arms: 3rd arabesque
position, croisé, right foot stretched   (the right arm in
back, pointe tendue.   front).

Begin from corner No. 2.

Off-beat *(2nd, 3rd)* *fourth*	CHASSÉ with the right leg back, croisé with a half-turn to the right.	3rd arabesque, 2nd allongée.
1 bar, *1st, 2nd* *fourth*	JETÉ ENTRELACÉ (Grand jeté en tournant) croisé (end in 3rd arabesque facing corner No. 2).	A - 1st - 3rd, end position arms in 3rd arabesque (right arm in front).
3rd, 1st, 2nd *fourth*	SISSONNE TOMBÉE EN TOURNANT EN DEHORS with the right leg, and with a half turn to the right (end facing corner No. 6).	The right arm opens as the body turns to the front (hands turned out).
3rd, 1st, 2nd *fourth*	COUPÉ DESSOUS left foot. GRAND ROND DE JAMBE (90°) EN TOURNANT EN DEHORS SAUTÉ with the right leg back, and a half turn to the right (end in 3rd arabesque facing corner No. 2).	A Through the 1st position, reach 3rd arabesque (right arm is in front).
3rd fourth *1 bar,* *1st, 2nd* *fourth*	CHASSÉ with the right leg back, croisé, and a half turn to the right. JETÉ ENTRELACÉ croisé (end in 3rd arabesque facing corner No. 2).	3rd arabesque, 2nd allongée. A - 1st - 3rd, end in 3rd arabesque (the right arm in front).
3rd, 1st, 2nd *3rd, 1st, 2nd* *fourth*	CHASSÉ right leg back, croisé. CHASSÉ left leg front, croisé	2nd (hands turned out) follow arm position A. A - 1st - 2nd (hands turned out) - A.

3rd fourth, *1 bar*	PAS COURU to the front diagonally (corner No. 2).	2nd allongée, then the hands come down.
1st, 2nd *fourth*	GRAND ASSEMBLÉ with the left leg front, croisé.	A - 1st - 3rd
3rd, 1st, 2nd *fourth*	FAILLI with the right foot, ending in front croisé.	2nd (hands turned out), the right arm moves down-forward, the left arm is open to the side (palms turned down).

CONCLUDING EXERCISE FOR THE MEN'S CLASS:

3rd fourth, *1 bar*	STEP - COUPÉ with the left foot, to the side (No. 7).	A
	GRAND ASSEMBLÉ with the right leg front, croisé.	1st - 3rd
1 bar	PRÉPARATION POUR PIROUETTES EN DEHORS with the right foot (in 2nd position).	2nd - 6th (right arm is bent), and opens during the course of the movement; both
2 bars *1st fourth*	PIROUETTES EN DEHORS (End in 4th position croisé, the right foot back, the left leg in front in plié à quart.)	arms meet between A and 1st, ending in 1st position (wide), hands turned out.

CONCLUDING EXERCISE FOR THE WOMEN'S CLASS:

3rd, 1st, 2nd *fourth*	STEP - COUPÉ with the left foot to the side (No. 7).	A
	ASSEMBLÉ with the right foot front, croisé.	1st - 3rd
	PRÉPARATION POUR CHAÎNÉS-DÉBOULÉS *Breakdown of the movement:*	
5th eighth	Step on the left foot to the side, to corner No. 6, bringing the right foot front, pointe tendue, croisé.	2nd, follow the right arm to the front, bent at the elbow: 6th arm position.

6th eighth,
3 bars
1st fourth

CHAÎNÉS-DÉBOULÉS
to the front diagonally (corner No. 2).
End in position effacée, left foot
back, pointe tendue.

The right arm opens
during the course of
the movement, both
arms meet between
A and 1st, end with
both arms front
(right arm higher
than the left).

Total accompaniment
16 bars

(*Pause*)
Repeat the exercise once more.

(*Pause*)
Repeat the whole combination on the
other leg (beginning from corner No.
8).

Pose in effacé "two arms in front"

Tatiana Archangelskaya

Measure 2/4
Tempo
moderate
Introduction
(2 bars)

13. JUMPS
(FOR THE MEN'S CLASS)

Preparation
Starting position of the feet: 5th position en face, right foot front.

Starting position of arms: A.

Begin from corner No. 5.

Off-beat (4th), 1st, 2nd eighth	CHASSÉ with the right leg front (corner No. 1).	A - 1st - 3rd
3rd, 4th, 1st eighth	SISSONNE TOMBÉE with the right leg front. The left leg rises back and from this lifted position of the leg	2nd
	PETIT ASSEMBLÉ with the left leg back (en face).	6th (right arm is bent).
2nd, 3rd eighth	DOUBLE TOUR EN L'AIR EN DEHORS (end the last relevé in 5th position,	The right arm opens during the course of the movement, followed with 3rd position, and then 2nd position.
4th eighth, 3 bars, 1st, 2nd, 3rd eighth	Repeat the combination 2 more consecutive times.	
4th eighth	PRÉPARATION POUR PIROUETTES EN DEHORS with the left foot (in 2nd position).	2nd - 6th (left arm is bent).
1 bar, 1st, 2nd, 3rd eighth	PIROUETTES EN DEHORS (end in 4th position, croisé, left foot back, right leg front in plié à quart).	The left arm opens during the course of the movement, both arms meet between A and 1st, ending in 1st position (wide).

Total accompaniment
8 bars

(Pause)
Repeat the exercise once more.

(Pause)
Repeat the combined exercises on the other leg.

Measure 2/4
Tempo lively
Introduction
(1 bar)

14.   PETITS CHANGEMENTS DE PIEDS
(FOR THE MEN'S CLASS)

Preparation Starting position of the feet: 5th position, croisé, right foot front.	Starting position of arms - A.
16 PETITS CHANGEMENTS DE PIEDS.	A

Off-beat
(4th)
eighth,
7 bars,
1st, 2nd, 3rd
eighth

Total accompaniment
8 bars

Measure 3/4
(Waltz)
Tempo slow
Introduction
(2 bars)

15.   PORT DE BRAS AND BENDING
OF THE BODY
(FOR THE MEN'S CLASS)

Preparation Starting position of the feet: 1st position (turned out halfway).	Starting position of arms: 2nd position.
The body bends forward (down).	2nd - A
The body returns to the starting position.	A - 1st - 3rd
The body bends backward (the head leans to the right). The body returns to the starting position (the head turns en face).	3rd 3rd - 2nd
Repeat the movements once more (turning the head to the left, etc.).	

2 bars

2 bars

2 bars
2 bars

8 bars

2 bars	The body bends to the left side (the head turns to the left).	5th (right arm up).
2 bars	The body returns to the starting position (the head turns en face).	2nd
2 bars	The body bends to the right side. The head turns to the right.	5th (left arm up).
2 bars	The body returns to the starting position (the head turns en face).	2nd
4 bars	Bring the right shoulder forward, pull the left shoulder back, the feet remain in 1st position (not fully turned out). The body bends forward (down) and follows the circular movement of bending (to the right, etc.) then straightens out, returning to the starting position, en face.	Lift the right arm up, 5th position arms the right arm lowers and is met by the left arm, then the right arm moves to the side, as the left arm comes up and moves in a wide circular movement (left), end in 2nd arm position.
4 bars	Bring the left shoulder forward, pull the right shoulder back, the feet remain in 1st position (not fully turned out). The body bends forward (down) and follows the circular movement of bending (to the left, etc.), then straightens out, returning to the starting position, en face.	Lift the left arm up, 5th position arms. The left arm lowers and is met by the right arm, then the left arm moves to the side, simultaneously the right arm comes up and moves in a wide circular movement (right) : 2nd - A.

Total accompaniment
32 bars

Measure 2/4
Tempo lively
Introduction
(1 bar)

16.   FIRST EXERCISE ON POINTES

Preparation
Starting position of the feet: 1st   Starting position of
position.   arms: A.

Off-beat
(4th)   8 RELEVÉS   A
eighth,   in 1st position.
7 bars,
1st, 2nd, 3rd
eighth

4th eighth,   8 RELEVÉS   A
7 bars,   in 2nd position
1st, 2nd, 3rd   (end the last relevé in 5th position,
eighth   the right foot front).
4th eighth,
15 bars,

1st, 2nd, 3rd   16 ÉCHAPPÉS
eighth   in 2nd position (change).

Total accompaniment
32 bars

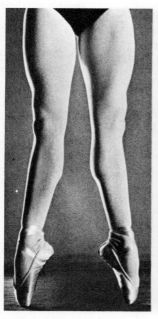
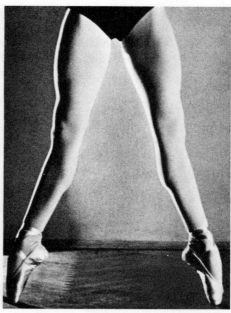

Relevé in 1st position   Relevé in 2nd position

Measure 3/4
Tempo
moderate
Introduction
(2 bars)

17. SECOND EXERCISE ON POINTES

Preparation

	Starting position of the feet: 4th position, croisé, left foot stretched to the back, pointe tendue.	Starting position of arms: 6th (right arm is bent).

Off-beat *(6th) eighth*	DEMI-PLIÉ on the right leg (the left leg bends back slightly).	6th (the right arm is bent).
1st, 2nd, 3rd *fourth*	COUPÉ-DESSOUS on the left leg (stand on pointe). BALLONNÉ with the right leg to the side (45°), end sur le cou-de-pied back.	2nd, 6th (left arm is bent).
1st, 2nd *fourth*	PETIT DÉVELOPPÉ (45°) with the right leg to the side (simultaneously the left leg rises on pointe)	The left arm opens to the side: 2nd.
3rd fourth	TOMBER PIED DESSUS with the right leg, the left leg bends sur le cou-de-pied back.	6th (right arm is bent).
1st, 2nd, 3rd *fourth*	PAS DE BOURRÉE EN DEHORS (changing feet).	2nd - 6th (left arm is bent).
1st, 2nd *fourth*	STEP - PIQUÉ SUR LA POINTE with the right foot to the side, PETIT DÉVELOPPÉ (45°) with the left leg to the front, croisé.	The left arm opens to the front, simultaneously the arms move in a circular manner outward.
5th eighth	TOMBER PIED DESSUS with the left leg, right foot sur le cou-de-pied.	6th (left arm is bent).

4 bars	Repeat the exercise on the other leg.
8 bars	Repeat the whole combination once more.

Total accompaniment
16 bars

Measure 3/4
Tempo lively
Introduction
(2 bars)

18.   THIRD EXERCISE ON POINTES

Preparation
Starting position of the feet: 4th
position croisé, right foot front, pointe
tendue.

Starting position of
arms: A.

Off-beat
(6th)
eighth

DEMI-PLIÉ
on the left leg, simultaneously lift the
right leg front (45°), croisé (the body
and head leaning slightly forward).

A - 1st, with a slight
stroke of hands
upward, then

1st, 2nd, 3rd
fourth

GRAND ROND DE JAMBE JETÉ EN
DEDANS
with the left leg, right leg sur la pointe
(straighten the body, turn the head to
the left), ending with the following
movement.

The hands make a
circular movement:
go down, to the side,
then up (palms
turned out), then
the hands lower to
the front and down.

1st, 2nd
fourth

TOMBER PIED DESSUS
on the left leg, épaulement croisé, the
right foot sur le cou-de-pied back (the
body and head leaning slightly
forward).

3rd fourth

DEMI-PLIÉ
on the right leg, simultaneously
DÉGAGÉ
with the left leg front (45°), croisé
(the body and the head leaning slightly
forward)

A - 1st, with a slight
stroke of hands
upward, then

1st, 2nd, 3rd
fourth

GRAND ROND DE JAMBE JETÉ EN
DEDANS
with the right leg, the left leg sur la
pointe (straighten the body, turn the
head to the right), ending with the
following movement.

The hands make a
circular movement:
go down, to the side,
then up (palms
turned out). Then
the hands lower to
the front and down.

1st, 2nd
fourth

TOMBER PIED DESSUS
on the right leg, épaulement croisé,
the left foot sur le cou-de-pied back
(the body and head leaning slightly
forward).

Grand rond de jambe jeté en dedans, ending tomber pied dessus

Nina Sorokina

3rd, 1st *fourth*	DEMI-PLIÉ on the left leg. RENVERSÉ EN DEHORS in attitude right leg, the left leg on pointe.	A - then the left arm comes up through the 1st position. Simultaneously the right arm opens to the side: 5th arm position.
2nd, 3rd *1st, 2nd* *fourth*	PAS DE BOURRÉE EN TOURNANT EN DEHORS (stepping to the back twice). On the third step over, hold the right leg in demi-plié, the left leg bends back.	2nd - 6th (the right arm is bent).
3rd fourth	DEMI-PLIÉ on the left leg, simultaneously the right leg stretches to the front diagonally to corner No. 2 (raised at 45°).	As above.
1st, 2nd, *3rd fourth*	TOUR PIQUÉ EN DEDANS EN ATTITUDE EFFACÉE (the turn is on the right leg), ending with the following movement.	The right arm opens during the course of the movement, the left arm comes up: 5th position of arms.
1st, 2nd *fourth*	TOMBÉ on the left leg front, croisé (lean the head slightly to the left).	The left arm lowers to the side (hands turned out).
5th eighth	DEMI-PLIÉ on the right leg, simultaneously DÉGAGÉ left leg front, at 45°, croisé (the body and head slightly leaning forward).	A - 1st, with a slight stroke of hands forward and upward.
8 bars	Repeat the exercise on the other leg (starting with the movement grand rond de jambe jeté en dedans, etc.).	
16 bars	Repeat the whole combination.	

Total accompaniment
32 bars

19. FOURTH EXERCISE ON POINTES

Preparation

Starting position of the feet: 4th position, croisé, the right leg stretched front, pointe tendue.

Starting position of arms: 6th position (the right arm is bent).

Begin from corner No. 6
(traveling diagonally forward to corner No. 2).

Off-beat *(4th) eighth*	DEMI-PLIÉ on the left leg, simultaneously the right leg (with a passing movement) rises up slightly and moves to corner No. 2.	6th (right arm bent), the right arm opens during the course of the movement, then both arms meet between A and 1st position.
1st, 2nd, 3rd eighth	TOUR PIQUÉ EN DEDANS (during the turn on the right leg, left leg sur le cou-de-pied back, end on demi-plié of the left leg, right foot sur le cou-de-pied front). Follow with	
4th eighth	DÉGAGÉ with the right leg 45° front diagonally to corner No. 2.	The arms open to the side through 1st position, then meet
1st, 2nd, 3rd eighth	TOUR PIQUÉ EN DEDANS	between A and 1st position.
4th eighth	DÉGAGÉ with the right leg.	As above.
1st, 2nd, 3rd eighth	TOUR PIQUÉ EN DEDANS	
4th eighth	DÉGAGÉ with the right leg.	As above.
1st, 2nd, 3rd eighth	TOUR PIQUÉ EN DEDANS	
4th, 1st 2nd, 3rd eighth	STEP - COUPÉ right foot to the side. ASSEMBLÉ SOUTENU EN TOURNANT EN DEDANS with the left leg. Follow with	As above.

4th, 1st, *2nd, 3rd* *eighth*	STEP - COUPÉ right foot to the side. ASSEMBLÉ SOUTENU EN TOURNANT EN DEDANS with the left leg.	As above.
4th, 1st, *2nd, 3rd* *eighth*	STEP - COUPÉ with the right foot to the side. ASSEMBLÉ SOUTENU EN TOURNANT EN DEDANS with the left leg.	As above.
4th, 1st, *2nd, 3rd* *eighth*	STEP - COUPÉ with the right foot to the side. ASSEMBLÉ SOUTENU EN TOURNANT EN DEDANS with the left leg.	As above.

8 bars	Repeat the exercise once more (continuing to travel forward diagonally to corner No. 2) with the following change at the end of the combination. After the third assemblé soutenu en tournant en dedans make a step tombé with the right leg diagonally (to corner No. 2), then relevé on pointe, in 1st arabesque, effacé.

Total accompaniment
16 bars

(*Pause*)
Repeat the exercise on the other leg
(starting from corner No. 4, traveling
diagonally forward to corner No. 8).

Tour piqué en dedans (position of the leg in retiré back, supporting leg on pointe)

Rimma Karelskaya

Measure 2/4
Tempo lively
Introduction
(2 bars)

20. FIFTH EXERCISE ON POINTES

Preparation
Starting position of the feet: 5th
position, en face, right foot front.

Starting position of
arms - 2nd position.

Off-beat
2nd, 3rd,
4th eighth,
15 bars,
1st eighth

DEMI-PLIÉ
in 5th position.

TOUR EN DEHORS.
Execute 16 times consecutively. After
each turn, the right leg steps in 5th
position front (demi-plié in 5th
position, excluding the last tour, when
the leg steps in 5th position back)
(demi-plié in 5th position) and
follows a relevé in 5th position.

6th (right arm is
bent).

The right arm opens
during the course of
the movement, both
hands meet between
A and 1st, then open
to the side going
through the 1st
position and meet
between A and 1st,
etc. End in the 1st
arm position (wide).

Total accompaniment
16 bars

(Pause)
Repeat the exercise once more.

(Pause)
Repeat the combined exercise on the
other leg.

Tour en dehors

Measure 3/4
Tempo lively
Introduction
(2 bars)

21. SIXTH EXERCISE ON POINTES

Preparation
Starting position of the feet: 5th   Starting position
position croisé, right foot front.   arms: A.

Begin from corner No. 6.

Off-beat
(2nd, 3rd)
fourth

DEMI-PLIÉ   A
in 5th position.

4 bars

PAS SUIVI   The right arm
travel forward diagonally to corner   comes up through
No. 2 (the head leans slightly forward,   the 1st position,
look to the right, under the arm):   simultaneously the
when completing pas suivi, make a   left arm moves to the
quarter turn to the left, continuing   side: 5th arm
with the following movement.   position.

2 bars

PAS COURU   The arms move down
travel backward to corner No. 2 in the   and go through to
course of the movement (the body is   the back (hands
leaning slightly forward, the head is   lowered).
turned to the right); when completing
pas couru, make a half turn to the
right, continuing with the following
movement.

Rimma Karelskaya

2 bars	PAS COURU travel forward diagonally to corner No. 2 facing in the course of the movement (the body straightened out, the head slightly raised).	The arms move up front until they reach the 1st position (palms turned down).
4 bars	PAS SUIVI EN TOURNANT EN DEHORS (right leg front) three turning steps to the right (the body and head slightly leaning to the right, looking over the right shoulder and down).	6th (right arm bent).
1 bar	STEP - PIQUÉ SUR LA POINTE with the right leg forward to corner No. 2. Lift the left leg back 45° in effacé, stand in this pose.	1st arabesque (right arm front) then remaining in the same position.
1 bar	BRING the left leg (through 1st position) front, in croisé, and come down in 4th position demi-plié.	3rd arabesque (right arm front).
1 bar *1st fourth*	PIROUETTES EN DEHORS (end in 4th position, croisé, right foot back, the left leg front in plié à quart).	The right arm opens during the course of the movement, the arms move into the 3rd position, ending in 2nd position (hands turned out).

Total accompaniment
16 bars

(*Pause*)
Repeat the exercise on the other leg
(starting from corner No. 4, traveling
forward diagonally to corner No. 8).

Measure 2/4
Tempo lively
Introduction
(1 bar)

22.   SEVENTH EXERCISE ON POINTES

Preparation
Starting position of the feet: Starting position of
5th position, en face, right foot front.   arms: A.

Off-beat
(4th)
eighth,
7 bars,
1st, 2nd, 3rd
eighth

16 PETITS CHANGEMENTS DE   A - 1st - 3rd - 2nd -
PIEDS SUR LES POINTES   A

Total accompaniment
8 bars

Measure 3/4
(Waltz)
Tempo slow
Introduction
(2 bars)

23.   PORT DE BRAS AND BENDING
OF THE BODY

Preparation
Starting position of the feet: Starting position of
1st position (halfway turned out).   arms: 2nd position.

This combination corresponds to
exercise 15 (in the center of the room).
See page 108.

Total accompaniment
32 bars

PHOTO BY JENNIE WALTON

Second Class

EXERCISES AT THE BARRE

Musical-rhythmical accompaniment	DANCING EXERCISES

Measure 3/4 (Waltz) Tempo slow Introduction (2 bars)

1. GRANDS PLIÉS

Preparation
Starting position of the feet: ·
1st position.

Starting position of the right arm: 2nd position.

This exercise corresponds to exercise 1 (at the barre) of the first class (see page 55).

Total accompaniment 32 bars

Measure 2/4
Tempo
moderate
Introduction
(1 bar)

2.   BATTEMENTS TENDUS

Preparation
Starting position of the feet: 5th
position, right foot front.

Starting position of
the right arm: 2nd
position.

Off-beat	BATTEMENT TENDU	2nd position.

Off-beat
(4th),
1st eighth

BATTEMENT TENDU
front, right foot front.

2nd position.

2nd, 3rd
eighth

BATTEMENT TENDU
to the side (change), right foot.

4th eighth

DÉGAGÉ
to the back, with the right foot,
pointe tendue.

1st, 2nd
eighth

BRING
the right leg (through 1st position)
front, pointe tendue, in demi-plié of
the left leg.

3rd eighth

Place the right foot in 5th position,
simultaneously stretch from demi-
plié.

4th, 1st
eighth

BATTEMENT TENDU
to the side (change) with the right
foot.

2nd, 3rd
eighth

BATTEMENT TENDU
to the side (change) with the right
foot.

BATTEMENT TENDU
to the side, with a demi-plié in 2nd
position, right foot
   Breakdown of the movement:

4th eighth

Dégagé with the right foot to the
side (pointe tendue).

2nd

1st eighth

Come down in demi-plié in 2nd
position.

2nd - 1st

2nd eighth

Come up from demi-plié,
simultaneously stretch out the right
leg to pointe tendue.

1st - 2nd

3rd eighth	Bring the leg to 5th position back.	2nd
4 bars	Repeat the exercise in the reverse direction.	
8 bars	Repeat the whole combination once more.	

Total accompaniment
16 bars

Turn to the other side and repeat the exercise on the other leg.

3. BATTEMENTS TENDUS JETÉS

Measure 2/4 *Tempo lively* *Introduction* *(1 bar)*	Preparation Starting position of the feet: 5th position, right foot front.	Starting position of arms: 2nd position.
Off-beat *(4th),* *1st eighth*	BATTEMENT TENDU JETÉ to the front, right foot.	2nd position.
2nd, 3rd *eighth*	BATTEMENT TENDU JETÉ to the side (change), right foot.	2nd position.
4th, 1st, 2nd, *3rd eighth*	BATTEMENT TENDU JETÉ to the back, right foot.	2nd position.
	BATTEMENT TENDU JETÉ to the side (change), right foot.	
	BATTEMENT TENDU JETÉ to the side (change), right foot.	
2 bars	Repeat the exercise in the reverse direction.	
4 bars	Repeat the whole combination once more.	

Total accompaniment
8 bars

Turn to the other side and repeat the exercise on the other leg.

Measure 3/4
Tempo
moderate   **4. RONDS DE JAMBE À TERRE**
Introduction
(2 bars)   Preparation
                    Starting position of the feet[1]

                                                    Starting position of
                                                    arms: 2nd position.

8 bars   8 RONDS DE JAMBE À TERRE EN   2nd
                    DEHORS
                    right leg.

1 bar   1 ROND DE JAMBE À TERRE IN   A - 1st - 2nd
                    DEMI-PLIÉ

1 bar   1 ROND DE JAMBE À TERRE   2nd

1 bar   1 ROND DE JAMBE À TERRE IN   A - 1st - 2nd
                    DEMI-PLIÉ

1 bar   1 ROND DE JAMBE À TERRE   2nd

3 bars   3 GRANDS RONDS DE JAMBE JETÉS

1 bar   BRING
                    the right leg (through 1st position)
                    front, pointe tendue.

16 bars   Repeat this combination to the reverse
                    side en dedans (with the following
                    change at the end of the combination:
                    end the last grand rond de jambe
                    jeté en dedans in 5th position front).

                    Immediately follows:

Tempo slow   PORT DE BRAS ET BATTEMENTS
32 bars   RELEVÉS LENTS (90°)
                    (This exercise corresponds to the
                    second part of exercise 5, exercises
                    at the barre, of the first class. See
                    page 62.)

Total accompaniment
64 bars
                    Turn to the other side and repeat
                    the exercise on the other leg.

---

[1] Ronds de jambe à terre is executed immediately after preparation, continuing the movement of the preparatory rond.

Measure 2/4	**5. BATTEMENTS FONDUS**	
Tempo slow		
Introduction		
(2 bars)	Preparation	
	Starting position of the feet:	Starting position of
	2nd position, right foot pointe tendue.	the right arm: 2nd
		position.

Off-beat	BATTEMENT FONDU	2nd - A - 1st - 2nd
(4th),	to the front (45°), right leg.	
1st, 2nd, 3rd		
eighth		
4th, 1st	DEMI-PLIÉ	2nd
eighth	on the left leg.	
2nd, 3rd	MOVE[1]	
eighth	the right leg to the side (45°),	
	simultaneously stretch out from the	
	demi-plié of the left leg.	
4th, 1st	DEMI-PLIÉ	
eighth	on the left leg	
2nd, 3rd	BRING[1]	
eighth	the right leg back (45°).	
	Simultaneously stretch out from the	
	demi-plié of the left leg.	
4th, 1st, 2nd,	BATTEMENT FONDU	2nd - A - 1st - 2nd
3rd eighth	to the side, with the right leg.	

4 bars	Repeat the exercise in the reverse
	direction.
8 bars	Repeat the whole combination once
	more (on half toe).

Total accompaniment
16 bars

Turn to the other side and repeat the
exercise on the other leg.

[1] Demi-rond de jambe en dehors (45°).

Measure 2/4
Tempo
moderate
Introduction
(1 bar)

6.   BATTEMENTS FRAPPÉS ET RONDS DE JAMBE EN L'AIR

Preparation

Starting position of the feet: 2nd position, right foot pointe tendue.	Starting position of the right arm: 2nd position.

Off-beat (4th), 1st, 2nd, 3rd eighth	3 BATTEMENTS FRAPPÉS to the front (45°) with the right foot.	2nd position.
4th, 1st, 2nd, 3rd eighth	3 BATTEMENTS FRAPPÉS to the side (45°), (change) with the right foot.	
4th, 1st, 2nd, 3rd eighth	2 RONDS DE JAMBE EN L'AIR (45°) EN DEHORS with the right leg (each rond ends in demi-plié).	
4th, 1st, 2nd, 3rd eighth	1 ROND DE JAMBE EN L'AIR (45°) EN DEHORS with the right leg (without demi-plié).	
	2 RONDS DE JAMBE EN L'AIR (45°) EN DEHORS with the right leg.	

4 bars	Repeat the exercise in the reverse direction.
8 bars	Repeat the whole combination once more on half toe.

Total accompaniment
16 bars

Turn to the other side and repeat the exercise on the other leg.

Measure 3/4
(Waltz)
Tempo slow   **7.   ADAGIO**
Introduction
(2 bars)   Preparation
                   Starting position of the feet: 5th   Starting position of
                   position, right foot front.   the right arm: 2nd
                                                              position.

3 bars	DÉVELOPPÉ with the right leg front.	A - 1st - 2nd
1 bar	PASSER LA JAMBE $(90°)$ right leg.	A
3 bars	DÉVELOPPÉ with the right leg back.	A - 1st - 2nd arabesque arm position.
1 bar	PASSER LA JAMBE $(90°)$ right leg.	A
2 bars	DÉVELOPPÉ with the right leg à la seconde $(90°)$.	A - 1st - 2nd
2 bars	BRING the right leg to the front $(90°)$ in demi-plié of the left leg.	2nd - 1st
3 bars	GRAND ROND DE JAMBE EN DEHORS with the right leg, simultaneously stretch out from the demi-plié of the left leg.	1st - 2nd, then the right arm comes down and stretches to the front: 2nd arabesque arm position.
1 bar	Lower the right leg in 5th position back.	A
16 bars	Repeat the exercise in the reverse direction.	

Total accompaniment
32 bars

Turn to the other side and repeat
the exercise on the other leg.

Measure 2/4
Tempo
moderate   ## 8.   BATTEMENTS DOUBLES FRAPPÉS
Introduction
(1 bar)   Preparation
                   Starting position of the feet: 2nd   Starting position of
                   position, right foot pointe tendue.   the right arm: 2nd
                                                                position.

Off-beat
(4th)   4 BATTEMENTS DOUBLES FRAPPÉS   2nd position.
eighth,   ending front, back, front, back with
1 bar,   the right foot, pointe tendue.
1st, 2nd, 3rd
eighth

4th eighth,   4 BATTEMENTS DOUBLES FRAPPÉS
1 bar,   ending to the side (change), with the
1st, 2nd, 3rd   right foot, pointe tendue.
eighth

4 bars   Repeat the exercise in the reverse
                   direction.

8 bars   Repeat the whole combination once
                   more on half toe.

Total accompaniment
16 bars

                   Turn to the other side and repeat the
                   exercise on the other leg.

Measure 2/4
Tempo fast
Introduction
(2 bars)

9. PETITS BATTEMENTS SUR LE COU-DE-PIED

Preparation

Starting position of the feet: right
foot sur le cou-de-pied front (wrapping
the ankle).

Starting position of
the right arm: A.

Off-beat
(4th),
1st, 2nd, 3rd,
4th, 1st
eighth

3 PETITS BATTEMENTS
(accent front) right foot.

Arms - A

2nd, 3rd
eighth

Stand (pause).

4th, 1st, 2nd,
3rd, 4th, 1st
eighth

3 PETITS BATTEMENTS
accent back, right foot.

2nd, 3rd
eighth

Stand (pause).

---

4 bars

Repeat the exercise once more.

8 bars

Repeat the combination once more
on half toe.

16 bars

Then balance on half toe of the left
foot in varied poses. Read the
description in the second part of
exercise 11 (exercises at the barre) of
the first class, see page 71.

Total accompaniment
32 bars

Turn to the other side and repeat the
exercise on the other leg.

Measure 2/4
Tempo
moderate
Introduction
(*1 bar*)

10.   GRANDS BATTEMENTS JETÉS

Preparation
Starting position of the feet: 5th
position, right foot front.

Starting position of
the right arm: 2nd
position.

Off-beat
(*4th*),
1st eighth

GRAND BATTEMENT JETÉ
front, right leg.

2nd position.

2nd, 3rd
eighth

GRAND BATTEMENT JETÉ
to the side, (change) right leg.

GRANDS BATTEMENTS JETÉ
BALANÇOIRE
right leg.
   Breakdown of the movement:

4th eighth   Kick backward,
1st eighth   kick front through the 1st position.
2nd, 3rd   Swift développé back, through
eighth   passer la jambe (90°).
4th, 1st   Kick front through 1st position.
eighth
2nd, 3rd   Bring the leg down in 5th position
eighth   front.

4th eighth   GRAND BATTEMENT JETÉ
                 to the side, kick to the front, with the
                 right leg, then
1st eighth   bend the leg in retiré front (90°).
2nd eighth   Swift développé to the side with the
                 right leg.
3rd eighth   Bring down the leg in 5th position
                 back.

2nd position.

4 bars   Repeat the exercise to the reverse side.

8 bars   Repeat the whole combination once
                 more.

Total accompaniment
16 bars

Turn to the other side and repeat the
exercise on the other leg.

Measure 3/4
(Waltz)
Tempo slow
Introduction
(2 bars)

11. PORT DE BRAS AND BENDING OF THE BODY

Preparation
Starting position of the feet: 1st position, facing the barre.

Starting position of the arms: both hands on the barre.

This exercise corresponds to exercise 13 (exercises at the barre) of the first class (see page 75).

Total accompaniment
32 bars

Measure 3/4
(Waltz)
Tempo slow
Introduction
(2 bars)

11a. STRETCHING OF THE LEGS AND BENDING OF THE BODY

Preparation
Starting position of the feet: the right leg is raised in front (lying on the barre with the heel turned outward).

Starting position of arms: the right arm in 3rd position, the left arm on the barre.

STRETCHING FORWARD
Breakdown of the movement:

2 bars	The right leg slides forward on the barre (heel turned outward), simultaneously the body leans forward to the right leg.	The right arm lowers in front, with the palm of the hand turning down.
2 bars	The body returns to the starting position, simultaneously the right leg pulls back.	The right arm goes up in 3rd position.
2 bars *1 bar*	The body bends backward, the body returns to the starting position.	The right arm in 3rd position.

PREPARATION
Breakdown of the movement:

1 bar Without taking the right leg off from the barre, rise on half toe of the left foot and turn to the left, simultaneously the right leg turns in, lying on the inside of the heel, come down from half toe.

Place the right arm on the barre, bring the left arm forward.

STRETCHING BACKWARD
Breakdown of the movement:

2 bars The body leans forward, simultaneously the right leg slides backward on the barre.

The left arm comes down.

2 bars The body returns to the starting position, simultaneously the right leg pulls in.

The left arm lifts in 3rd position.

2 bars The body bends backward.

The left arm in 3rd position.

1 bar The body returns to the starting position.

PREPARATION
Breakdown of the movement:

1 bar Without taking the right leg off the barre, rise on half toe of the left foot and turn to the right, simultaneously the right leg turns out lying on the outside heel.

Place the left arm on the barre, raise the right arm in 3rd position.

16 bars Repeat the exercise once more (on half toe).
End the stretching on half toe in arabesque, lift the right leg above the barre, and hold it, then lower it in 5th position back.

Arm position 4th arabesque (left arm in front), then A.

Total accompaniment
32 bars

(Pause)
Repeat the exercise on the other leg.

Initial position for stretching the legs

Stretching the legs in front (the body bends forward)
Elena Tcherkaskaya

Stretching the legs in front (the body bends backward)

Stretching the legs to the back

Elena Tcherkaskaya

Measure 2/4
Tempo lively
Introduction
(1 bar)

12. RELEVÉS

Preparation
Starting position of the feet: 1st position facing the barre.

Starting position of the arms: both arms on the barre.

The given exercise corresponds to exercise 14 (exercises at the barre) of the first class (see page 78).

Total accompaniment
16 bars

Temps lié to the front and to the side

Ekaterina Maximova

EXERCISES IN THE CENTER

Measure 3/4
(Waltz)
Tempo slow
Introduction
(2 bars)

1. SMALL ADAGIO

Preparation
Starting position of the feet: 5th
position, croisé, right foot front.

Starting position of
arms: A.

TEMPS LIÉ
forward and backward.
Breakdown of the movement:

Off-beat
(3rd)
fourth
1 bar

Demi-plié in 5th position, glide the
right leg to the front (pointe tendue on
the floor) to croisé and through demi-
plié in 4th position (passing
movement) step on the right leg,
simultaneously stretch the left leg back,
pointe tendue.

A - 1st
5th (left arm up).

1 bar

Carry the body onto the left leg
through demi-plié in 4th position
(passing movement) stretch from
demi-plié, simultaneously bring the
right leg to the front, pointe
tendue, position under the arm.

5th (right arm up).

2 bars

ROND DE JAMBE À TERRE EN
DEHORS
with the right leg, in demi-plié of
the left leg, end the movement in
effacé back.

The right arm opens
to the side, lowers
and rises forward, the
left arm to the side
(palms down).

1 bar,
1st, 2nd
fourth

LIFT
stretched out right leg back on effacé
(90°)
simultaneously come up from demi-
plié of the left leg.

Arm position: 2nd
arabesque.

3rd fourth	**DEMI-PLIÉ** on the left leg.	5th (right arm up).
2 bars	**MOVE BACK** onto the right leg. **LIFT** the left leg stretched out in the front in effacé (90°).	
1 bar, *1st, 2nd* *fourth*	**LOWER** the left leg and through the 1st position. **LIFT** the left leg back (90°) in croisé, 3rd arabesque position.	The left arm comes down, rises to the front, simultaneously the right arm lowers to the side: position 3rd arabesque.
3rd fourth *2 bars*	**DEMI-PLIÉ** on the right leg. **MOVE BACK** onto the left leg. **LIFT** the right leg stretched out in the front, in croisé (90°).	5th (left arm up).
3 bars	**GRAND ROND DE JAMBE EN** **DEHORS** with the right leg, end back in croisé, 3rd arabesque (facing corner No. 2).	The left arm lowers to the side, then the right arm comes down, rises to the front, arm position 3rd arabesque.
1st, 2nd *fourth*	Lower the right leg in 5th position back.	A

16 bars	Repeat the exercise on the other leg.

Total accompaniment
32 bars

(*Pause*)
Repeat the exercise in the reverse
direction.

Measure 2/4
Tempo
moderate
Introduction
(1 bar)

2. BATTEMENTS TENDUS

Preparation
Starting position of the feet: 5th
position croisé, right foot front.

Starting position of
arms: 2nd position.

Off-beat *(4th),* *1st, 2nd, 3rd* *eighth*	2 BATTEMENTS TENDUS front, croisé, with the right foot.	6th (right arm bent).
4th, 1st, *2nd, 3rd* *eighth*	2 BATTEMENTS TENDUS front, effacé, with the right foot.	6th (left arm bent).
4th, 1st, *2nd, 3rd* *eighth*	2 BATTEMENTS TENDUS to the side (change), with the right foot.	2nd
4th, 1st, *2nd, 3rd* *eighth*	1 BATTEMENT TENDU to the side (change) with demi-plié in 5th position, with the right foot (then come up from demi-plié).	2nd
4th eighth, *1 bar,* *1st, 2nd, 3rd* *eighth*	7 BATTEMENTS TENDUS JETÉS to the side (change), with the right foot.	2nd

CONCLUDING EXERCISES FOR THE MEN'S CLASS:

4th eighth *1 bar*	PRÉPARATION POUR PIROUETTES EN DEHORS with the right leg (in 2nd position).	2nd - 6th (right arm bent).
1st, 2nd, 3rd *eighth*	PIROUETTES EN DEHORS (end in 4th position, croisé, right foot back, left leg in front in plié à quart).	The right arm opens during the course of the movement, then both arms meet between A and 1st, end in 2nd position.

CONCLUDING EXERCISE FOR THE WOMEN'S CLASS:

4th eighth, *1 bar* *1st, 2nd, 3rd* *eighth*	PRÉPARATION POUR PIROUETTES EN DEHORS with the right foot (in 4th position, croisé).	A - 1st - 3rd arabesque (right arm front).
	PIROUETTES EN DEHORS (end in 4th position croisé, right foot back, left leg in front in plié à quart).	The right arm opens during the course of the movement, then both arms meet between A and 1st, end in 2nd position.

---

8 bars	Repeat the exercise on the other leg.

Total accompaniment
16 bars

(*Pause*)
Repeat the exercise in the reverse
direction (the pirouettes remain en
dehors).

Measure 3/4
Tempo slow
Introduction
(*2 bars*)

3.   BATTEMENTS FONDUS

Preparation Starting position of feet: 5th position croisé, right foot front.	Starting position of arms: 2nd position.

Off-beat (*3rd*) *fourth* *1 bar*	BATTEMENT FONDU front (45°), effacé, right leg on half toe of the left foot.	2nd - A, then (through 1st position) the right arm moves to the front, the left arm moves simultaneously to the side (hands turned out).

FOUETTÉ EN TOURNANT EN DEDANS

Breakdown of the movement:

1 bar Tombé with the right leg forward in effacé. Simultaneously kick the left leg front (45°) in croisé, then the left leg ends the turn fouetté back (45°) in croisé, the right foot rises simultaneously on half toe.

1st position, end in 3rd arabesque (left arm raised in front).

BATTEMENT FONDU TOMBÉ
right leg.

Breakdown of the movement:

1 bar Tombé with the left leg back, simultaneously bend the right leg sur le cou-de-pied front, then stretch the right leg to the side (45°) on half toe of the left foot.

A

A - 1st, 2nd

BATTEMENT FONDU

1 bar with the right leg back (45°) in effacé on half toe of the left foot.

A - 1st - 6th (right arm bent).

FOUETTÉ EN TOURNANT EN DEHORS

Breakdown of the movement:

1 bar Tombé with the right leg backward, in effacé, simultaneously kick the left leg back (45°) in croisé, then the left leg ends the turn fouetté front (45°) in croisé, the right foot rises simultaneously on half toe.

3rd arabesque arm position (the left arm is stretched forward), then through 1st position to 6th position of arms (left arm bent).

BATTEMENT FONDU TOMBÉ
right leg.

Breakdown of the movement:

1 bar Tombé on the left leg front, simultaneously bend the right leg sur le cou-de-pied back, stretch the right leg to the side (45°) à la seconde, on half toe of the left foot.

A

A - 1st - 2nd

PAS DE BOURRÉE EN DEDANS

Breakdown of the movement:

1st, 2nd
fourth Demi-plié on the left leg, bend the right leg front, then step on it on half toe.

A

Bend the left leg sur le cou-de-pied back, then

3rd, 1st, 2nd fourth	STEP OVER with the left foot to the side, step on half toe, bend the right leg sur le cou-de-pied back, then bring back in croisé and come down on it in demi-plié, stretch the left leg front, croisé, on pointe tendue.	1st - 6th (left arm bent).
3rd fourth	PRÉPARATION TEMPS RELEVÉ EN DEHORS left leg.	3rd
1st, 2nd, 3rd fourth	PIROUETTES EN DEHORS (during the turn on the right leg, the left foot is sur le cou-de-pied back), then	
1st fourth	DEMI-PLIÉ on the right leg, following with	
2nd, 3rd fourth	BATTEMENT FONDU with the left leg back (45°) in effacé, on the half toe of the right foot.	3rd - 5th (left arm up).
1st fourth	TOMBÉ with the left leg back, in effacé.	The left arm moves to the side (hands turned out).
2nd, 3rd fourth *1st, 2nd fourth*	PAS DE BOURRÉE EN DEDANS stepping over twice, end in 4th position, croisé, right foot back, left leg front in plié à quart.	A - 1st 6th (left arm bent).
3rd fourth	DÉGAGÉ with the right leg to the side (45°) on demi-plié of the left leg.	The left arm opens during the course of the movement.
1st, 2nd, 3rd, 1st fourth	PIROUETTES EN DEDANS (after the turn end in demi-plié of the left leg, right foot sur le cou-de-pied front) follow with	3rd
2nd, 3rd fourth	BATTEMENT FONDU with the right foot front (45°) in effacé, on half toe of the left foot. Then	The right arm opens front, simultaneously the left arm moves to the side (hand turned out).

1st fourth	TOMBÉ right leg front, in effacé.	
2nd, 3rd, *1st, 2nd* *fourth*	PAS DE BOURÉE EN DEHORS (changing feet), end in 5th position, left foot front, épaulement croisé.	2nd - hands turn in and the arms come down, ending in position of arms - A.

---

16 bars	Repeat the exercise on the other leg.

Total accompaniment
32 bars

(*Pause*)
Repeat the exercise once more.

Measure 2/4
Tempo
moderate
Introduction
(*1 bar*)

4. BATTEMENTS FRAPPÉS ET RONDS DE JAMBE EN L'AIR

	Preparation Starting position of the feet: 2nd position, right foot pointe tendue.	Starting position of arms: 2nd position.

Off-beat (*4th*) *eighth* *1 bar,* *1st, 2nd, 3rd* *eighth*	7 BATTEMENTS FRAPPÉS to the side (change), with the right foot pointe tendue.	2nd
4th eighth *1 bar,* *1st, 2nd, 3rd* *eighth* *4th eighth*	LIFT the right leg (45°) following with 7 RONDS DE JAMBE EN L'AIR (45°) EN DEHORS with the right leg, end the last rond on demi-plié of the left leg, then bend the right leg sur le cou-de-pied back.	A

1 bar	PAS DE BOURRÉE EN DEHORS (stepping to the side twice), simultaneously demi-plié on the left leg.	A
	DÉGAGÉ with the left leg to the side (45°).	A - hands turned out to the side.
1st, 2nd eighth	SOUTENU EN TOURNANT EN DEDANS with the left foot, end in 5th position half toe, right foot front, épaulement croisé.	A - 1st
	PRÉPARATION POUR CHAÎNÉS-DÉBOULÉS *Breakdown of the movement:*	
3rd eighth	Step to the side with the left foot (to the direction of corner No. 6), bring the right foot front, in croisé, pointe tendue.	6th (right arm bent).
4th eighth, 1 bar, 1st, 2nd, 3rd eighth	CHAÎNÉS-DÉBOULÉS diagonally front (corner No. 2), end in effacé (left foot pointe tendue back).	The right arm opens during the course of the movement, then the arms meet between A and 1st. End in position "two arms in front" (the right arm higher than the left).

8 bars	Repeat the exercise on the other leg.

Total accompaniment
16 bars

(*Pause*)
Repeat the exercise in the reverse direction (chaînés-déboulés are done in the same direction: diagonally front).

Measure 3/4
(Waltz)
Tempo slow
Introduction
(2 bars)

5. GRAND ADAGIO

Preparation
Starting position of the feet: 5th
position, croisé, right foot front.

Starting position of
arms: A.

---

4 bars

GRAND PLIÉ
in 5th position.
Moving down
(the head turns gradually to the right
and leans slightly front, looking under
the arm).

A
Lift arms slowly to
the side, the right
arm follows the
movement upward,
the left arm
simultaneously moves
front, bent at the
elbow: 4th position
arms.

2 bars

Moving up.

The right arm comes
down in front: 1st,
subsequently the left
arm comes up: 4th
position arms.

2 bars

COME UP
on half toe in 5th position (turn the
head to the right), then come down
from half toe in 5th position.

4th (left arm up).

2 bars

DÉVELOPPÉ À LA SECONDE $(90°)$
with the right leg (en face).

Through 1st position.
The hands turn out
into the 2nd position.

2 bars

BRING
the right leg front $(90°)$, in croisé
(lean the head slightly front, looking
to the right under the arm).

4th (right arm up).

2 bars

GRAND ROND DE JAMBE EN
DEHORS
with the right leg, end in attitude
croisée (lean the head slightly to the
front, looking to the left under the
arm), then
DEMI-PLIÉ
on the left leg (in attitude).

The right arm moves
to the side and
follows the movement
front, the left arm
opens simultaneously
to the side and
follows the movement
up: 4th position arms.

Pose in attitude croisée, position "under the arm"

Elena Tcherkaskaya

2 bars	**PAS DE BOURRÉE EN TOURNANT EN DEHORS** (stepping under twice on half toe) with the passage follow into the movement.	A
	TEMPS LIÉ front, with the right foot, step in croisé left foot back pointe tendue.	1st - 5th (left arm up).
3 bars, *1st, 2nd* *fourth* *5th eighth* *6th eighth*	**GRAND PORT DE BRAS** leaning the body front and bending back, end in 4th position (wide), croisé (right foot front in plié à quart). **DEMI-PLIÉ**	1st - 5th (right arm up), then the right arm moves to the side in a circular movement, front, and ends in 6th position (right arm bent).

2 bars	TOURS EN DEDANS À LA SECONDE (90°) left leg, then (without lowering the leg) at the end of the turn go into	3rd
2 bars	FOUETTÉ EN TOURNANT EN DEDANS left leg, end back (90°) in croisé (lean the head slightly to the front, looking to the right under the arm).	4th (right arm up).
3 bars *1st, 2nd* *fourth* *5th eighth*	GRAND ROND DE JAMBE EN DEDANS (90°) with the left leg, end front (90°) in croisé (lean the head slightly to the front, looking to the left under the arm), lower the left leg in plié à quart in 4th position, in the preparatory position for tours en dehors.	Through 1st position, the arms move into the 2nd position, ending in 4th (left arm up). The left arm moves to the front and continues the movement to the side, the right arm stretched forward: arm position: 3rd arabesque.
6th eighth	DEMI-PLIÉ	
4 bars	TOURS EN DEHORS À LA SECONDE (90°) right leg, then (at the end of the turn)	3rd
	BRING the right leg back (90°) in croisé (come down from half toe on the left foot on a flat foot), end in 4th arabesque position.	2nd, then the left arm moves down and forward into 4th arabesque arm position.

Total accompaniment
32 bars

(*Pause*)
Repeat the exercise on the other leg.

Measure 2/4
Tempo
moderate
Introduction
(1 bar)

6. GRANDS BATTEMENTS JETÉS

Preparation
Starting position of the feet: 5th   Starting position of
position, croisé, right foot front.   arms: 2nd position.

Off-beat
(4th),
1st, 2nd, 3rd
eighth

2 GRANDS BATTEMENTS JETÉS   5th (left arm up).
front, with the right leg, croisé.

GRANDS BATTEMENTS JETÉS
BALANÇOIRE
with the right leg.
  Breakdown of the movement:

4th eighth   Kick the right leg front, in croisé   5th (left arm up).
1st eighth   through 1st position.   The left arm lowers
2nd eighth   Kick the right leg back in effacé.   to the side,
                                                               simultaneously the
                                                               right arm lowers and
                                                               continues the
                                                               movement forward.
                                                               Arm position: 2nd
3rd eighth   Lower the leg in 5th position back.   arabesque - A.

4th, 1st,   2 GRANDS BATTEMENTS JETÉS   Through 1st position
2nd, 3rd   front, with the left leg, in effacé   to 5th position (right
eighth   (lean the body slightly backward, turn   arm up).
                  the head slightly to the right).

GRANDS BATTEMENTS JETÉS
BALANÇOIRE
left leg.
  Breakdown of the movement:

4th eighth   Kick the left leg forward in effacé,   5th (right arm up).
1st eighth   through the 1st position (passing   The right arm moves
                  movement).   to the side,
2nd eighth   Throw the left leg backward, in   simultaneously the
                  croisé.   left arm lowers and
                                                                continues the
                                                                movement forward.
                                                                Arm position: 3rd
3rd eighth   Lower the leg in 5th position back.   arabesque - A.

4th, 1st *eighth*	GRAND BATTEMENT JETÉ to the side (change), with the right leg.	Through 1st position to 2nd position.
2nd, 3rd *eighth*	GRAND BATTEMENT JETÉ to the side (change), with the left leg, end in demi-plié in 5th position.	2nd - A

CONCLUDING EXERCISE FOR THE MEN'S CLASS:

4th, 1st, *2nd, 3rd* *4th eighth*	PRÉPARATION POUR PIROUETTES EN DEHORS right leg (in 2nd position).	A - 1st - 2nd - 6th (right arm bent).
1 bar, *1st, 2nd, 3rd* *eighth*	PIROUETTES EN DEHORS (end in 4th position, croisé, right foot back, the left leg in front in plié à quart).	The right arm opens during the course of the movement, then the arms meet between A and 1st, end in 1st position (wide) (hands turned out).

CONCLUDING EXERCISE FOR THE WOMEN'S CLASS:

4th, 1st, *2nd, 3rd, 4th* *eighth*	PRÉPARATION POUR PIROUETTES EN DEHORS right leg (in 4th position, croisé).	A - 1st - 3rd arabesque arm position (right arm in front).
1 bar, *1st, 2nd, 3rd* *eighth*	PIROUETTES EN DEHORS (end in 4th position, croisé, right foot back, the left leg in front in plié à quart).	The right arm opens during the course of the movement, then the arms meet between A and 1st, end in 1st position (wide) (hands turned out).

8 bars	Repeat the exercise on the other leg.

Total accompaniment
16 bars

(Pause)
Repeat the exercise in the reverse
direction (pirouettes remain en
dehors).

Measure 2/4
Tempo
moderate   **7. SMALL JUMPS**
Introduction
(1 bar)   Preparation
                     Starting position of the feet: Starting position of
                     5th position, croisé, left foot front.   arms: A.

Off-beat *(4th),* *1st eighth*	ASSEMBLÉ with the right leg to the side (change), changing épaulement croisé.	A
2nd, 3rd *eighth*	ASSEMBLÉ with the left leg to the side (change), changing épaulement croisé.	A
4th, 1st *eighth*	GLISSADE with the right leg to the side (No. 3) (do not change).	A (open hands slightly to the side and close in).
2nd, 3rd *eighth*	ASSEMBLÉ with the right leg to the side (change), changing épaulement croisé.	A
4th, 1st *eighth*	SISSONNE OUVERTE with the right leg to the side (45°). Then	1st - 2nd (hands turned out).
2nd eighth	LOWER the right leg (in the back of the left leg) in demi-plié, following with	2nd
3rd eighth	STEP - COUPÉ with the left foot to the side (No. 7).	6th (right arm bent), then A.
4th, 1st *eighth*	ASSEMBLÉ with the right leg forward, in croisé (through 1st position) (ending in 5th	
2nd, 3rd *eighth*	position demi-plié). Come up from demi-plié.	

4 bars	Repeat the exercise on the other leg.
8 bars	Repeat the whole combination once more.

Total accompaniment
16 bars   *(Pause)*
                     Repeat the exercise in the reverse
                     direction.

Measure 2/4
Tempo
moderate
Introduction
(2 bars)

8. SMALL JUMPS WITH BEATS

Preparation

Starting position of the feet: 5th position, croisé, right foot front.	Starting position of arms: A.

Off-beat (4th), 1st eighth	SISSONNE OUVERTE BATTUE with the left leg back (45°) in effacé.	A - 1st - 1st arabesque arm position (right arm in front).
2nd eighth	COUPÉ DESSUS with the left foot (traveling forward).	2nd allongée, and position A.
3rd eighth	ASSEMBLÉ BATTU with the right leg to the side, in écarté front (to corner No. 2), end with the right foot in 5th position front.	
4th, 1st eighth	SISSONNE OUVERTE BATTUE with the right leg back (45°), in croisé.	A - 1st - 3rd arabesque arm position (right arm in front).
2nd eighth	STEP - COUPÉ with the right foot front directing to corner No. 2.	6th (left arm bent), then A.
3rd eighth	ASSEMBLÉ with the left leg front, in croisé.	
4th, 1st eighth	SISSONNE OUVERTE BATTUE with the right leg to the side (45°) (lean the body slightly to the right, turn the head to the right).	Reach 2nd position through the 1st (hands turned out).
2nd eighth	COUPÉ DESSUS with the right foot.	2nd (the hands turn in), then hands come down: position A.
3rd eighth	ASSEMBLÉ BATTU with the left leg to the side, end in 5th position back, épaulement croisé.	
4th, 1st eighth	SISSONNE OUVERTE BATTUE with the left leg to the side (45°) (lean the body slightly to the right, turn the head to the right).	Reach 2nd position through the 1st (hands turned out).

2nd eighth	COUPÉ DESSUS with the left foot.	2nd (the hands turn in),
3rd eighth	ASSEMBLÉ BATTU with the right leg to the side, end in 5th position back, épaulement croisé.	then the hands come down: position A.

4 bars	Repeat the exercise on the other leg.
8 bars	Repeat the whole combination once more.

Total accompaniment
16 bars

Measure 2/4
Tempo
moderate
Introduction
(2 bars)

9. MEDIUM JUMPS

Preparation
Starting position of the feet: 5th   Starting position of
position, croisé, right foot front.   arms: A.

Start from corner No. 6.

Off-beat *(4th),* *1st eighth*	SISSONNE FERMÉE with the left leg back, in effacé, end with the left leg (sur le cou-de-pied back).	Through the 1st position reach 1st arabesque arm position (right arm in front), then A.
2nd, 3rd *eighth*	SISSONNE TOMBÉE with the left leg back, in effacé, continuing the movement with	Through the 1st position reach 5th (left arm up).
4th, 1st *eighth*	ASSEMBLÉ with the right leg front in effacé.	2nd, end in position A.
2nd, 3rd *eighth*	SISSONNE OUVERTE with the right leg back, in attitude croisée.	Through the 1st position reach 5th (right arm up).

4th, 1st *eighth*	SISSONNE TOMBÉE with the left leg front, in croisé.	The right arm lowers fluidly in front and continues the movement to the left, simultaneously the left arm as well moves fluidly slightly to the left (palms down). Then without stopping the arms move in the same fluid movement to the other side— right, the left arm opens to the front and side: 2nd position of arms.
2nd, 3rd, 4th *eighth*	CHASSÉ with the right leg front, in effacé.	
1st, 2nd, 3rd *eighth*	STEP - COUPÉ with the right foot to the side. ASSEMBLÉ with the left leg front, in croisé.	The right arm moves to the front (through A), left arm to the side (palms turned down make a slight stroke up), ending in position A.

4 bars	Repeat the exercise on the other leg.

Total accompaniment
8 bars

(*Pause*)
Repeat the exercise in the reverse direction.

Measure 3/4
(Waltz)
Tempo lively
Introduction
(2 bars)

10.   BIG JUMPS

Preparation
Starting position of the feet: 5th   Starting position of
position, croisé, right foot front.   arms: A.

Start from corner No. 6.

Off-beat
(2nd, 3rd)
fourth
1 bar,
1st, 2nd
fourth

GRANDE SISSONNE SOUBRESAUT
in attitude effacée-allongée of the left
leg to corner No. 2.

COUPÉ DESSUS
with the left foot (traveling forward
diagonally).

PETIT ASSEMBLÉ
with the right leg to the side, in
ecarté front to corner No. 2.

A - 1st - 5th allongée
(left arm up), hands
open to the front.

2nd allongée, end
position arms A.

3rd fourth
5 bars,
1st, 2nd
fourth

Repeat this combination three times
consecutively, traveling
diagonally front, to corner No. 2.

CONCLUDING EXERCISE FOR THE MEN'S CLASS:

3rd, 1st
fourth

SISSONNE TOMBÉE
with the left leg front, in effacé.

The left arm opens
to the front, through
1st position, the right
arm to the side
(hands turned out).

2nd, 3rd,
1st, 2nd
fourth

PAS DE BOURRÉE EN DEHORS
(changing feet).

2nd - end in 6th
(right arm bent).

3rd, 1st
fourth

PETIT ASSEMBLÉ
with the left leg back, in croisé.

2nd, 3rd,
1st, 2nd
fourth

DOUBLE TOUR EN L'AIR EN DEHORS
(end in 5th position, right foot back).

The right arm opens
in the course of the
movement, then the
arms meet between
A and 1st positions,
then 1st, 2nd, ending
in position A.

Grand sissonne soubresaut

Vladimir Nikonov

3rd, 1st *fourth*	SISSONNE TOMBÉE with the left leg in front, in effacé.	The left arm opens in the front through 1st position, the right arm to the side (hands turned out).
2nd, 3rd, *1st, 2nd* *fourth*	PAS DE BOURRÉE EN DEHORS (changing feet).	2nd, end
3rd, 1st *fourth*	PETIT ASSEMBLÉ with the left leg back, in croisé.	in the 6th position (right arm bent).
2nd, 3rd, *1st* *fourth*	DOUBLE TOUR EN L'AIR EN DEHORS position tire-bouchon (right foot back), end in 4th position effacé (wide), the left leg in front in demi- plié (the head turned to the right).	3rd, then 5th allongée (right arm up), palms facing front.

CONCLUDING EXERCISE FOR THE WOMEN'S CLASS:

3rd, 1st *fourth*	SISSONNE TOMBÉE with the left leg in front, in effacé.	The left arm opens to the front through the 1st position, the right arm to the side (hands turned out).
2nd, 3rd *fourth*	PAS DE BOURRÉE EN DEHORS (changing feet), stepping twice to the side.	2nd -
1st fourth	End in 4th position in croisé, right leg front in plié à quart.	6th (right arm bent).
2nd fourth	Stay in the preparatory position for pirouettes en dedans.	
3rd fourth	DÉGAGÉ with the left leg to the side (45°), the right leg lowers in demi-plié.	The right arm opens to the side.
1 bar, *1st, 2nd* *fourth*	PIROUETTES EN DEDANS (end in 5th position, left foot front).	4th (right arm up). End in arm position A.
3rd, 1st *fourth*	SISSONNE TOMBÉE with the left leg in front, in effacé.	The left arm opens to the front through 1st position, the right arm to the side (hands turned out).
2nd, 3rd *fourth*	PAS DE BOURRÉE EN DEHORS (changing feet) stepping twice to the side.	2nd -
1st fourth	End in 4th position croisé, right leg front in plié à quart.	6th (right arm bent).
2nd fourth	Stay in the preparatory position for pirouettes en dedans.	
3rd fourth	DÉGAGÉ with the left leg to the side (45°), the right leg lowers in demi-plié.	The right arm opens to the side.
1 bar	PIROUETTES EN DEDANS (end with a swift développé backward with the left leg.	4th (right arm up), then
1st fourth	Stop in arabesque on the right leg demi-plié facing corner No. 3).	the arms stretch forward (right higher than the left, palms down).

Total accompaniment
16 bars

(Pause)
Repeat the exercise once more.

(Pause)
Repeat the full combination on the other leg (starting from corner No. 4).

Measure 2/4
Tempo fast
Introduction
(2 bars)

11. SMALL JUMPS WITH BEATS

Preparation
Starting position of the feet: 5th position, croisé, left foot front.

Starting position of arms: A.

Off-beat *(4th)* *1st eighth*	JETÉ BATTU to the side, with the right leg, left foot ends sur le cou-de-pied back.	Position A.
2nd, 3rd *eighth*	JETÉ BATTU to the side, with the left leg, right foot ends sur le cou-de-pied back.	
4th, 1st *eighth*	JETÉ BATTU to the side, with the right leg, left foot ends sur le cou-de-pied back.	
2nd, 3rd *eighth*	BALLONNÉ BATTU to the side, with the left leg, end sur le cou-de-pied back.	A - end in 6th (right arm bent).

2 bars	Repeat the exercises on the other leg.
4 bars	Repeat the whole combination once more en tournant en dehors, with a quarter turn for each movement.

Total accompaniment
8 bars

(Pause)
Repeat the exercise in the reverse direction.

Chassé, jeté entrelacé, ending in 1st arabesque

Nina Sorokina

Measure 3/4
(Waltz)
Tempo lively
Introduction
(2 bars)

12. BIG JUMPS

Preparation

Starting position of the feet: 4th position, effacé, left foot back, pointe tendue.

Starting position of arms: 1st arabesque (right arm in front).

Start from corner No. 2.

Off-beat *2nd, 3rd* *fourth* *2 bars*	CHASSÉ with the left leg back, in effacé, turning halfway to the left.	1st arabesque arm position, then 2nd allongée.
	JETÉ ENTRELACÉ (end in 1st arabesque, effacé).	A - 1st - 3rd, end 1st arabesque arm position (right arm in front).
1 bar	Stand in 1st arabesque, rising on half toe, right foot.	
1 bar	CHASSÉ with the left leg back, in effacé turning halfway to the left.	1st arabesque arm position, then 2nd allongée.
2 bars	JETÉ ENTRELACÉ (end in 1st arabesque, effacé) and follow with	A - 1st - 3rd - 1st arabesque arm position (right arm in front).
2 bars	GLISSADE (do not change), with the left leg diagonally backward, to corner No. 6.	2nd allongée.
	STEP - PIQUÉ with the left foot (on half toe) to corner No. 6, lift the right leg back (at 45°). Stand in 2nd arabesque.	The right arm comes down, then rises and stretches to the front, the left arm to the side: 2nd arabesque arm position.

CONCLUDING EXERCISE FOR THE MEN'S CLASS:

2 bars

CHASSÉ
with the right leg back, turning
halfway to the right (end facing
corner No. 2).

2nd allongée, A - 1st -
3rd - 1st arabesque
arm position (left
arm in front).

REVOLTADE
(with half a turn to the left).
End in 1st arabesque (facing corner
No. 6).

2 bars

CHASSÉ
with the right leg back, turning
halfway to the right (end facing
corner No. 2).

A - 1st

SISSONNE TOMBÉE
with the right leg front, in effacé, the
left leg rises to the back (and from
this raised leg position), end with
following movement.

ASSEMBLÉ
with the left leg back in effacé.

The right arm opens
to the front,
simultaneously the
left arm moves to the
side (hands turned
out). Then (hands
turned in) the arms
come down.

1 bar

PRÉPARATION POUR PIROUETTES
EN DEHORS
with the right leg (in 2nd position).

A - 1st - 2nd - 6th
(right arm bent).

2 bars,
1st fourth

PIROUETTES EN DEHORS
(end in 4th position croisé, right leg
back, left leg front in plié à quart).

The right arm opens
during the course of
the movement, the
arms meet between
A and 1st: end in 1st
position (wide)
(hands slightly
turned out).

CONCLUDING EXERCISE FOR THE WOMEN'S CLASS:

2 bars	CHASSÉ with the right leg back, halfway turning to the right.	2nd arabesque arm position, then 2nd allongée.
	SAUT DE BASQUE with the right leg, diagonally front to corner No. 2.	A - 1st - 3rd
1 bar	CHASSÉ with the right leg front, in effacé.	The right arm comes down in front, simultaneously the left arm moves to the side (hands turned out).
1st, 2nd *fourth*	Step with the right foot front (to corner No. 2), end in demi-plié, lift the left leg back in effacé (90°).	
	Stand in 1st arabesque position, on demi-plié.	Then 1st arabesque arm position.
	PRÉPARATION POUR CHAÎNÉS-DÉBOULÉS *Breakdown of the movement:*	
5th eighth	Step with the left foot to the side (to corner No. 6), bring the right leg to the front, pointe tendue, in croisé.	6th (right arm bent).
6th eighth, *3 bars* *1st fourth*	CHAÎNÉS-DÉBOULÉS in diagonal front to corner No. 2. End in effacé position, the left leg stretched backward, pointe tendue.	The right arm opens during the course of the movement, then the arms join between A and 1st. End both arms forward, in position "right arm higher than the left."

Total accompaniment
16 bars

(*Pause*)
Repeat the exercise once more.

(*Pause*)
Repeat the whole combination on the other leg.

Measure 3/4
Tempo
moderate
Introduction
(2 bars)

13. BIG JUMPS
(FOR THE MEN'S CLASS)

Preparation
Starting position of feet: 5th position, en face, right foot front.

Starting position of arms: 2nd position.

Off-beat		
2nd, 3rd fourth	PRÉPARATION POUR TOUR EN L'AIR. Rise on half toe in 5th position.	2nd - 6th (right arm bent).
1st fourth	Come down in demi-plié.	
2nd, 3rd, 1st, 2nd fourth	DOUBLE TOUR EN L'AIR EN DEHORS (end in 5th position, right foot back).	The right arm opens in the course of the movement, then the arms meet between A and 1st, ending in 2nd position.
3rd fourth 1st fourth	PRÉPARATION POUR TOUR EN L'AIR. Rise on half toe in 5th position, come down in demi-plié.	2nd - 6th (left arm bent).
2nd, 3rd, 1st, 2nd fourth	DOUBLE TOUR EN L'AIR EN DEHORS. (End in 5th position, left foot back.)	The left arm opens in the course of the movement, then the arms meet between A and 1st, ending in 2nd position.
3rd fourth 8 bars	Repeat this combination consecutively 2 more times, then	
1 bar	PRÉPARATION POUR PIROUETTES EN DEHORS with the right leg (in 2nd position).	2nd - 6th (right arm bent).
2 bars 1st fourth	PIROUETTES EN DEHORS. (End in 4th position, croisé, right foot back, the left leg in front in plié à quart.)	The right arm opens in the course of the movement, then the arms meet between A and 1st, ending in 1st position (wide).

Total accompaniment
16 bars

Measure 2/4
Tempo slow
Introduction
(1 bar)

14. PETITS CHANGEMENTS DE PIEDS ET ENTRECHATS

Preparation
Starting position of the feet: 5th position, en face, right foot front.

Starting position of arms: A

Off-beat (4th), 1st, 2nd, 3rd eighth

3 PETITS CHANGEMENTS DE PIEDS.   Arm position A.

4th, 1st, 2nd, 3rd eighth

2 ENTRECHATS SIX.

4th, 1st, 2nd, 3rd eighth

3 PETITS CHANGEMENTS DE PIEDS.

4th, 1st, 2nd, 3rd eighth

2 ENTRECHATS SIX.

4 bars

Repeat the exercise once more.

Total accompaniment
8 bars

Measure 3/4
(Waltz)
Tempo slow
Introduction
(2 bars)

15. PORT DE BRAS AND BENDING OF THE BODY
(FOR THE MEN'S CLASS)

Preparation
Starting position of the feet: 1st position (turned out halfway).

Starting position of the arms: 2nd position.

This exercise corresponds to the exercise 15 (exercises in the center) of the first class (see page 108).

Total accompaniment
32 bars

Measure 2/4
Tempo lively   **16. FIRST EXERCISE ON POINTES**
Introduction
(1 bar)   Preparation
                           Starting position of the feet: 5th   Starting position of
                           position, en face, right foot front.   arms: A.

Off-beat   ÉCHAPPÉ   A
(4th) 1st,   in 2nd position with demi-plié in 2nd
2nd, 3rd,   position. (End in 5th position, right
4th, 1st, 2nd,   foot back.)
3rd
eighth

4th, 1st, 2nd,   ÉCHAPPÉ
3rd,   in 2nd position with demi-plié in
4th, 1st, 2nd,   2nd position (end in 5th position,
3rd   right foot front).
eighth

4th eighth,   4 ÉCHAPPÉS
3 bars,   in 2nd position (change).
1st, 2nd, 3rd
eighth

24 bars   Repeat the exercise 3 more times
                           consecutively.

Total accompaniment
32 bars

Measure 2/4 *Tempo lively* *Introduction* *(2 bars)*	**17. SECOND EXERCISE ON POINTES**

Preparation

Starting position of the feet: 4th position croisé, the left leg stretched back, pointe tendue.

Starting position of arms: 6th position (right arm bent).

Off-beat (4th) eighth

DEMI-PLIÉ
on the right leg (simultaneously bend the left foot back).

6th (right arm bent).

1st eighth

PIQUÉ SUR LA POINTE
with the left leg.
DÉGAGÉ
with the right leg front (45°), in effacé.

The right arm moves to the side, simultaneously the left arm bends in the front: 6th position arms.

2nd, 3rd eighth

DEMI-PLIÉ
on the left leg (traveling slightly forward diagonally to corner No. 2), simultaneously bend the right leg sur le cou-de-pied front.

6th (left arm bent).

4th, 1st eighth

RELEVÉ SUR LA POINTE
on the left leg (traveling slightly to corner No. 2). Simultaneously
DÉGAGÉ
with the right leg front (45°), in effacé.

2nd, 3rd eighth

DEMI-PLIÉ
on the left leg (traveling slightly to corner No. 2). Simultaneously bend the right leg sur le cou-de-pied front.

4th, 1st eighth

RELEVÉ SUR LA POINTE
on the left leg (traveling slightly to corner No. 2). Simultaneously
DÉGAGÉ
with the right leg front (45°), in effacé.

6th (left arm bent).

2nd, 3rd eighth

DEMI-PLIÉ
on the left leg (traveling slightly to corner No. 2). Simultaneously bend the right leg sur le cou-de-pied front.

4th, 1st *eighth*	RELEVÉ SUR LA POINTE on the left leg. Simultaneously DÉGAGÉ with the right leg à la seconde (45°).	2nd
2nd, 3rd *eighth*	DEMI-PLIÉ on the left leg, simultaneously bend the right leg sur le cou-de-pied back, épaulement effacé.	The right arm bends in front: 6th position.
4th, 1st *eighth*	RELEVÉ SUR LA POINTE on the left leg (traveling slightly backward diagonally to corner No. 4). Simultaneously DÉGAGÉ with the right leg back (45°), in effacé.	6th (left arm bent).
2nd, 3rd *eighth*	DEMI-PLIÉ on the left leg (traveling slightly to corner No. 4). Simultaneously bend the right leg sur le cou-de-pied back.	
4th, 1st *eighth*	RELEVÉ SUR LA POINTE on the left leg (traveling slightly to corner No. 4). Simultaneously DÉGAGÉ with the right leg back (45°), in effacé.	6th (left arm bent).
2nd, 3rd *eighth*	DEMI-PLIÉ on the left leg (traveling slightly to corner No. 4). Simultaneously bend the right leg sur le cou-de-pied back.	
4th, 1st *eighth*	RELEVÉ SUR LA POINTE on the left leg (traveling slightly to corner No. 4). Simultaneously DÉGAGÉ with the right leg back, in effacé (45°).	6th (left arm bent).
2nd, 3rd *eighth*	DEMI-PLIÉ on the left leg (traveling slightly to corner No. 4). Simultaneously bend the right leg sur le cou-de-pied back.	

Relevé on right pointe, left leg raised in front (45°) in effacé

4th, 1st eighth	RELEVÉ SUR LA POINTE on the left leg (traveling slightly to corner No. 4). Simultaneously DÉGAGÉ with the right leg back (45°) in effacé.
2nd, 3rd eighth	Then lower the right leg (back of the left leg) into demi-plié, bend the left leg sur le cou-de-pied front.
8 bars	Repeat the exercise on the other leg (starting from relevé on the right leg, traveling slightly to corner No. 8, etc.).

Total accompaniment
16 bars

(*Pause*)
Repeat the exercise once again.

Rimma Karelskaya

Pose with a half bent leg in front (90°)

Natalia Bessmertnova, Nina Sorokina

Measure 3/4
(Waltz)
Tempo
moderate
Introduction
(2 bars)

18.   THIRD EXERCISE ON POINTES

Preparation
Starting position of the feet: 4th
position croisé, left leg stretched to
the front, pointe tendue.

Starting position
arms: 5th position
(right arm up).

Off-beat
(6th) eighth

PLIÉ À QUART
on the left leg (with a passing
movement).

STEP - GLISSÉ
with the right leg front diagonally
(to corner No. 2), end in demi-plié
(the left leg stretched back pointe
tendue).

Reach 1st arabesque
arm position, through
1st position (right
arm in front).

1st, 2nd
fourth

RELEVÉ SUR LA POINTE
on the right leg, simultaneously

LIFT
the left leg back, in effacé (90°), stand
in 1st arabesque position sur la pointe
(lean the body slightly forward).

1st arabesque arm
position (right arm
in front).

3rd fourth

DEMI-PLIÉ
on the right leg, simultaneously lower
the left leg in 1st position (with a
passing movement).

Arm position A.

1st, 2nd
fourth

RELEVÉ SUR LA POINTE
on the right leg, simultaneously

LIFT
the left leg to the front (90°) halfway
bent, in croisé, stay in position, then

Reach 5th position
through 1st position
(right arm up).

3rd fourth

TOMBÉ
on the left leg front, croisé, right foot
sur le cou-de-pied back.

The right arm lowers
forward in 1st
position.

1st, 2nd
fourth

DÉVELOPPÉ À LA SECONDE (90°)
with the right leg, simultaneously rise
on left pointe.

The right arm moves
to the side, 2nd
allongée.

3rd, 1st, 2nd *fourth*	GRANDE FOUETTÉ EN TOURNANT EN DEDANS with the right leg (end in attitude croisée with the right leg, simultaneously rise on left pointe)	A - 1st - 5th (right arm up).
5th eighth	then tombé pied dessous with the right foot, left foot sur le cou-de-pied front (lean the body and the head slightly to the right).	The right arm lowers to the side, then arm position A.

4 bars	Repeat the exercise on the other leg (starting from step - glissé with the left leg diagonally front to corner No. 8, etc.).

Total accompaniment
8 bars

(*Pause*)
Repeat the exercise once more.

Grand fouetté en tournant en dedans, ending in attitude croisée

Nina Sorokina

Measure 2/4
Tempo
moderate   ## 19.   FOURTH EXERCISE ON POINTES
Introduction
(2 bars)   Preparation
Starting position of the feet: 4th   Starting position of
position, position croisé, right leg   arms: 6th position
stretched front, pointe tendue.   (right arm bent).

Start from corner No. 6, gradually traveling diagonally front to corner No. 2.

PRÉPARATION:

Off-beat   STEP FORWARD   The right arm opens
(4th)   with the right foot to the side.   to the side, then
eighth   In demi-plié, simultaneously
               DÉGAGÉ
               with the left leg to the side (45°).

1st, 2nd   TOUR PIQUÉ EN DEHORS   the arms meet
eighth   (during the turn on the left leg, the   between A and 1st
               right foot is sur le cou-de-pied   position.
               front).
               End with the right leg to the side, in   The arms open to the
               demi-plié. Simultaneously   side through the 1st
3rd, 4th   DÉGAGÉ   position, then
eighth   with the left leg to the side (45°).

1st, 2nd   TOUR PIQUÉ EN DEHORS   the arms meet
eighth   (turn on the left leg).   between A and 1st
               End with the movement   position.

3rd, 4th   DÉGAGÉ   The arms open to the
eighth   with the right leg to the side (45°) in   side through the 1st
               demi-plié of the left leg.   position.

1st, 2nd,   FOUETTÉ EN TOURNANT   The arms meet
3rd, 4th   EN DEHORS $(45°)$ between A and 1st
eighth   with the right leg.   position, then
               End à la seconde (45°) with the   through the 1st
               right leg, left leg in demi-plié.   position, they open
                                                   to the side.

1st, 2nd *eighth*	FOUETTÉ EN TOURNANT EN DEHORS (45°) with the right leg, end with the right leg to the side, in demi-plié, simultaneously	The arms meet between A and 1st position, then moving through the 1st position they open to the side.
3rd, 4th *eighth*	DÉGAGÉ with the left leg, to the side (45°).	
11 bars, *1st, 2nd, 3rd* *eighth*	Repeat the exercise three more times consecutively (gradually traveling diagonally to corner No. 2) ; the last fouetté en tournant en dehors ends in 4th position, croisé, the right foot back, the left leg front in plié à quart.	End in 1st position (wide), hands slightly turned out.

Total accompaniment
16 bars

(*Pause*)
Repeat the exercise on the other leg
(starting from corner No. 4,
gradually traveling diagonally
forward to corner No. 8).

Tour piqué en dehors

Rimma Karelskaya

Measure 2/4
Tempo fast
Introduction
(2 bars)

20.   FIFTH EXERCISE ON POINTES

Preparation

Starting position of the feet: 4th position, position croisé, right leg stretched to the front, pointe tendue.

Starting position of arms: 6th position (right arm bent).

Start from corner No. 8.

Off-beat
(2nd, 3rd,
4th)
eighth
11 bars,
1st, 2nd, 3rd
eighth

12 TOURS PIQUÉS EN DEDANS (gradually traveling in a circle, clockwise), then

The right arm opens in the course of the movement; subsequently the arms meet between A and 1st position. All the following arm movements move through 1st position to the side, then the arms meet between A and 1st position, etc.

4th eighth
3 bars

CHAÎNÉS-DÉBOULÉS traveling diagonally front to corner No. 2.

The arms open to the side, subsequently they join between A and 1st position.

1st eighth

End with tombé - relevé sur la pointe on the right leg, simultaneously lift the left leg back, in effacé, and stay in 1st arabesque position.

End (through the 1st position) with the 1st arabesque arm position (right arm bent).

Total accompaniment
16 bars

(Pause)

Repeat the exercise on the other leg (start from corner No. 2 with the following gradual traveling in a circle counterclockwise, end diagonally forward to corner No. 8).

Measure 3/4
Tempo lively
Introduction
(2 bars)

21. SIXTH EXERCISE ON POINTES

Preparation
Starting position of the feet: 5th
position, croisé, right foot front.

Starting position of
arms: A.

Start from corner No. 6.

Off-beat *(2nd, 3rd)* *fourth,* *4 bars*	PAS SUIVI traveling diagonally front to corner No. 2 (lean the head slightly forward, looking to the right under the arm). While ending pas suivi turn in a ¼ circle to the left and continue	Arm position - A - the arms move up gradually (through the 1st position) in 5th position (right arm up).
3 bars	PAS COURU traveling diagonally front to corner No. 2, "facing with your back" in the course of the movement (lean the	The arms move down, placed slightly backward (hands pulled down).
1 bar	body slightly forward and turn the head to the right), make a turn to ¾ circle to the left.	
4 bars	PAS COURU traveling diagonally front to corner No. 8 "facing" in the course of the movement (the body straightened, the head slightly raised).	The arms move to the front (to the level of the 1st position), the palms facing down.
3 bars	PAS SUIVI EN TOURNANT (the left leg in front in 5th position), two turns to the left (lean the body and the head slightly to the left, looking down over the left shoulder).	6th (left arm bent).
1st fourth	STEP - PIQUÉ SUR LA POINTE with the left foot to the front to corner No. 8, lift the right leg forward bent halfway in croisé (90°).	The left arm opens to the side, then comes up in the 5th arm position (accentuate the concluding movement by turning hands inward).

Total accompaniment
16 bars

(Pause)
Repeat the exercise on the other leg
(starting from corner No. 4, traveling
diagonally forward to corner No. 8).

Measure 2/4
Tempo lively
Introduction
(1 bar)

22. SEVENTH EXERCISE ON POINTES

Preparation
Starting position of the feet: 5th   Starting position of
position, en face, right foot front.   arms: A.

Off-beat
(4th) eighth,
7 bars,   16 PETITS CHANGEMENTS DE   A - 1st - 3rd - 2nd- A.
1st, 2nd, 3rd   PIEDS SUR LES POINTES.
eighth

Total accompaniment
8 bars

Measure 3/4
(Waltz)
Tempo slow
Introduction
(2 bars)

23. PORT DE BRAS AND BENDING
OF THE BODY

Preparation
Starting position of the feet: 1st   Starting position of
position (halfway turned out).   arms: 2nd position.

This exercise corresponds to exercise
15 (exercises in the center) of the first
class (see page 108).

Total accompaniment
32 bars

Third Class

EXERCISES AT THE BARRE

*Musical-
rhythmical
accompaniment*

DANCING EXERCISES

---

*Measure 3/4
(Waltz)
Tempo slow
Introduction
(2 bars)*

1. GRANDS PLIÉS

Preparation
Starting position of the feet: 1st
position.

Starting position of
the right arm: 2nd
position.

This practice corresponds to exercise
1 (exercises at the barre) of the first
class (see page 55).

---

*Total accompaniment
32 bars*

Measure 2/4
Tempo
moderate   **2.   BATTEMENTS TENDUS**
Introduction   Preparation
(1 bar)   Starting position of the feet: 5th   Starting position of
                        position, right foot front.   the right arm: 2nd
                                                                position.

Off-beat
(4th),   2 BATTEMENTS TENDUS   2nd position.
1st, 2nd, 3rd   with the right foot
eighth   to the front.

4th, 1st,   1 BATTEMENT TENDU
2nd, 3rd   with the right foot to the side
eighth   (change), in 5th position demi-plié
                        (then rise from demi-plié).

4th, 1st,   2 BATTEMENTS TENDUS
2nd, 3rd   with the right foot to the side
eighth   (change).

4th, 1st,   1 BATTEMENT TENDU
2nd, 3rd   with the right foot to the back in 5th
eighth   position demi-plié (then rise from
                        demi-plié).

4th, 1st,   2 BATTEMENTS TENDUS
2nd, 3rd   with the right foot back.
eighth

4th, 1st,   1 BATTEMENT TENDU
2nd, 3rd   with the right foot to the side
eighth   (change), in 5th position demi-plié
                        (then rise from demi-plié).

4th, 1st,   2 BATTEMENTS TENDUS
2nd, 3rd   with the right foot to the side
eighth   (change).

4th, 1st,   1 BATTEMENT TENDU
2nd, 3rd   with the right foot to the front, in
eighth   5th position demi-plié (then rise from
                        demi-plié).

8 bars   Repeat the exercise once more.

Total accompaniment
16 bars   Turn to the other side and repeat
                        the exercise on the other leg.

Measure 2/4
Tempo lively
Introduction
(1 bar)

3. BATTEMENTS TENDUS JETÉS

Preparation
Starting position of the feet: 5th position, right foot front.

Starting position of the right arm: 2nd position.

Off-beat
(4th),
1st, 2nd, 3rd
eighth

2 BATTEMENTS TENDUS JETÉS with the right foot to the front.

2nd position.

4th, 1st,
2nd, 3rd
eighth

BATTEMENTS TENDUS JETÉS DOUBLE PIQUÉ with the right foot to the front.

4th, 1st,
2nd, 3rd
eighth

2 BATTEMENTS TENDUS JETÉS with the right foot to the side (change).

4th, 1st,
2nd, 3rd
eighth

BATTEMENTS TENDUS JETÉS DOUBLE PIQUÉ with the right foot to the side (end in 5th position back).

4th, 1st,
2nd, 3rd
eighth

2 BATTEMENTS TENDUS JETÉS with the right foot to the back.

4th, 1st,
2nd, 3rd
eighth

BATTEMENTS TENDUS JETÉS DOUBLE PIQUÉ with the right foot to the back.

4th, 1st,
2nd, 3rd
eighth

2 BATTEMENTS TENDUS JETÉS with the right foot to the side (change).

4th, 1st,
2nd, 3rd
eighth

BATTEMENTS TENDUS JETÉS DOUBLE PIQUÉ with the right foot to the side (end in 5th position front).

2nd position.

8 bars

Repeat the exercise once more.

Total accompaniment
16 bars

Turn to the other side and repeat the exercise on the other leg.

4. RONDS DE JAMBE À TERRE

Preparation Starting position of the feet[1]	Starting position of the right arm: 2nd position.

	Preparation Starting position of the feet[1]	Starting position of the right arm: 2nd position.
2 bars	2 RONDS DE JAMBE À TERRE EN DEHORS with the right leg.	2nd
1 bar	1 ROND DE JAMBE À TERRE, IN DEMI-PLIÉ.	A - 1st - 2nd
3 bars	3 RONDS DE JAMBE À TERRE.	2nd
1 bar	1 ROND DE JAMBE À TERRE, IN DEMI-PLIÉ.	A - 1st - 2nd
1 bar	1 ROND DE JAMBE À TERRE.	2nd position.
1 bar	1 GRAND ROND DE JAMBE JETÉ.	
1 bar	1 ROND DE JAMBE À TERRE.	
1 bar	1 GRAND ROND DE JAMBE JETÉ.	
1 bar	1 ROND DE JAMBE À TERRE.	
3 bars	3 GRANDS RONDS DE JAMBE JETÉS.	
1 bar	Bring the leg through 1st position, front, pointe tendue.	
16 bars	Repeat the exercise in the reverse direction with the following change at the end of the combination: after the three grands ronds de jambe jetés en dedans, lower the right leg to 5th position front.	

[1] Execute the ronds de jambe à terre immediately after the preparation, continuing the movement of the preparatory rond.

Then immediately start the following
movements of the combination:

Tempo slow PORT DE BRAS ET BATTEMENTS
32 bars RELEVÉS LENTS (90°).
This part of the practice corresponds to
the port de bras and battements relevés
lents of exercise 5 (exercises at the
barre) of the first class (see page
62).

Total accompaniment
64 bars

Turn to the other side and repeat the
exercise on the other leg.

Measure 2/4
Tempo slow
Introduction
(2 bars)

5. BATTEMENTS FONDUS

Preparation
Starting position of the feet: 2nd
position, right foot pointe tendue.

Starting position of
the right arm: 2nd
position.

Off-beat
(4th),
1st, 2nd, 3rd
eighth

BATTEMENT FONDU
with the right leg to the front (45°).

2nd position.

4th, 1st
eighth

LOWER
the right leg to the floor, pointe
tendue, in demi-plié of the left leg.

2nd, 3rd
eighth

LIFT
the right leg upward (45°),
simultaneously come up from
demi-plié.

4th, 1st
eighth

BRING
the right leg through 1st position
back (45°), in demi-plié of the
left leg.

2nd, 3rd
eighth

MOVE
the leg to the side (45°) simultaneously
come up from demi-plié.

4th, 1st,
2nd, 3rd
eighth

BATTEMENT FONDU
with the right leg to the side.

---

4 bars

Repeat the exercise in the reverse
direction.

8 bars

Repeat the whole combination once
more on half toe.

Total accompaniment
16 bars

Turn to the other side and repeat the
exercise on the other leg.

6. BATTEMENTS FRAPPÉS ET RONDS DE JAMBE EN L'AIR

Measure 2/4
Tempo
moderate
Introduction
(1 bar)

Preparation
Starting position of the feet: 2nd position, right foot pointe tendue.

Starting position of the right arm: 2nd position.

Off-beat
(4th),
1st, 2nd, 3rd
eighth
4th eighth

3 BATTEMENTS FRAPPÉS
to the front, with the right foot on the floor.
Lift the right leg (25°), then

2nd position.

1st eighth
2nd, 3rd
eighth

FLIC
with the right foot front, opening the leg to the side, on the floor.

4th, 1st, 2nd
eighth

LIFT
the right leg (45°), following with
2 RONDS DE JAMBE EN L'AIR
(45°) EN DEHORS
with the right leg.

3rd, 4th
eighth

1 ROND DE JAMBE EN L'AIR
(45°) EN DEHORS
with the right leg, ending in demi-plié of the left leg.

1st, 2nd
eighth
3rd eighth

PIROUETTES EN DEHORS.
During the turn on the left leg, the right foot is sur le cou-de-pied back, end with the right leg to the side à la seconde at (45°).

The arms meet between A and 1st, the right arm moves into the 2nd, the left arm at the barre.

4 bars

Execute the exercise in the reverse direction.

8 bars

Repeat the whole combination once more (on half toe).

Total accompaniment
16 bars

Turn to the other side and repeat the exercise on the other leg.

Measure 3/4		
(Waltz)	7. ADAGIO	
Tempo slow		
Introduction	Preparation	
(2 bars)	Starting position of the feet: 5th	Starting position of
	position, right foot front.	the right arm: 2nd
		position.

3 bars	DÉVELOPPÉ with the right leg front.	A - 1st - 2nd
1 bar	PASSER LA JAMBE (90°) with the right leg.	2nd - A
2 bars	DÉVELOPPÉ with the right leg front, in demi-plié of the left leg.	A - 1st
1 bar	MOVE the right leg to the side à la seconde (90°), simultaneously come up from demi-plié of the left leg.	1st - 2nd
1 bar	PASSER LA JAMBE (90°) with the right leg.	2nd - A
3 bars	DÉVELOPPÉ À LA SECONDE (90°) with the right leg.	A - 1st - 2nd
1 bar	PASSER LA JAMBE (90°) with the right leg.	2nd - A
2 bars	DÉVELOPPÉ A LA SECONDE (90°) with the right leg, left leg demi-plié.	A - 1st - 2nd
1 bar	BRING the right leg back (90°) simultaneously come up from the demi-plié of the left leg.	The right arm comes down, then rises and stretches forward: 2nd arabesque arm position.
1 bar	PASSER LA JAMBE (90°) with the right leg	A

| 16 bars | Repeat the exercise in the reverse
direction. | |

Total accompaniment
32 bars

Turn to the other side and repeat the
exercise on the other leg.

Measure 2/4
Tempo
moderate
Introduction
(1 bar)

8. BATTEMENTS DOUBLES FRAPPÉS

Preparation
Starting position of the feet: 2nd
position, right foot pointe tendue.

Starting position of
the right arm: 2nd
position.

Off-beat *(4th),* *1st eighth*	BATTEMENT DOUBLE FRAPPÉ ending front, on the floor, with the right foot.	2nd position.
2nd, 3rd *eighth*	BATTEMENT DOUBLE FRAPPÉ ending to the side, on the floor, with the right foot.	
4th, 1st	BATTEMENT DOUBLE FRAPPÉ ending backward, on the floor, with the right foot.	
2nd, 3rd *eighth*	BATTEMENT DOUBLE FRAPPÉ ending to the side, on the floor, with the right foot.	

2 bars — Repeat the exercise in the reverse direction.

4 bars — Repeat the whole combination once more on half toe.

Total accompaniment
8 bars

Turn to the other side and repeat the
exercise on the other leg.

Measure 2/4
Tempo lively
Introduction
(2 bars)

9.   PETITS BATTEMENTS SUR LE COU-DE-PIED

Preparation
Starting position of the feet: right foot
sur le cou-de-pied front (wrapping the
ankle).

Starting position of
the right arm: A.

Off-beat
(4th)
eighth,
15 bars

16 PETITS BATTEMENTS SUR LE
COU-DE-PIED
(accent front), with the right foot.

Arm position A.

1st, 2nd, 3rd
eighth

16 PETITS BATTEMENTS SUR LE
COU-DE-PIED
(accent front), with the right foot,
on half toe of the left leg.

16 bars

At the end of this practice, balance on
half toe of the left foot in various poses.
Look for the description in the second
part of exercise 11, exercises at the
barre, of the first class, (page 71).

Total accompaniment
32 bars

Turn to the other side and repeat the
exercise on the other leg.

Measure 2/4
Tempo
moderate
Introduction
(1 bar)

10.   GRANDS BATTEMENTS JETÉS

Preparation
Starting position of the feet: 5th position right foot front.

Starting position of the right arm: 2nd position.

GRANDS BATTEMENTS JETÉS PIQUÉ AVEC DEMI-ROND DE JAMBE JETÉ (90°) with the right leg.

Breakdown of the movement:

Off-beat (4th) eighth

Kick the leg forward.

2nd position.

1st eighth

Lower the leg to the floor, pointe tendue, then

2nd eighth

kick the leg forward and to the side (in one movement).

3rd eighth

Lower the leg to the floor, pointe tendue in 2nd position, then

4th eighth

kick the leg to the side and back (in one movement).

1st eighth

Lower the leg to the floor, pointe tendue, then

2nd eighth

kick the leg back.

3rd eighth

Bring down the leg to 5th position back.

2 bars

Repeat the exercise in the reverse direction.

4 bars

Repeat the whole combination once more.

Total accompaniment
8 bars

Turn to the other side and repeat the exercise on the other leg.

Measure 3/4
(Waltz)
Tempo slow
Introduction
(2 bars)

11.   PORT DE BRAS AND BENDING OF THE BODY

Preparation
Starting position of the feet: 1st
position, facing the barre.

Starting position of
the arms: both hands
on the barre.

This practice corresponds to exercise
13 (exercises at the barre) of the first
class (see page 75).

Total accompaniment
32 bars

Measure 3/4
(Waltz)
Tempo slow
Introduction
(2 bars)

11a.   STRETCHING OF THE LEGS AND BENDING OF THE BODY

Preparation
Starting position of the feet: the right
leg is raised to the side (placed on the
barre, with the heel turned out) facing
the barre.

Starting position of
arms: both hands at
the barre.

STRETCHING TO THE SIDE
Breakdown of the movement:

2 bars
The right leg slides to the right along
the barre (with the heel turned out),
simultaneously the body leans toward
the right leg.

The left arm opens
to the side, moves up,
and simultaneously
with the leaning of
the body proceeds to
the right.

2 bars
The body returns to the starting
position, simultaneously the right leg
slides back into the starting position.

The left arm returns
to the starting
position (at the
barre).

STRETCHING TO THE SIDE.
Breakdown of the movement:

2 bars	The body bends to the left, simultaneously the right leg slides along the barre to the right.	The right arm opens to the side, moves up, and simultaneously with the leaning of the body proceeds to the left.
2 bars	The body returns to the starting position, simultaneously the right leg slides back into the starting position.	The right arm returns to the starting position (at the barre).
4 bars	The body bends in a circular way (right, back, left) and returns to the starting position.	The left arm moves up and simultaneously makes a circular movement with the bending of the body, then returns to the barre.
4 bars	The body bends in a circular way to the opposite side (left, back, right) and returns to the starting position.	The right arm moves up and simultaneously makes a circular movement with the bending of the body, then returns to the barre.
16 bars	Repeat the exercise once more on half toe.	Hands on the barre.
	At the end of the stretching on half toe, lift the right leg above the barre and hold awhile, then lower slowly the leg to 1st position.	

Total accompaniment
32 bars

(*Pause*)
Repeat the exercise on the other leg.

Measure 2/4
Tempo lively
Introduction
(1 bar)

12.   RELEVÉS

Preparation
Starting position of the feet: 1st   Starting position of
position, facing the barre.   the arms: both hands
                                            on the barre.

This practice corresponds to exercise
14 (exercises at the barre) of the first
class (see page 78).

Total accompaniment
16 bars

EXERCISES IN THE CENTER

1. SMALL ADAGIO

Preparation
Starting position of the feet: 2nd
position, en face.

Starting position of
arms: 2nd position.

GRAND PLIÉ
in 2nd position.
Breakdown of the movement:

2 bars

Moving downward (at the end of the
squatting, the body leans slightly to
the left).

2nd
The arms come **down**,
then move slightly to
the left.

2 bars

Moving upward, the body straightens
out and then continues with a flowing
turn to the right (ending the
movement with a turn facing side No.
3), simultaneously the left leg stretches
out to the back, pointe tendue and
rises (90°) in 2nd arabesque.

The right arm rises,
continues the
movement to the
side, simultaneously
the left arm moves
down and front: 2nd
arabesque arm
position.

4 bars

TOUR LENT[1] EN DEHORS
(turn to the left, in 2nd arabesque,
ending in 1st arabesque).

2nd arabesque arm
position (the left
arm in front), end in
1st arabesque arm
position (right arm
in front).

1 bar,

PASSER LA JAMBE (90°)
with the left leg.

A

1st, 2nd
fourth

DÉVELOPPÉ
with the left leg in front, croisé (lean
the head forward slightly, looking to
the left under the arm).

1st
5th (left arm up).

---

[1] Tour lent: turn slowly on the fully stretched supporting leg, pushing the heel slightly
in the direction of the movement.

3rd fourth, *2 bars*	DEMI-PLIÉ on the right leg. STEP OVER on the left leg in front. LIFT the right leg back (90°), croisé, in 3rd arabesque.	The left arm lowers to the side, simultaneously the right arm moves down and front (3rd arabesque arm position).
3 bars	TOUR LENT EN DEHORS turn to the right, three quarters of a turn in 3rd arabesque position, end the turn facing side No. 7, in 2nd arabesque position.	3rd arabesque arm position (right arm in front) and, remaining in this same position, move to 2nd arabesque.
1 bar	The body turns to the right, to position en face, simultaneously the right leg moves à la seconde (90°).	The right arm opens to the side, through 1st position: 2nd position arms.
16 bars	Repeat the exercise on the other leg.	
32 bars	Repeat the whole combination in the reverse direction.	

Total accompaniment
64 bars

Measure 2/4 *Tempo slow* *Introduction* *(1 bar)*	**2. BATTEMENTS TENDUS**	
	Preparation Starting position of the feet: 5th position croisé, right foot forward.	Starting position of arms: 2nd position.
Off-beat *(4th),* *1st, 2nd, 3rd* *eighth*	2 BATTEMENTS TENDUS to the front, with the right leg in croisé.	5th (right arm up).
4th, 1st, *2nd, 3rd* *eighth*	BATTEMENT TENDU to the front, with the right leg in croisé, and demi-plié in 5th position.	5th (right arm up).
4th, 1st, *2nd, 3rd* *eighth*	2 BATTEMENTS TENDUS to the back, with the left leg in croisé.	5th (left arm up).
4th, 1st, *2nd, 3rd* *eighth*	BATTEMENT TENDU to the back, with the left leg in croisé, and demi-plié in 5th position.	5th (left arm up).
4th, 1st, *2nd, 3rd* *eighth*	3 BATTEMENTS TENDUS JETÉS to the side, with the right leg (change).	2nd
4th, 1st, *2nd, 3rd* *eighth*	3 BATTEMENTS TENDUS JETÉS to the side, with the left leg (change).	2nd

CONCLUDING EXERCISE FOR THE MEN'S CLASS:

4th eighth	PRÉPARATION POUR PIROUETTES EN DEHORS with the right foot (in 2nd position).	2nd - 6th (right arm bent).
1 bar, *1st, 2nd, 3rd* *eighth*	PIROUETTES EN DEHORS (end in 5th position, croisé, right foot back).	The right arm opens during the course of the movement, then the arms meet between A and 1st position, end in 2nd arabesque.

CONCLUDING EXERCISE FOR THE WOMEN'S CLASS:

4th eighth *1 bar*	PRÉPARATION POUR PIROUETTES EN DEHORS with the right foot (in 4th position croisé, right foot back).	A - 1st - 3rd arabesque position (right arm in front).
1st, 2nd, *3rd eighth*	PIROUETTES EN DEHORS (end in 5th position, croisé, right foot back).	The right arm opens during the course of the movement, then the arms meet between A and 1st position, end in 2nd position.
8 bars	Repeat the exercise on the other leg.	

Total accompaniment
16 bars

(*Pause*)
Repeat the exercise in the reverse direction (pirouettes remain en dehors).

Measure 3/4
Tempo slow
Introduction
(*2 bars*)

3. BATTEMENTS FONDUS

	Preparation Starting position of the feet: 2nd position, right foot pointe tendue.	Starting of arms: 2nd position.
Off-beat (*3rd*), *1st, 2nd, 3rd* *fourth*	BATTEMENT FONDU to the front (45°), croisé, with the right leg (on half toe of the left foot).	A - 1st - 6th (right arm bent).
1st fourth .	DEMI-PLIÉ with the left leg.	6th (right arm bent).

2nd, 3rd *fourth*	ROND DE JAMBE EN DEHORS with the right leg, end back in croisé (45°), rise from demi-plié on half toe of the left foot.	The right arm opens to the side: 2nd position arms.
1st fourth	DEMI-PLIÉ with the left leg, bend the right leg to the back (lean the body slightly to the right, turning the head to the left).	6th (left arm bent).
2nd, 3rd *fourth* *1st fourth*	PAS DE BOURRÉE EN TOURNANT EN DEHORS stepping to the back twice. The final demi-plié on the right leg (the left foot sur le cou-de-pied back) starts simultaneously the beginning of the following movement.	A
2nd, 3rd *fourth*	BATTEMENT FONDU to the side, with the left leg (on half toe of the right foot).	A - 1st - 2nd
1st fourth	TOMBER PIED DESSUS on the left leg, with the right foot sur le cou-de-pied back.	A
2nd, 3rd *fourth*	BATTEMENT FONDU to the side, with the right leg (on half toe of the left foot).	A - 1st - 2nd
1st fourth	TOMBER PIED DESSUS on the right leg, the left foot sur le cou-de-pied back.	A
2nd, 3rd *fourth*	BATTEMENT FONDU to the back, in effacé, with the left leg (on half toe of the right leg).	Reach 6th position through 1st (left arm bent).
1st fourth	TOMBÉ backward, in effacé, with the left leg.	The left arm opens to the side (hands turned out slightly).
2nd, 3rd *fourth* *2nd fourth*	PAS DE BOURRÉE EN DEDANS stepping over twice. End in 4th position (wide) croisé, right leg back, left leg in front in plié à quart. Stay in the preparatory position for tours en dedans.	A Reach 6th position through the 1st (left arm bent).

3rd fourth	DEMI-PLIÉ in 4th position.	
2 bars	TOURS EN DEDANS EN ATTITUDE EFFACÉE with the right leg, then ALLONGÉE with the right leg, in effacé back on demi-plié of the left leg.	5th (right arm up). 5th allongée (hands stretch out and the palms turn outward).
1st, 2nd *fourth* *3rd fourth* *1st, 2nd* *fourth*	PAS DE BOURRÉE EN DEHORS (stepping under twice, end in 4th position, wide, croisé, the left leg back, the right leg in front in plié à quart). Stand in the preparatory position for tours en dehors.	The arms lower to the side, continue downward: position A, then 3rd arabesque position (left arm stretched out to the front).
3rd fourth	DEMI-PLIÉ in 4th position.	
2 bars	TOURS EN DEHORS EN ATTITUDE CROISÉE with the left leg, then ALLONGÉE with the left leg, in croisé back, on demi-plié of the right leg.	5th (left arm up). 5th allongée (hands stretch out and the palms turn outward).
1 bar *1st, 2nd* *fourth*	PAS DE BOURRÉE EN TOURNANT EN DEHORS (end in 5th position, with the left foot front). Stand in 5th position (pause).	The hands come down, position A. A

16 bars	Repeat the exercise on the other leg.

Total accompaniment
32 bars

(*Pause*)
Repeat the exercise in the reverse
direction.

Measure 2/4
Tempo
moderate
Introduction
(1 bar)

4. BATTEMENTS FRAPPÉS

Preparation
Starting position of the feet: Starting position of
2nd position, right foot pointe tendue.   arms: 2nd position.

Off-beat (4th), 1st, 2nd, 3rd eighth	3 BATTEMENTS FRAPPÉS to the front, in croisé, with the right foot, pointe tendue.	5th (right arm up).
4th, 1st, 2nd, 3rd eighth	2 BATTEMENTS DOUBLES FRAPPÉS to the side (change), en face, with the right foot, pointe tendue.	2nd
4th, 1st, 2nd, 3rd eighth	LIFT the right leg (45°) and follow with	2nd
	3 RONDS DE JAMBE EN L'AIR (45°), EN DEHORS with the right leg, end the third rond in demi-plié.	2nd
4th, 1st, 2nd eighth	PAS DE BOURRÉE EN TOURNANT EN DEHORS stepping under twice (on half toe).	A
3rd eighth	Then step on the right leg, simultaneously	
	DÉGAGÉ with the left leg to the side (45°).	1st - 2nd
4th, 1st, 2nd, 3rd eighth	3 RONDS DE JAMBE EN L'AIR (45°), EN DEDANS with the left leg, end the third rond in demi-plié.	2nd
4th, 1st, 2nd eighth	PAS DE BOURRÉE EN TOURNANT EN DEDANS (stepping over twice, on half toe), then	A
3rd eighth	PRÉPARATION POUR CHAÎNÉS-DÉBOULÉS. (Step on the left foot to corner No. 6, bring the right leg to the front in croisé, pointe tendue.)	6th (right arm bent).

4th eighth, *1 bar,* *1st, 2nd, 3rd* *eighth*	CHAÎNÉS-DÉBOULÉS diagonally forward to corner No. 2, end in position effacée (left leg stretched backward, pointe tendue).	The right arm opens during the course of the movement, then the arms meet between A and 1st. End in 5th position (left arm up).

---

8 bars	Repeat the exercise on the other leg.

Total accompaniment
16 bars

(*Pause*)
Repeat the exercise in the reverse direction. (Chaînés-déboulés remain in the same direction: diagonally front.)

Measure 3/4
(*Waltz*)
Tempo slow
Introduction
(*2 bars*)

5.   GRAND ADAGIO

	Preparation Starting position of the feet: 5th position, croisé, right foot front.	Starting position of arms: A.

Off-beat (*2nd, 3rd*) *fourth,* *1st, 2nd* *fourth*	GLISSADE diagonally forward to corner No. 2 (do not change) with the right leg.	Position A, then the arms open slightly to the side and close again.
3rd fourth	STEP with the right foot forward diagonally to corner No. 2.	A
2 bars *1st, 2nd* *fourth*	DÉVELOPPÉ with the left leg front, in croisé (looking to the left under the arm).	A - 1st- 5th (left arm up).

3rd fourth	DEMI-PLIÉ on the right leg.	5th (left arm up).
	PRÉPARATION GRAND TEMPS RELEVÉ EN DEHORS with the left leg.	As above.
1 bar, *1st, 2nd* *fourth*	PIROUETTES TIRE-BOUCHON EN DEHORS (The left foot is placed in retiré back.) End with the left leg back, in croisé, 4th arabesque (come down flat from half toe of the right foot).	3rd, then 4th arabesque arm position (right arm in front).
3rd fourth	DEMI-PLIÉ on the right leg.	4th arabesque arm position.
	PRÉPARATION GRAND TEMPS RELEVÉ EN DEDANS with the left leg.	
1 bar	PIROUETTES TIRE-BÒUCHON EN DEDANS (the left foot is placed in retiré front).	3rd
1 bar	End with the left leg à la seconde, at 90° (come down flat from half toe of the right foot).	
1st, 2nd, *3rd,* *1st, 2nd* *fourth*	RISE˙ on half toe of the right foot, stay in à la seconde position with the left leg (90°).	3rd
3rd fourth	TOMBÉ with the left foot, turning to the left (facing corner No. 7), right foot sur le cou-de-pied back.	1st - A
1 bar, *1st, 2nd* *fourth*	DÉVELOPPÉ with the right leg (to corner No. 8) in écarté front, simultaneously stretching out the left leg (the head turned to the right).	The hands move down and to the side (palms turned down) : 2nd allongée.
3rd fourth,	RELEVÉ on half toe of the left foot.	A stroke with the hands, then

2 bars	GRAND FOUETTÉ EN TOURNANT EN DEDANS with the right leg, end 1st arabesque in effacé (facing corner No. 8).	A - 1st - 3rd - 1st arabesque arm position (left arm in front).
1st, 2nd fourth	PAS DE BOURRÉE EN DEHORS (stepping under twice, with a passing movement into)	A
3rd, 1st, 2nd, 3rd fourth	TEMPS LIÉ to the front, in croisé, with the right leg. Stay in croisé position, the left leg stretched out to the back, pointe tendue.	A - 1st - 5th (left arm up).
3 bars, 1st, 2nd fourth	PORT DE BRAS leaning the body to the front then bending back: end in 4th position (wide), croisé, right foot front in plié à quart.	5th (left arm up), 1st, 5th (right arm up), then the right arm makes a circular movement (to the side, to the front), ending in 6th position (right arm bent).
3rd fourth	DEMI-PLIÉ in 4th position.	
2 bars 1 bar, 1st, 2nd fourth	TOURS EN DEDANS the left leg stretched to the front (90°), when ending the turn, stop in attitude effacée position with the left leg. (Come down flat from half toe of the right foot.) Stand in this position.	4th (right arm up). Reach 5th position through 1st (left arm up).
3rd fourth	PASSER LA JAMBE (90°) with the left leg (the head leans slightly downward).	The left arm lowers to the front in 1st position.
1 bar, 1st, 2nd fourth	DÉVELOPPÉ À LA SECONDE (90°) with the left leg (the head rises to the starting position).	The left arm opens to the side: 2nd position.
3rd fourth	DEMI-PLIÉ on the right leg.	
1st, 2nd fourth	PAS DE BOURRÉE EN DEHORS (stepping to the side twice).	The arms come down. A

Pose in attitude effacée

Maya Plisetskaya

3rd fourth	End in 4th position croisé (wide), left leg in front in plié à quart.	A - 1st - 3rd arabesque arm position (right arm front).
1st, 2nd fourth	Stand in the preparatory position for tours en dehors.	
3rd fourth	DEMI-PLIÉ in 4th position.	3rd arabesque arm position.
2 bars	TOURS EN DEHORS the right leg stretched to the front (90°), then, when ending the turn come down from half toe of the left foot, continuing the following movement with the right leg.	4th (left arm up, right arm bent).
1 bar, 1st fourth	GRAND ROND DE JAMBE EN DEHORS (end in attitude croisée position, with the right leg).	The arms move into 2nd position, then the right arm rises, the left arm simultaneously bends in the front: 4th arm position.

Total accompaniment
32 bars

(*Pause*)
Repeat the exercise on the other leg.

6. GRANDS BATTEMENTS JETÉS

Measure 2/4
Tempo slow
Introduction
(1 bar)

	Preparation	
	Starting position of the feet: 5th position, croisé, right foot front.	Starting position of arms: 2nd position.

Off-beat (*4th*) *1st eighth*	GRAND BATTEMENT JETÉ with the right leg to the front in croisé.	5th (right arm up).
2nd, 3rd eighth	GRAND BATTEMENT JETÉ with the left leg to the back in croisé, 4th arabesque position.	The right arm comes down and stretches forward: 4th arabesque arm position.
4th, 1st eighth	GRAND BATTEMENT JETÉ with the right leg to the side, in écarté back (to corner No. 4). (End in 5th position back.)	The right arm moves upward: 5th position, then 2nd position.
2nd, 3rd eighth	Stand in 5th position.	The arms come down, position A, then 1st.
4th, 1st eighth	GRAND BATTEMENT JETÉ with the left leg to the front in croisé.	5th position of arms (left arm up).
2nd, 3rd eighth	GRAND BATTEMENT JETÉ with the right leg back in croisé, 4th arabesque position.	The left arm comes down and stretches forward: 4th arabesque arm position.
4th, 1st eighth	GRAND BATTEMENT JETÉ with the left leg to the side, in écarté back (to corner No. 6). (End in 5th position back.)	The left arm moves upward: 5th position, then 2nd position.
2nd, 3rd eighth	Stand in 5th position.	The arms come down, position A.
4th, 1st eighth	GRAND BATTEMENT JETÉ with the right leg to the side (change), en face.	Reach 2nd position through 1st position.
2nd, 3rd eighth	GRAND BATTEMENT JETÉ with the left leg to the side (change).	2nd

CONCLUDING EXERCISE FOR THE MEN'S CLASS:

4th eighth, *1 bar*	PRÉPARATION POUR PIROUETTES EN DEHORS with the right foot (in 2nd position).	2nd - 6th (right arm bent).
1 bar, *1st, 2nd, 3rd* *eighth*	PIROUETTES EN DEHORS. (End in 5th position, croisé, right foot back.)	The right arm opens during the course of the movement, then the arms meet between A and 1st; end in 2nd position.

CONCLUDING EXERCISE FOR THE WOMEN'S CLASS:

4th eighth, *1 bar*	PRÉPARATION POUR PIROUETTES EN DEHORS with the right foot (in 4th position, croisé).	A - 1st - 3rd arabesque arm position (right arm in front).
1 bar, *1st, 2nd, 3rd* *eighth*	PIROUETTES EN DEHORS. (End in 5th position croisé, right foot back.)	The right arm opens during the course of the movement, then the arms meet between A and 1st, end in 2nd position.

8 bars   Repeat the exercise on the other leg.

Total accompaniment
16 bars

(*Pause*)
Repeat the exercise in the reverse
direction. (The execution of the
pirouettes remains en dehors.)

Measure 2/4
Tempo
moderate
Introduction
(1 bar)

7. SMALL JUMPS

Preparation
Starting position of the feet: 5th
position, croisé, left foot front.

Starting position of
arms: A.

Off-beat *(4th)*, *1st eighth*	ASSEMBLÉ with the right leg to the side (change), changing épaulement croisé.	A
2nd, 3rd *eighth*	ASSEMBLÉ with the left leg to the side (change) changing épaulement croisé.	
4th, 1st *eighth*	ASSEMBLÉ with the right leg to the side (change) changing épaulement croisé.	
2nd, 3rd *eighth*	SISSONNE SIMPLE with the right leg, left foot sur le cou-de-pied back.	
4th, 1st *eighth*	BALLOTTÉ with the right leg to the side (No. 3).	Reach 2nd position through 1st.
2nd eighth	Lower the right leg (back of the left leg) in demi-plié.	2nd
3rd eighth	STEP - COUPÉ with the left leg to the side (No. 7).	
4th, 1st *eighth*	ASSEMBLÉ with the right leg in front, croisé (through 1st position). (End in demi-plié.)	6th (right arm bent), then arm position A.
2nd, 3rd	Come up from demi-plié.	

4 bars   Repeat the exercise on the other leg.

Total accompaniment
8 bars

(*Pause*)
Repeat the exercise in the reverse
direction.

Measure 2/4
Tempo
moderate
Introduction
(2 bars)

8. SMALL JUMPS WITH BEATS

Preparation
Starting position of the feet:
5th position, croisé, right foot front.

Starting position of
arms: A.

Off-beat *(4th)*, *1st eighth*	ENTRECHAT-TROIS. (Right foot ends sur le cou-de-pied back, change the épaulement croisé, and turn the head to the left.)	A - 6th (left arm bent).
2nd, 3rd *eighth*	BALLOTTÉ with the left leg to the side (No. 7), then	The left arm opens to the side: 2nd position (hands turned out).
4th eighth	the left foot lowers (in the back of the right leg) in demi-plié.	2nd (hands turned in).
1st eighth	STEP - COUPÉ with the right leg to the side (No. 3).	6th (left arm bent),
2nd, 3rd *eighth*	ASSEMBLÉ with the left leg front (through 1st position), croisé.	then - A.
4th, 1st *eighth*	ENTRECHAT-CINQ. (Right foot ends sur le cou-de-pied back.)	A - 6th (left arm bent).
2nd, 3rd *eighth*	GLISSADE (do not change) with the right foot to the side (No. 3).	The arms open slightly to the side and turn in again - position A.
4th, 1st *eighth*	BRISÉ with the right foot forward diagonally (to corner No. 2), right foot ends in 5th position back.	6th (right arm bent).
2nd, 3rd *eighth*	ENTRECHAT-QUATRE. (Épaulement croisé, left foot front.)	A

4 bars   Repeat the exercise on the other leg.

Total accompaniment
8 bars

(*Pause*)
Repeat the exercise in the reverse
direction.

Measure 2/4
Tempo
moderate   **9.   MEDIUM JUMPS**
Introduction   Preparation
(2 bars)   Starting position of the feet: 5th   Starting position of
                  position, croisé, right foot front.   arms: A.

Start from corner No. 6.

Off-beat   FAILLI   A, 2nd allongée, left
(4th),   with the left foot, ending front in   arm moves down and
1st eighth   croisé.   front (palms down).

2nd, 3rd, 4th   CHASSÉ   The right arm opens
eighth   with the right leg in front, in effacé.   in front, the left arm
                                                        moves to the side
                                                        (hands turned out),
                                                        then 2nd.

1st, 2nd, 3rd   STEP - COUPÉ   6th (left arm bent).
eighth   with the right leg to the side (No. 3).
                  CABRIOLE
                  with the left leg front, in croisé.

4th, 1st, 2nd, COUPÉ DESSUS   A - 1st
3rd   with the left foot.
eighth   SISSONNE TOMBÉE EN TOURNANT   then the right arm
                  EN DEHORS   moves to the side,
                  with the right leg (end front croisé, simultaneously the
                  facing corner No. 8)   left arm stretches
                  CABRIOLE   forward: 3rd
                  with the left leg back, in croisé.   arabesque arm
                                                        position.

4th eighth   TOMBER PIED DESSOUS   A
                  with the left foot, right foot sur le
                  cou-de-pied front.

1st, 2nd, 3rd   STEP - COUPÉ   6th (left arm bent).
eighth   with the right leg to the side (No. 3).
                  ASSEMBLÉ
                  with the left leg front (through 1st
                  position) in croisé.

---

4 bars   Repeat the exercise on the other leg.

Total accompaniment
8 bars   (*Pause*)
                  Repeat the exercise once more.

Measure 3/4
(Waltz)
Tempo
moderate
Introduction
(2 bars)

10. BIG JUMPS

	Preparation Starting position of the feet: 5th position, croisé, right foot front.	Starting position of the arms: A.

Start from corner No. 6.

Off-beat (2nd, 3rd), 1st, 2nd, 3rd fourth	GLISSADE (do not change) with the right foot, diagonally forward (to corner No. 2). GRANDE CABRIOLE with the right leg front, in effacé.	Position A, from below the arms open to the side, then the right arm closes in the front, bent at the elbow: 6th position of arms.
1st, 2nd fourth	TOMBÉ on the right foot front, in effacé, then	The right arm opens fluidly to the front (hands turned out), then the right arm moves to the side:
3rd fourth	pull the left leg to the right leg in a small jump (turn slightly to the right).	2nd position of arms.
1st, 2nd, 3rd fourth	STEP - COUPÉ with the right leg to the side. GRANDE CABRIOLE with the left leg front, in croisé.	The left arm closes in front, bent at the elbow: 6th position of arms.
1st, 2nd fourth *3rd fourth*	TOMBÉ on the left foot front, croisé, then pull the right leg to the left in a small jump (turn slightly to the left).	The left arm opens fluidly to the front (hands turned out), then the left arm moves to the side: 2nd position of arms.
1st, 2nd, 3rd fourth	STEP - COUPÉ with the left leg to the side. GRANDE CABRIOLE with the right leg front, in effacé.	The right arm closes in front, bent at the elbow: 6th position of arms.

Glissade-double cabriole, in effacé

Maris Liepa

1st, 2nd *fourth*	TOMBÉ on the right foot front, in effacé.	The right arm opens in front (hands turned out).
3rd fourth	STEP with the left foot forward diagonally (to corner No. 2).	2nd allongée.
1st fourth *2nd, 3rd,* *1st, 2nd* *fourth*	STEP - PIQUÉ on the right leg forward diagonally (to corner No. 2), rise on half toe, simultaneously lift the left leg (45°), in back effacé, stand in 2nd arabesque (on half toe), then	The left arm (from below) rises and stretches to the front: 2nd arabesque arm position.
3rd fourth	DEMI-PLIÉ on the right leg, continuing with CHASSÉ with the left foot back, in effacé, turning halfway to the left. STEP - COUPÉ with the left leg moving to corner No. 6.	2nd allongée.
1 bar, *1st, 2nd* *fourth*	GRANDE CABRIOLE FOUETTÉE EN TOURNANT EN DEDANS. (End with the right leg back, in croisé, 4th arabesque position.)	A - 1st - 4th arabesque position (arm in front).
3rd fourth, *1 bar,* *1st, 2nd* *fourth*	COUPÉ DESSOUS with the right foot. PETIT ASSEMBLÉ with the left leg front, in croisé. ENTRECHAT-SIX. (Change épaulement croisé.)	A A - 1st - 3rd
3rd, 1st *fourth*	SISSONNE TOMBÉE with the left leg front, in effacé (to corner No. 8).	The left arm opens front, simultaneously the right arm moves to the side (hands turned out).
2nd, 3rd *fourth*	PAS DE BOURRÉE EN DEHORS stepping under twice.	2nd (hands turned in).

CONCLUDING EXERCISE FOR THE MEN'S CLASS:

1st, 2nd *fourth*	End in 5th position croisé on demi-plié, right foot front.	A
3rd fourth	PRÉPARATION POUR TOURS EN L'AIR EN DEHORS. Rise on half toe in 5th position.	6th (right arm bent).
1st fourth	Demi-plié.	
2nd, 3rd, 1st *fourth*	DOUBLE TOUR EN L'AIR EN DEHORS. (End in 5th position, right foot back, épaulement croisé.)	The right arm opens during the course of the movement, then the arms join between A and 1st; end in 2nd (hands slightly turned out).

CONCLUDING EXERCISE FOR THE WOMEN'S CLASS:

1st fourth   End (pas de bourrée en dehors) in 4th   6th (right arm bent).
position, croisé, right foot front in
plié à quart.

2nd fourth   Stand in the preparatory position for
pirouettes en dedans.

3rd fourth   DÉGAGÉ   The right arm opens
with the left leg to the side (45°),   to the side, then
on the demi-plié of the right leg.

1 bar   PIROUETTES EN DEDANS.   continues the
1st fourth   (End in 5th position, left foot front,   movement upward,
épaulement croisé.)   the left arm bends in
the front, 4th
position of arms.
End with the position
"two arms in front,"
right arm higher than
the left.

Total accompaniment
16 bars

(*Pause*)
Repeat the exercise once more.

(*Pause*)
Repeat the exercise on the other leg
(starting from corner No. 4).

11. SMALL JUMPS

Measure 2/4
Tempo lively
Introduction
(1 bar)

Preparation
Starting position of the feet: 4th position, croisé, left foot stretched backward, pointe tendue.

Starting position of arms: 6th (right arm bent).

Off-beat (4th) eighth

DEMI-PLIÉ
on the right leg, simultaneously the left leg bends in the back.

6th (right arm bent).

1st, 2nd, 3rd eighth

COUPÉ-DESSOUS
with the left foot.

PETITE CABRIOLE
with the right leg front, in effacé.

6th (left arm bent).

4th, 1st eighth

TOMBER PIED DESSUS
on the right foot, the left leg bends sur le cou-de-pied back.

The left arm opens to the side, 2nd position of arms (hands slightly turned out).

2nd, 3rd eighth

JETÉ BATTU
with the left leg to the side (No. 7), the right foot ends sur le cou-de-pied back.

The hands turn in, the arms come down to position A.

4th, 1st, 2nd eighth

BALLOTTÉ
with the left leg to the side, in écarté back, to corner No. 6
(turn the head to the right).

The arms open to the side (through the 1st position): 2nd position (hands slightly turned out).

3rd, 4th eighth,

LOWER
the left leg in the back of the right leg in demi-plié, continuing with

The hands turn in.

1st, 2nd, 3rd eighth

STEP - COUPÉ
with the right leg to the side (No. 3).

PETITE CABRIOLE
with the left leg front, in croisé.

6th (left arm bent).

4th, 1st, 2nd eighth

BALLOTTÉ
with the right leg to the side, in écarté front, to corner No. 2 (turn the head to the right).

The left arm opens to the side (hands move with palms turned in) 2nd allongée.

3rd, 4th eighth

TOMBER PIED DESSUS
on the right foot, continuing with

A

1st, 2nd, 3rd eighth	STEP - COUPÉ with the left leg to the side (No. 7). PETITE CABRIOLE with the right leg back, in croisé then	Reach 3rd arabesque going through 1st position (right arm in front).
4th eighth	the right foot bends in the back.	A
1st, 2nd, 3rd eighth	COUPÉ-DESSOUS with the right leg. PETITE CABRIOLE with the leg to the side (No. 7), then	The arms open to the side going through the 1st position, 2nd position of arms (hands slightly turned out).
4th eighth	the left foot bends in the back.	
1st, 2nd, 3rd eighth	COUPÉ-DESSOUS with the left leg. PETITE CABRIOLE with the right leg to the side (No. 3).	

8 bars	Repeat the exercise on the other leg.

Total accompaniment
16 bars

(*Pause*)
Repeat the exercise once more.

Measure 3/4
(Waltz brillante)

12. BIG JUMPS

Tempo lively Introduction (2 bars)

Preparation Starting position of the feet: 4th position, effacé, left foot stretched in the back, pointe tendue.	Starting position of arms: 1st arabesque, right arm in the front.

Start from corner No. 2.

Off-beat (2nd, 3rd) fourth

CHASSÉ
with the left leg back, in effacé, turning halfway to the left.

1st arabesque, then 2nd allongée.

1 bar, 1st, 2nd fourth

JETÉ ENTRELACÉ
(end in 1st arabesque, effacé).

A - 1st - 3rd, end in 1st arabesque position (right arm in front).

3rd fourth, 1 bar, 1st, 2nd fourth

CHASSÉ
with the left leg backward, in effacé, turning halfway to the left.

2nd allongée.

STEP - COUPÉ
with the left leg (to corner No. 6).

GRANDE CABRIOLE FOUETTÉE
EN TOURNANT EN DEDANS
with the right leg, end in 3rd arabesque position.

A - 1st - 3rd, end in 3rd arabesque position (right arm in front).

3rd fourth, 1 bar, 1st, 2nd fourth

TOMBER PIED DESSOUS
on the right foot.

A

SISSONNE TOMBÉE
with the left leg front (with a half turn to the left) to corner No. 6.

The left arm opens to the front moving through the 1st position, simultaneously the right arm moves to the side (hands turned out).

CABRIOLE FAILLI
with the right leg, end in front, croisé (facing corner No. 6).

The left arm moves to the side, simultaneously the hands turn in, making a stroke upward, 2nd allongée, then A.

3rd fourth, *1 bar*	PAS DE BASQUE to the back, with the left leg, and a half turn to the right (end facing corner No. 2).	A - 1st - 2nd - A
1st, 2nd *fourth,*	SISSONNE TOMBÉE with the left leg front, in croisé.	1st (wide) position.
3rd fourth, *1 bar*	GLISSADE (do not change) with the right foot diagonally forward (to corner No. 2).	The arms open to the side and turn in, closing in position A.
	GRANDE CABRIOLE[1] with the right leg front, in effacé.	A - 1st - 5th (left arm up).
1st, 2nd *fourth,*	TOMBÉ on the right foot front, in effacé.	2nd (hands turned out).
3rd fourth, *2 bars*	PAS DE BOURRÉE EN DEHORS (changing feet) traveling forward diagonally to corner No. 2.	A
	GRAND ASSEMBLÉ ENTRECHAT-SIX DE VOLÉ with the right leg to the side, in écarté front (to corner No. 2).	2nd allongée (right arm raised slightly higher than the left), end position A.

[1] Execution of double cabriole for the men's class.

Glissade, grand fouetté sauté en tournant en dehors, ending in 1st arabesque

Rimma Karelskaya

CONCLUDING EXERCISE FOR THE MEN'S CLASS:

1 bar	PRÉPARATION POUR PIROUETTES EN DEHORS with the right foot (in 2nd position).	A - 1st - 2nd - 6th (right arm bent).
2 bars, 1st fourth	PIROUETTES EN DEHORS. (End in 3rd arabesque, left leg in demi-plié.)	The right arm opens during the course of the movement, then the arms meet between A and 1st, end 3rd arabesque position of arms (right arm in front).

CONCLUDING EXERCISE FOR THE WOMEN'S CLASS:

1st, 2nd fourth	PRÉPARATION POUR CHAÎNÉS-DÉBOULÉS. (Step on the left leg to the side, toward corner No. 6, bring the right foot in front croisé, pointe tendue.)	6th (right arm bent).
3rd fourth, 2 bars, 1st fourth	CHAÎNÉS-DÉBOULÉS forward diagonally to corner No. 2 (end in arabesque effacé, the left leg raised in the back, 90°), the right leg in demi-plié.	The right arm opens during the course of the movement, then the arms meet between A and 1st. End in position "two arms in front" (right arm higher than the left).

Total accompaniment
16 bars

(*Pause*)
Repeat the exercise once more.

(*Pause*)
Repeat the whole combination on the other leg.

Measure 3/4
Tempo lively
Introduction
(2 bars)

13. JUMPS
(FOR THE MEN'S CLASS)

Preparation
Starting position of the feet: 4th position, croisé, left foot stretched in the back, pointe tendue.

Starting position of the arms: 6th (left arm bent).

Start from corner No. 4.

Off-beat
(2nd, 3rd),
1st, 2nd
fourth

DEMI-PLIÉ
on the right leg, the left leg bends sur le cou-de-pied back.

6th (left arm bent).

SISSONNE TOMBÉE
with the left leg, in effacé front.

6th (right arm bent).

3rd, 1st, 2nd
fourth

SISSONNE TOMBÉE
with the right leg, in front croisé, continuing with

6th (right arm bent).

3rd, 1st
fourth

PETIT ASSEMBLÉ
with the left leg back in croisé.

6th (right arm bent).

2nd, 3rd,
1st, 2nd
fourth

DOUBLE TOUR EN L'AIR EN DEHORS
(position tire-bouchon, right foot back), end in 1st arabesque effacé (facing corner No. 8).

3rd position of arms, end in 1st arabesque position (left arm in front).

3rd fourth,
11 bars,
1st fourth

Repeat the combination again 3 times consecutively, traveling diagonally forward to corner No. 8. End the last double tour en l'air in the position "on the knee" (land down on the right knee after the jump) épaulement effacé (turn the head to the right).

The enumeration of the arm movements are executed again 3 times consecutively, end in 5th position (right arm up).

Total accompaniment
16 bars

(Pause)
Repeat the exercise once more.

(Pause)
Repeat the exercise on the other leg (start from corner No. 6, then travel forward diagonally to corner No. 2).

Measure 2/4
Tempo lively
Introduction
(2 bars)

14.   PETITS CHANGEMENTS DE PIEDS
ET ENTRECHATS

Preparation
Starting position of the feet: 5th   Starting position of
position, croisé, right foot front.   arms: A.

Off-beat   4 ENTRECHATS-SIX[1].   A, then the arms rise
(4th) eighth,   slightly to the side
7 bars   and come down - A.

1st, 2nd, 3rd   7 PETITS CHANGEMENTS DE PIEDS.   Position A.
eighth

---

8 bars   Repeat the exercise once more.

Total accompaniment
16 bars

Measure 3/4
(Waltz)
Tempo slow
Introduction
(2 bars)

15.   PORT DE BRAS AND BENDING
OF THE BODY
(FOR THE MEN'S CLASS)

Preparation
Starting position of the feet: 1st   Starting position of
position (halfway turned out).   arms: 2nd position.

This given exercise corresponds to
exercise 15 (exercises in the center) of
the first class (see page 108).

Total accompaniment
32 bars

---

[1] Change épaulement croisé on entrechat six.

Measure 2/4
Tempo lively
Introduction
(2 bars)

16.   FIRST EXERCISE ON POINTES

Preparation
Starting position of feet: 5th position,   Starting position of
croisé, right foot front.   arms: A.

Off-beat *(4th) eighth,* *1 bar,* *1st, 2nd, 3rd* *eighth*	ÉCHAPPÉ SUR LES POINTES in 4th position, with demi-plié in 4th position, épaulement croisé.	A - 1st - 3rd arabesque arm position (left arm in front), end A.
4th eighth, *1 bar,* *1st, 2nd, 3rd* *eighth*	ÉCHAPPÉ SUR LES POINTES in 2nd position, with demi-plié in 2nd position (en face), end with the right foot back, in 5th position.	A - 1st - 2nd - A
4 bars	Repeat the exercise on the other leg.	Arms position A.
8 bars	Repeat the whole combination once more.	
8 bars	Échappés in 4th and 2nd position (do not come down in demi-plié).	

Total accompaniment
24 bars

17. SECOND EXERCISE ON POINTES

Measure 2/4
Tempo
moderate
Introduction
(2 bars)

Preparation
Starting position of the feet:
4th position, croisé, right foot
stretched in the back, pointe tendue.

Starting position of
arms: A.

Off-beat *(4th),* *1st eighth*	PETIT PAS DE CHAT (a kick of the legs forward), diagonally to corner No. 2.	A - 1st, 6th (right arm bent).
2nd, 3rd *eighth*	PETIT JETÉ with the right leg to the side, left foot ends sur le cou-de-pied back (not on pointe).	The right arm opens to the side, simultaneously the left arm bends in front: 6th position of arms.
4th, 1st, 2nd *eighth*	STEP - PIQUÉ SUR LA POINTE with the left leg to the side (No. 7). PETIT DÉVELOPPÉ (45°) with the right leg in front, croisé.	The left arm opens in front (hands outward).
3rd, 4th *eighth*	TOMBER PIED DESSUS on the right foot.	A
1st, 2nd, 3rd, *4th, 1st, 2nd* *eighth*	COUPÉ DESSOUS with the left leg. BALLONNÉ with the right leg to the side (end with the right foot sur le cou-de-pied back). Then continue with FOUETTÉ EN TOURNANT EN DEHORS (45°) with the right leg (end with the right leg front, 45°, croisé, on left pointe).	A - 1st - 2nd 6th (left arm bent). 1st - 6th (right arm bent).
3rd eighth	TOMBÉ on the right foot front, croisé.	The right arm opens in front (hands slightly turned out).

---

4 bars   Repeat the exercise on the other leg.

8 bars   Repeat the whole combination once
more.

Total accompaniment
16 bars

Measure 3/4
(Waltz)
Tempo slow
Introduction
(2 bars)

18.   THIRD EXERCISE ON POINTES

Preparation

Starting position of the feet: 4th position, croisé, right foot stretched in the front, pointe tendue.	Starting position of arms: 6th position (right arm bent).

Off-beat *(3rd) fourth* *1st, 2nd* *fourth*	TOMBÉ on the right foot, front, in effacé. TOUR EN DEDANS in 1st arabesque.	The right arm stretches forward (hands turn outward): 1st arabesque arm position.
3rd fourth *1st, 2nd* *fourth*	DEMI-PLIÉ on the right leg. TOUR EN DEDANS in 1st arabesque.	1st arabesque arm position (right arm in front).
3rd fourth *1st, 2nd* *fourth*	DEMI-PLIÉ on the right leg. TOUR EN DEDANS in 1st arabesque.	1st arabesque arm position (right arm in front).
3rd fourth *1st, 2nd* *fourth*	DEMI-PLIÉ on the right leg. GRAND TEMPS RELEVÉ EN DEDANS with the left leg, continue with TOUR EN DEDANS with the left leg bent halfway in front (90°).	1st arabesque, then 4th (right arm up).
3rd fourth *1st, 2nd* *fourth*	TOMBÉ on the left foot front, croisé. TOUR EN DEHORS in 3rd arabesque.	3rd arabesque arm position (right arm in front).
3rd fourth *1st, 2nd* *fourth*	DEMI-PLIÉ on the left leg. TOUR EN DEHORS in 3rd arabesque.	3rd arabesque arm position (right arm in front).
3rd fourth *1st, 2nd* *fourth*	DEMI-PLIÉ on the left leg. TOUR EN DEHORS in 3rd arabesque.	As above.

Tour en dedans in 1st arabesque

Rimma Karelskaya

3rd fourth	DEMI-PLIÉ on the left leg.	3rd arabesque arm position (right arm
1st, 2nd *fourth*	TOUR EN DEHORS with the right leg bent halfway in front (90°).	in front), then 4th (left arm up).
3rd fourth	TOMBÉ on the right foot front, in effacé, then	1st arabesque arm position (right arm in front).
7 bars, *1st, 2nd* *fourth*	repeat the execution of the whole combination from the beginning (starting with tour en dedans in 1st arabesque, etc.).	

Total accompaniment
16 bars

(*Pause*)
Repeat the exercise on the other leg.

Measure 3/4
Tempo
moderate
Introduction
(2 bars)

19. FOURTH EXERCISE ON POINTES

Preparation
Starting position of the feet: 4th   Starting position of
position, croisé, right foot stretched in   arms: 6th position
the front, pointe tendue.   (right arm bent).

Start from corner No. 6, then
travel forward diagonally to corner No. 2.

Off-beat	DEMI-PLIÉ	The right arm opens
(3rd)	on the left leg, simultaneously lift	during the course of
fourth	the right leg in front (25°) and bring	the movement, then
	it in the direction of corner No. 2.	the arms meet
1st, 2nd	DOUBLE TOUR PIQUÉ EN DEDANS	between A and 1st
fourth	(during the turn on the right leg, the	position.
	left foot is sur le cou-de-pied back).	
5th eighth	End on demi-plié of the left leg (right	
	foot sur le cou-de-pied front).	
6th eighth	TOMBÉ	The arms open to the
	on the right foot to the side,	side going through
	simultaneously	the 1st position.
	DÉGAGÉ	
	with the left leg to the side (45°).	
1st, 2nd	DOUBLE TOUR PIQUÉ EN DEHORS	The arms meet
fourth	(during the turn of the left leg, the	between A and 1st
	right foot is sur le cou-de-pied front.	position, then
	Then stretch the right leg in front	
	(45°) croisé, the left leg remains on	6th (right arm bent).
	pointe.	
5th eighth	STEP	The right arm opens
	on the right foot to corner No. 2.	during the course of
		the movement.
6th eighth	STEP OVER	The arms meet
	on the left leg (in the same direction),	between A and 1st.
	with a full turn to the right, and come	
	on it in demi-plié, the right leg bent	
	in front sur le cou-de-pied, épaulement	
	croisé.	

5 bars, *1st, 2nd* *fourth*	Repeat the whole combination 3 more times consecutively. End the last double tour piqué en dehors in 4th position croisé, right foot back, the left leg in front in plié à quart.	Arm movements as above. End in 3rd arabesque arm position (right arm in front).

Total accompaniment
8 bars

(*Pause*)

Repeat the exercise on the other leg
(start from corner No. 4, travel
forward diagonally, to corner No. 8).

Measure 2/4
Tempo
moderate
Introduction
(*1 bar*)

20. FIFTH EXERCISE ON POINTES

	Preparation Starting position of the feet: 4th position, croisé, left leg stretched in the back, pointe tendue.	Starting position of arms: 6th position (right arm bent).
Off-beat (*4th*) *eighth*	DEMI-PLIÉ on the right leg, left leg bent in the back.	6th (right arm bent).
2 bars	8 SAUTÉS SUR LA POINTE on the left leg, the right leg bent in front 45° (execute two turns to the right).	6th (left arm bent).
2 bars	8 SAUTÉS SUR LA POINTE on the right leg, the left leg bent in the back 45° (execute two turns to the right).	6th (right arm bent).

2 bars	8 SAUTÉS SUR LA POINTE on the left leg, the right leg bent in front, 90° (execute one turn to the right).	5th (left arm up).
1 bar, *1st eighth*	5 SAUTÉS SUR LA POINTE on the right leg, the left leg bent in the back, in attitude effacée (lean the head slightly forward, looking to the right under the arm), execute one turn to the right.	5th (right arm up).
2nd eighth	Come down in demi-plié on the right leg after the fifth sauté, then	The right arm lowers in front: 6th position arms.
3rd eighth	RELEVÉ SUR LA POINTE on the right leg, simultaneously stretch the left leg back (90°), in effacé.	1st arabesque arm position (right arm in front).

Total accompaniment
8 bars

(Pause)
Repeat the exercise on the other leg.

Measure 3/4
Tempo fast
Introduction
(2 bars)

21. SIXTH EXERCISE ON POINTES

Preparation
Starting position of the feet: 5th   Starting position of
position, croisé, right foot front.   arms: A.

Start from corner No. 7.

Off-beat *(3rd) fourth,* *3 bars*	PAS SUIVI traveling to side No. 3 lean the head slightly forward (looking to the right under the arm).	A - 1st - 5th (right arm up).
1 bar	STEP on the right foot to side (No. 3), coming down in demi-plié, bring the left leg front croisé, pointe tendue (lean the head slightly forward, looking to the left under the arm).	5th (left arm up).

Pose croisé front (right foot pointe tendue, the left leg in demi-plié) position "under the arm," 5th position arms

Pose croisé front, 4th position arms

Pose croisé to the back, 4th position arms

Pose croisé to the back (left foot pointe tendue, the right leg in demi-plié) position "under the arm," 5th position arms

Nina Sorokina

3 bars	PAS SUIVI left foot in front, traveling to side No. 7 (lean the head slightly forward, looking to the left under the arm).	5th (left arm up).
1 bar	STEP on the left foot to side (No. 7), coming down in demi-plié, bring the right leg in front croisé, pointe tendue (lean the head slightly forward, looking under the arm).	5th (right arm up).
4 bars	PAS COURU traveling forward diagonally to corner No. 2 (lean the body slightly front, then gradually straighten out, with the head slightly raised).	The arms come down (hands turn inward), then the arms gradually rise in front, to the level of the forward-looking face; end the movement with a fluid stroke of the hands upward.
3 bars	PAS COURU traveling in a straight line to side No. 7, "backward" during the course of the movement (the body leans slightly forward, turn the head to the left, and at the end of the movement the body straightens out and turns to the left).	The arms gradually come down and move slightly backward.
1st fourth	STEP - PIQUÉ on the left foot front, to side No. 7, lift the right leg to the back in 2nd arabesque.	The right arm (from below) moves up, simultaneously the left arm moves to the side: 2nd arabesque arm position.
2nd fourth	Stand in 2nd arabesque position.	2nd arabesque arm position.

Total accompaniment
16 bars

(*Pause*)
Repeat the exercise on the other leg
(start from side No. 3).

22.   SEVENTH EXERCISE ON POINTES

Measure 2/4
Tempo
moderate
Introduction
(2 bars)

Preparation
Starting position of the feet: 4th position, en face, left leg front in plié à quart.

Starting position of arms: 2nd arabesque arm position (right arm forward).

Off-beat
(2nd, 3rd,
4th)
eighth,

DEMI-PLIÉ
in 4th position.

2nd arabesque arm position (right arm in front).

TOUR EN DEHORS
then continue, after the turn, with

The right arm opens during the course of the movement, then the arms meet between A and 1st position.

15 bars

15 FOUETTÉS EN TOURNANT EN DEHORS (45°)
each time, open the right leg in front croisé (45°). After the concluding fouetté en tournant en dehors, the right leg moves in 5th position back (demi-plié in 5th position). Then

The arms open to the side through the 1st position, then join between A and 1st, etc.

1st eighth

RELEVÉ
in 5th position.

1st - 2nd (hands turned out).

Total accompaniment
16 bars

(*Pause*)
Repeat the exercise once more.

Fouetté en tournant en dehors, the working leg opens to the front from (45°) in croisé ending in 4th position, croisé

Nina Sorokina

Measure 2/4
Tempo lively
Introduction
(1 bar)

23. EIGHTH EXERCISE ON POINTES

Preparation
Starting position of the feet:
5th position, en face, right foot front.

Starting position of arms: A.

Off-beat
(4th) eighth,
7 bars,
1st, 2nd, 3rd
eighth

16 PETITS CHANGEMENTS DE
PIEDS SUR LES POINTES.

A - 1st - 3rd - 2nd - A.

Total accompaniment
8 bars

Measure 3/4
(Waltz)
Tempo slow
Introduction
(2 bars)

24. PORT DE BRAS AND BENDING OF THE BODY

Preparation
Starting position of the feet: 1st
position (halfway turned out).

Starting position of arms: 2nd position.

This exercise corresponds to exercise 15
(exercises in the center) of the first
class (see page 108).

Total accompaniment
32 bars

Fourth Class

EXERCISES AT THE BARRE

DANCING EXERCISES

---

*Measure 3/4
(Waltz)
Tempo slow
Introduction
(2 bars)*

1. GRANDS PLIÉS

Preparation
Starting position of the feet: 1st
position.

Starting position of
the right arm: 2nd
position.

This exercise corresponds to exercise 1
(exercises at the barre) of the first
class (see page 55).

---

*Total accompaniment
32 bars*

Measure 2/4
Tempo
moderate   ## 2.   BATTEMENTS TENDUS
Introduction
(1 bar)   Preparation
                     Starting position of the feet: 5th   Starting position of
                     position, right foot front.   the right arm: 2nd
                                                                 position.

Off-beat *(4th),* *1st, 2nd, 3rd* *eighth*	2 BATTEMENTS TENDUS with the right foot to the front.	2nd, end in position A.
4th, 1st, 2nd, *3rd* *eighth*	2 BATTEMENTS TENDUS with the left foot to the back.	The right arm rises and stretches forward (palm facing down).
4th, 1st, 2nd, *3rd* *eighth*	2 BATTEMENTS TENDUS with the right foot to the side (change).	2nd
4th, 1st, 2nd, *3rd* *eighth*	BATTEMENT TENDU with the right foot to the side, in demi-plié in 2nd position. End in 5th position back.	2nd - 1st - 2nd

4 bars	Repeat the exercise in the reverse direction.
8 bars	Repeat the whole combination once more.

Total accompaniment
16 bars

              Turn to the other side and repeat the
              exercise on the other leg.

3. BATTEMENTS TENDUS JETÉS

Measure 2/4
Tempo lively
Introduction
(1 bar)

Preparation

	Starting position of the feet: 5th position, right foot front.	Starting position of right arm: 2nd position.

Off-beat (4th), 1st, 2nd, 3rd eighth	3 BATTEMENTS TENDUS JETÉS with the leg to the front.	2nd, end in position A.
4th, 1st, 2nd, 3rd eighth	3 BATTEMENTS TENDUS JETÉS with the left leg to the back.	The right arm rises and stretches forward (palm facing down).
4th, 1st, 2nd, 3rd, 4th, 1st, 2nd, 3rd eighth	7 BATTEMENTS TENDUS JETÉS with the right leg to the side (change).	2nd

4 bars	Repeat the exercise in the reverse direction.
8 bars	Repeat the whole combination once more.

Total accompaniment
16 bars

Turn to the other side and repeat the exercise on the other leg.

Measure 3/4
Tempo lively
Introduction
(2 bars)

4. RONDS DE JAMBE À TERRE

Preparation
Starting position of the feet[1]

Starting position of
the right arm: 2nd
position.

4 bars

4 RONDS DE JAMBE À TERRE
EN DEHORS
with the right leg.

2nd position.

3 bars

3 GRANDS RONDS DE JAMBE JETÉS.

1 bar
8 bars

1 ROND DE JAMBE À TERRE.
Repeat the exercise once en dehors
(with the following change at the end
of the combination: do not execute
the last rond de jambe à terre—the
right leg slides through 1st position
front, pointe tendue).

8 bars

Repeat the exercise in the reverse
direction: en dedans.

8 bars

Repeat the exercise once more en
dedans (with the following change at
the end of the combination: do not
execute the last rond de jambe à
terre—bring the right leg in 5th
position front).
Start immediately thereafter the
following combination of movements:

Tempo slow
32 bars

PORT DE BRAS ET BATTEMENTS
RELEVÉS LENTS (90°).
(This exercise corresponds to the
second part of exercise 5, exercises at
the barre, of the first class. See page
62).

Total accompaniment
64 bars

Turn to the other side and repeat the
exercise on the other leg.

[1] Execute the ronds de jambe immediately after preparation, following the movement of the
preparatory rond.

Measure 2/4
Tempo slow
Introduction
(2 bars)

5. BATTEMENTS FONDUS

Preparation

Starting position of the feet: 2nd position, right foot pointe tendue.	Starting position of the right arm: 2nd position.

Off-beat *(4th)*, *1st, 2nd, 3rd* *eighth*	BATTEMENT FONDU with the right leg in front (45°).	2nd - A - 1st - 2nd
4th, 1st, 2nd, *3rd* *eighth*	TOMBÉ with the third leg front, following with BATTEMENT FONDU with the left leg to the back (45°).	A, then the right arm rises in front (palm facing down).
4th, 1st, 2nd, *3rd* *eighth*	TOMBÉ with the left leg to the back, following with BATTEMENT FONDU with the right leg to the side (45°).	A - 1st - 2nd
4th, 1st *eighth*	DEMI-PLIÉ on the left leg.	2nd
2nd, 3rd *eighth*	BRING the right leg to the back (45°), simultaneously come up from demi-plié on the left leg.	2nd

4 bars	Repeat the exercise in the reverse direction.
8 bars	Repeat the whole combination once more (on half toe).

Total accompaniment
16 bars

Turn to the other side and repeat the exercise on the other leg.

Measure 2/4
Tempo
moderate
Introduction
(1 bar)

6. BATTEMENTS FRAPPÉS ET RONDS DE JAMBE EN L'AIR

Preparation
Starting position of the feet: 2nd position, right foot pointe tendue.

Starting position of the right arm: 2nd position.

Off-beat *(4th)* *eighth* *1 bar*	BATTEMENT FRAPPÉ with the right leg front, pointe tendue. BATTEMENT FRAPPÉ with the right leg, to the side. BATTEMENT FRAPPÉ with the right leg, to the back. BATTEMENT FRAPPÉ with the right leg to the side.	2nd position.
1st, 2nd, 3rd *eighth*	3 BATTEMENTS FRAPPÉS with the right leg to the side (change).	
4th, 1st, 2nd *3rd eighth*	LIFT the right leg fully stretched (45°), following with 3 RONDS DE JAMBE EN L'AIR EN DEHORS (45°) with the right leg.	
4th, 1st *eighth*	TOMBER PIED DESSOUS on the right foot, the left foot sur le cou-de-pied front.	A
2nd, 3rd *eighth*	Stand on the left leg, bring the right leg to the side, pointe tendue.	1st - 2nd
4 bars	Repeat the exercise in the reverse direction.	
8 bars	Repeat the whole combination (on half toe).	

Total accompaniment
16 bars

Turn to the other side and repeat the exercise on the other leg.

	7. ADAGIO	
Measure 3/4 *(Waltz)* *Tempo slow* *Introduction* *(2 bars)*	**Preparation** Starting position of the feet: 5th position, right foot front.	Starting position of the right arm: 2nd position.
3 bars	DÉVELOPPÉ with the right leg front.	A - 1st - 2nd
1 bar	PASSER LA JAMBE $(90°)$ right leg.	A
2 bars	DÉVELOPPÉ À LA SECONDE with the right leg.	A - 1st - 2nd
1 bar	BRING the right leg front $(90°)$, in demi-plié on the left leg.	1st
1 bar	STEP OVER onto the right leg in front on half toe, lift the stretched left leg back $(90°)$.	Stretch the right arm forward (simultaneously, the hand turns with the palm down).
2 bars	TOUR EN DEHORS (a half turn to the left), the left leg raised back at $90°$.	Place the right arm on the barre, stretch the left arm to the front (palm down).
2 bars	BRING the left leg à la seconde $90°$, right foot on half toe.	Bring the left arm in 2nd position (through 1st position).
2 bars	BEND the body toward the right side.	2nd - 3rd (for the left arm).
1 bar	Straighten out the body.	3rd, 2nd (for the left arm).
1 bar	Lower the left leg to 5th position front.	2nd - A (for the left arm).
16 bars	Repeat the exercise on the other leg.	
32 bars	Repeat the whole combination in the reverse direction.	

Total accompaniment
64 bars

Measure 2/4
Tempo
moderate
Introduction
(1 bar)

8.   BATTEMENTS DOUBLES FRAPPÉS

Preparation
Starting position of the feet: 2nd
position, right foot pointe tendue.

Starting position of
right arm: 2nd
position.

Off-beat
(4th)
eighth,
7 bars,
1st, 2nd, 3rd
eighth

16 BATTEMENTS DOUBLES
FRAPPÉS
with the right foot, pointe tendue,
in turn ending in front, back, etc.

2nd position.

4th eighth,
7 bars,
1st, 2nd, 3rd
eighth

16 BATTEMENTS DOUBLES
FRAPPÉS
with the right foot, ending to
the side, pointe tendue (coming
up on half toe and down on the left
foot on each battement double
frappé).

Total accompaniment
16 bars

Turn to the other side and repeat the
exercise on the other leg.

Measure 2/4
Tempo lively
Introduction
(2 bars)

9. PETITS BATTEMENTS SUR LE COU-DE-PIED

Preparation
Starting position of the feet:
right foot sur le cou-de-pied, front
(wrapping the ankle).

Starting position of
the right arm: A.

Off-beat
(4th)
eighth,
7 bars,
1st, 2nd, 3rd
eighth

16 PETITS BATTEMENTS SUR LE
COU-DE-PIED
accent front, with the right foot.

A

4th eighth,
7 bars,
1st, 2nd, 3rd
eighth

32 BATTEMENTS BATTUS
on half toe, with the right leg
in front.

16 bars

At the end of the combination
balance on half toe in any varied poses.
(Look for the description in the second
part of exercise 11, exercises at the
barre, of the first class. See page 71).

Total accompaniment
32 bars

Turn to the other side and repeat the
exercise on the other leg.

Measure 2/4
Tempo
moderate   ## 10.   GRANDS BATTEMENTS JETÉS
Introduction
(1 bar)   Preparation
                     Starting position of the feet: 5th   Starting position of
                     position, right foot front.   the right arm: 2nd
                                                                 position.

Off-beat *(4th),* *1st, 2nd, 3rd* *eighth*	2 GRANDS BATTEMENTS JETÉS with the right leg front.	2nd, end in A position.
4th, 1st, 2nd, *3rd* *eighth*	2 GRANDS BATTEMENTS JETÉS with the left leg back.	The right arm moves forward (palm facing down).
4th, 1st, 2nd, *3rd, 4th, 1st* *eighth*	3 GRANDS BATTEMENTS JETÉS with the right leg to the side (change).	2nd
2nd, 3rd *eighth*	Stand still, right foot in 5th position back.	2nd

4 bars	Repeat the exercise in the reverse direction.
8 bars	Repeat the whole combination (on half toe).

Total accompaniment
16 bars

Turn to the other side and repeat the
exercise on the other leg.

Measure 3/4
(Waltz)
Tempo slow
Introduction
(2 bars)

11. PORT DE BRAS AND BENDING OF THE BODY

Preparation
Starting position of the feet: 1st position, facing the barre.

Starting position of the arms: both hands on the barre.

This exercise corresponds to exercise 13 (exercises at the barre) of the first class (see page 75).

Total accompaniment
32 bars

Measure 3/4
(Waltz)
Tempo slow
Introduction
(2 bars)

11a. STRETCHING OF THE LEGS AND BENDING OF THE BODY

Preparation
Starting position of the feet: lift the right leg in front and place it on the barre with the heel turned outward.

Starting position of the arms: right arm up in 3rd position, left arm on the barre.

STRETCHING TO THE FRONT
Breakdown:

2 bars
The right leg slides forward (heel turned outward), simultaneously the body leans toward the right leg.

The right arm lowers to the front, simultaneously with the bending of the body (palm down).

2 bars
The body returns to the starting position, simultaneously the right leg slides back to the starting position.

The right arm rises in the 3rd position.

2 bars
The body bends backward.

The right arm in 3rd position

1 bar
The body returns to the starting position.

	PRÉPARATION *Breakdown:*	
1 bar	Move the right leg backward in a large circle (grand rond de jambe en dehors 90°) (place the leg on the barre on the inside of the heel).	The left arm remains holding the barre, the right arm comes down to the side, then all the way down, and moves forward (palm down).

	STRETCHING TO THE BACK *Breakdown:*	
2 bars	The body bends forward and all the way down, simultaneously the right leg slides back on the barre (on the inside of the heel).	The right arm to the front and all the way down.
2 bars	The body returns to the starting position simultaneously with the right leg.	The right arm rises in the 3rd position.
2 bars	The body bends backward.	
1 bar	The body returns to the starting position.	The right arm in 3rd position.

	PRÉPARATION *Breakdown:*	
1 bar	Move the right leg forward in a large circle (grand rond de jambe en dedans 90°) and place the right leg on the barre on the outside of the heel.	The right arm lowers in the front to 1st position, moves to the side, and rises in 3rd position. The right arm in 3rd position.

16 bars	Repeat the exercise on half toe. At the end of the stretching on half toe, lift the right leg above the barre and hold for a while in the air, lower gently in 5th position front.	The right arm in 3rd position, then the right arm lowers to the side and down: position A.

Total accompaniment
32 bars

Turn to the other side and repeat the exercise on the other leg.

Stretching of the legs (the body bends backward)
Elena Tcherkaskaya

Measure 2/4
Tempo lively
Introduction
(1 bar)

12.   RELEVÉS

Preparation
Starting position of the feet: 1st
position, facing the barre.

Starting position of
the arms: both hands
on the barre.

This exercise corresponds to exercise
14 (exercises at the barre) of the first
class (see page 78).

Total accompaniment
16 bars

Position of the raised leg in croisé front (90°)
5th arm position, "under the arm"

Position of the raised leg in croisé front (90°)
in demi-plié, 5th arm position, "under the arm"

Nina Sorokina

EXERCISES IN THE CENTER

1. SMALL ADAGIO

Preparation
Starting position of the feet:
5th position, croisé, right foot front.

Starting position of
the arms: 2nd
position.

GRAND PLIÉ
in 5th position.
> *Breakdown:*

2 bars	Moving down,	2nd - A
1 bar	moving up.	A - 1st
1 bar	Rise on half toe.	1st - 2nd
	Then come down from half toe.	2nd - A

2 bars
1st, 2nd
fourth

DÉVELOPPÉ
with the right leg front, croisé
(lean the head slightly forward looking
to the right under the arm).

A -1st - 5th (right
arm up).

3rd fourth

DEMI-PLIÉ
on the left leg.

5th (right arm up).

2 bars,
1st, 2nd
fourth

STEP OVER
on the right leg forward.

LIFT
the left leg in attitude croisée.

5th (left arm up).

3rd fourth

DEMI-PLIÉ
on the right leg.

5th (right arm up).

2 bars

STEP OVER
on the left leg backward.

LIFT
the extended right leg to the front
(90°) in croisé.

3 bars

GRAND ROND DE JAMBE EN
DEHORS
with the right leg, end in 3rd
arabesque position.

The right arm opens
to the side and
moving down comes
to the front 3rd
arabesque.

1 bar	Lower the right leg to 5th position back.	The arms come down to position A.
16 bars	Repeat the exercise on the other leg.	
32 bars	Repeat the whole combination in the reverse direction.	

Total accompaniment
64 bars

Measure 2/4
Tempo
moderate
Introduction
(1 bar)

2. BATTEMENTS TENDUS

Preparation
Starting position of the feet: 5th
position, croisé, right foot
front.

Starting position of
the arms: 2nd
position.

Off-beat *(4th),* *1st, 2nd, 3rd* *eighth*	2 BATTEMENTS TENDUS with the right foot front, croisé.	6th (right arm bent).
	BATTEMENTS TENDUS JETÉS BALANÇOIRE $(25°)$ with the right leg. *Breakdown:*	
4th, 1st, 2nd, *3rd* *eighth*	Kick front. Kick back, in effacé. Kick front. Bring the leg to 5th position front.	As above.
4th, 1st, 2nd *3rd* *eighth*	2 BATTEMENTS TENDUS with the left leg back, croisé. BATTEMENTS TENDUS JETÉS BALANÇOIRE $(25°)$ with the left leg.	6th (left arm bent).

	Breakdown:	
4th eighth	Kick back.	
1st eighth	Kick front, effacé.	
2nd eighth	Kick back.	
3rd eighth	Bring the leg to 5th position back.	
4th, 1st, 2nd, 3rd eighth	3 BATTEMENTS TENDUS JETÉS to the side with the right leg (change).	2nd
4th, 1st, 2nd, 3rd eighth	3 BATTEMENTS TENDUS JETÉS to the side, with the left leg (change).	2nd

CONCLUDING EXERCISE FOR THE MEN'S CLASS:

4th eighth, 1 bar	PRÉPARATION POUR PIROUETTES EN DEHORS with the right foot (in 2nd position).	2nd - 6th (right arm bent).
1st, 2nd, 3rd eighth	PIROUETTES EN DEHORS (end in 4th position, croisé, right foot back, the left leg in front in plié à quart).	The right arm opens during the movement, then the arms meet between A and 1st; end in 1st position (wide).

CONCLUDING EXERCISE FOR THE WOMEN'S CLASS:

4th eighth, 1 bar	PRÉPARATION POUR PIROUETTES EN DEHORS with the right foot (in 4th position croisé, right foot back).	A - 1st - 3rd arabesque (right arm in front).
1st, 2nd, 3rd eighth	PIROUETTES EN DEHORS (end in 4th position, croisé, right foot back, the left leg in front in plié à quart).	The right arm opens during the movement then the arms meet between A and 1st: end in 1st position (wide).

8 bars	Repeat the exercise on the other leg.

Total accompaniment
16 bars   (*Pause*)
Repeat the exercise in the reverse
direction (pirouettes remain en
dehors).

Measure 3/4 *Tempo slow* *Introduction* *(2 bars)*	### 3. BATTEMENTS FONDUS

Preparation
Starting position of the feet: 2nd | Starting position of
position, right foot pointe tendue. | the arms: 2nd
position.

Off-beat *(3rd), 1st,* *2nd fourth*	BATTEMENT FONDU with the right leg front, croisé (45°), on half toe.[1]	The right arm comes down, then moves forward, bent at the elbow: 6th position.
3rd fourth	TOMBÉ on the right foot front, follow with	
1st, 2nd *fourth*	BATTEMENT FONDU with the left leg to the side, in écarté front (to corner No. 8).	A, then 2nd allongée.
3rd fourth	TOMBÉ on the left foot front, in effacé, follow with	A
1st, 2nd *fourth*	BATTEMENT FONDU with the right leg back, in effacé.	2nd arabesque (right arm in front).
3rd fourth	TOMBÉ on the right foot back, follow with	A
1st, 2nd *fourth*	BATTEMENT FONDU with the left leg to the side à la seconde (45°).	A - 1st - 2nd
3rd fourth	DEMI-PLIÉ on the right leg, the left foot sur le cou-de-pied back, follow with	
1st, 2nd *fourth*	BATTEMENT FONDU with the left leg back, in croisé.	3rd arabesque (left arm in front).
3rd fourth	TOMBÉ on the left foot back, follow with	A
1st, 2nd *fourth*	BATTEMENT FONDU with the right leg to the side à la seconde (45°).	A - 1st - 2nd
3rd fourth	DEMI-PLIÉ on the left leg, the right foot sur le cou-de-pied back.	6th (left arm bent).

[1] All consecutive battements fondus are executed at 45°, on half toe.

1st, 2nd *fourth*	PAS DE BOURRÉE EN DEHORS stepping to the side twice (changing feet).	The left arm opens to the side, then
3rd fourth	End in 4th position, croisé, (wide) the right leg in front in plié à quart.	6th (right arm bent).
1st, 2nd *fourth*	Stand in the preparatory position for tour en dedans.	6th (right arm bent).
3rd fourth	DÉGAGÉ with the left leg to the side (45°), simultaneously demi-plié on the right leg.	The right arm opens to the side.
1st, 2nd, *3rd,* *1st, 2nd* *fourth*	TOUR EN DEDANS with the left leg bent halfway front (90°), end on the right leg demi-plié. Simultaneously extend the left leg in croisé front (90°). Lean the head slightly forward, looking to the left "under the arm."	4th (right arm up), end in 5th position going through 1st position (left arm up).
3rd fourth	Bend the left leg sur le cou-de-pied front.	
1st, 2nd, *3rd* *fourth*	PAS DE BOURRÉE EN TOURNANT EN DEDANS (stepping over twice, on the third step stand on half toe of the left foot, simultaneously dégagé with the right leg front in croisé (25°).	2nd - A A - 1st, then 3rd arabesque (left arm front).
1st fourth	Step in 4th position (wide), the right leg in plié à quart.	
2nd fourth	Stand in the preparatory position for tours en dehors.	3rd arabesque (left arm in front).
3rd fourth	DEMI-PLIÉ in 4th position.	As above.
1st, 2nd, *3rd,* *1st, 2nd,* *3rd* *fourth*	TOUR EN DEHORS EN ATTITUDE CROISÉE with the left leg. End on the right leg in demi-plié, stretching the left leg back, in croisé (90°).	4th (left arm up).

1 bar	PAS DE BOURRÉE EN TOURNANT EN DEHORS (stepping under twice), end in 5th position, left leg in front.	2nd A
1st, 2nd fourth	Stand in 5th position (pause).	A

16 bars	Repeat the exercise on the other leg.

Total accompaniment
32 bars

(*Pause*)

Repeat the exercise in the reverse direction.

Measure 2/4
Tempo
moderate
Introduction
(*1 bar*)

4.   RONDS DE JAMBE EN L'AIR

	Preparation Starting position of the feet: 5th position, en face, right foot front.	Starting position of the arms: A.

Off-beat (*4th*), *1st,* *2nd* *eighth*	DEMI-PLIÉ in 5th position, then DÉGAGÉ with the right leg to the side (45°), rise on half toe of the left foot, continuing with	A - 1st - 2nd
	2 RONDS DE JAMBE EN L'AIR EN DEHORS with the right leg (remaining on half toe of the left foot), then	2nd

3rd, 4th eighth,	FOUETTÉ EN TOURNANT EN DEHORS with the right leg (come down first on the left leg demi-plié, then rise on half toe) end with	A, then 6th position through 1st position (right arm bent).
1st, 2nd eighth	DÉGAGÉ with the right leg front (45°) in croisé (remaining on left foot half toe).	
3rd eighth	TOMBÉ on the right foot front, in croisé, the left foot sur le cou-de-pied back.	The right arm opens in front and moves to the side: 2nd position.
4th, 1st, 2nd eighth	DÉGAGÉ with the left leg to the side (45°) rise on half toe (right foot,) continuing with	
	2 RONDS DE JAMBE EN L'AIR EN DEDANS with the left leg (remaining on half toe of the right leg), then	2nd
3rd, 4th eighth	FOUETTÉ EN TOURNANT EN DEDANS with the left leg (come down first on the right leg demi-plié, then rise on half toe) end with	A, then 3rd arabesque through 1st position (left arm in front).
1st, 2nd eighth	DÉGAGÉ with the left leg back (45°), in croisé (remaining on half toe right foot).	
3rd eighth,	TOMBÉ on the left foot back, in croisé, the right foot sur le cou-de-pied front, continuing with	A, then 6th position through 1st position (right arm bent).
4th, 1st, 2nd eighth	BATTEMENT FONDU with the right leg front, in effacé (on half toe of the left foot).	
3rd, 4th eighth	TOMBÉ on the right foot to the side, simultaneously DÉGAGÉ with the left leg to the side (45°).	The right arm opens to the side: 2nd position.

1st, 2nd *eighth,*	TOUR PIQUÉ EN DEHORS (during the turn on the left leg, the right foot is sur le cou-de-pied front, and without coming down the half toe of the left foot), end with	The arms meet between A and 1st, then
3rd eighth	DÉGAGÉ with the right leg front (45°), in croisé, then follow with	6th position through 1st position (right arm bent).
4th eighth, *1 bar* *1st, 2nd, 3rd* *eighth*	CHAÎNÉS-DÉBOULÉS diagonally forward, to corner No. 2. (End in effacé, the left foot extended to the back, pointe tendue, lean the head slightly forward, looking to the left "under the arm".)	The right arm opens during the movement, then the arms meet between A and 1st. End in 3rd position.

8 bars	Repeat the exercise on the other leg.

Total accompaniment
16 bars

(*Pause*)
Repeat the exercise.

Measure 3/4
(Waltz)
Tempo
moderate
Introduction
(2 bars)

5.   GRAND ADAGIO

	Preparation Starting position of the feet: 5th position, croisé, right foot front.	Starting position of the arms: A.
Off-beat *(6th) eighth* *1 bar*	GLISSADE with the right foot (do not change) diagonally to corner No. 2, end in demi-plié.	A, then the arms open slightly to the side and close again.
1 bar	PETIT DÉVELOPPÉ (45°) with the right leg forward, in effacé, in demi-plié on the left leg.	A - 1st

2 bars	STEP on the right foot.	1st arabesque (right arm front).
	LIFT the left leg back, in effacé, stand in 1st arabesque.	
3 bars, *1st, 2nd* *fourth*	TOUR LENT EN DEDANS in 1st arabesque.	1st arabesque
3rd fourth	PASSER LA JAMBE (90°) the left leg.	A
1 bar, *1st, 2nd* *fourth*	DÉVELOPPÉ the left leg front, in croisé.	1st - 5th (left arm up).
3rd fourth	STEP OVER on the left leg front, in croisé.	The left arm lowers in front in 1st position and follows the movement to the side.
1 bar, *1st, 2nd* *fourth*	DÉVELOPPÉ with the right leg to the side, in écarté front (to corner No. 2).	2nd allongée (palms down).
3rd fourth,	RELEVÉ on half toe of the left foot, carry on with	2nd allongée (a slight stroke with the hands) then
1 bar, *1st, 2nd* *fourth*	GRAND FOUETTÉ EN TOURNANT EN DEDANS with the right leg, end croisé back (90°), in 3rd arabesque.	A - 1st - 3rd; end in 3rd arabesque (right arm in front).
3rd fourth	PASSER LA JAMBE (90°) the right leg (on half toe of the left foot), then a quick	The right arm bends front and carries the movement up: 5th position, then the right arm opens to the side.
1 bar	DÉVELOPPÉ with the right leg front, in croisé, carry on with	
	CHASSÉ with the right leg front, in croisé.	
1 bar	TEMPS LIÉ with the right leg front, end croisé, the left leg extended back, pointe tendue.	A - 1st - 5th (left arm up).

3 bars, *1st, 2nd* *fourth*	PORT DE BRAS leaning the body forward and then backward. End in 4th position, croisé (wide), the right leg in front in plié à quart preparing for tours en dedans.	1st - 5th (right arm up), then the right arm makes a circular movement to the side and the front. End in 6th position (right arm bent).
3rd fourth	DEMI-PLIÉ in 4th position.	
3 bars	TOURS EN DEDANS in 1st arabesque (end facing corner No. 3), then	1st arabesque (right arm in front).
1 bar	bring the leg down to 5th position back, simultaneously turn en face.	A
2 bars	DÉVELOPPÉ À LA SECONDE (90°) with the right leg.	A - 1st - 2nd
1 bar, *1st, 2nd*	RELEVÉ on half toe of the left foot.	3rd
fourth	LOWER the right leg in 2nd position.	2nd
3rd fourth	DEMI-PLIÉ in 2nd position.	6th (right arm bent).
3 bars, *1st, 2nd* *fourth,* *5th eighth*	TOURS EN DEHORS À LA SECONDE (90°) with the right leg, then bring the right leg to back croisé, and stand in 3rd arabesque.	3rd position, end in 3rd arabesque (right arm up).

32 bars	Repeat the exercise on the other leg.

Total accompaniment
64 bars

6. GRANDS BATTEMENTS JETÉS

Measure 2/4
Tempo
moderate
Introduction
(1 bar)

	Preparation Starting position of the feet: 5th position, croisé, right foot front.	Starting position of the arms: 2nd position.
Off-beat *(4th),* *1st eighth*	GRAND BATTEMENT JETÉ with the right leg front, croisé.	5th (left arm up).
2nd eighth,	GRAND BATTEMENT JETÉ with the right leg front, in effacé (on half toe of the left leg), then	As above.
3rd, 4th *eighth*	TOMBÉ on the right foot front, in effacé, lift the left leg back in effacé (45°), turn the head to the left and carry on with	5th allongée (hands turn outward).
1st, 2nd, 3rd *eighth*	PAS DE BOURRÉE EN DEHORS (changing feet), end with the left foot in 5th position front, épaulement croisé.	The arms come down A.
4th, 1st *eighth*	GRAND BATTEMENT JETÉ with the left leg front, croisé.	5th position going through 1st position (right arm up).
2nd eighth,	GRAND BATTEMENT JETÉ with the left leg front, in effacé (on half toe of the right foot), then	5th (right arm up).
3rd, 4th *eighth*	TOMBÉ on the left foot front, in effacé, lift the right leg back in effacé (45°), turn the head to the right and carry on with	5th allongée (hands turn outward).
1st, 2nd, 3rd *eighth*	PAS DE BOURRÉE EN DEHORS (changing feet), end with the right foot front in 5th position, en face.	The hands come down - A.
4th, 1st *eighth*	GRAND BATTEMENT JETÉ with the right leg to the side (change).	2nd going through 1st position.
2nd, 3rd *eighth*	GRAND BATTEMENT JETÉ with the left leg to the side (change), end in 5th position demi-plié.	2nd End in A position.

CONCLUDING EXERCISE FOR THE MEN'S CLASS:

4th eighth, *1 bar*	PRÉPARATION POUR PIROUETTES EN DEHORS with the right foot in 2nd position.	A - 1st - 2nd - 6th (right arm bent).
1 bar, *1st, 2nd, 3rd* *eighth*	PIROUETTES EN DEHORS end in 4th position croisé, in demi-plié, right foot back.	The right arm opens during the movement, then the arms meet between A and 1st. End in 1st position (wide).

CONCLUDING EXERCISE FOR THE WOMEN'S CLASS:

4th eighth, *1 bar*	PRÉPARATION POUR PIROUETTES EN DEHORS with the right foot in 4th position croisé.	A - 1st - 3rd arabesque (right arm in front).
1 bar, *1st, 2nd, 3rd* *eighth*	PIROUETTES EN DEHORS end in 4th position croisé, in demi-plié, right foot back.	The right arm opens during the movement, then the arms meet between A and 1st. End in 1st position (wide).

8 bars   Repeat the exercise on the other leg.

Total accompaniment
16 bars

(*Pause*)
Repeat the exercise in the reverse
direction (pirouettes remain en
dehors).

Measure 2/4
Tempo
moderate
Introduction
(1 bar)

7. SMALL JUMPS

Preparation

Starting position of the feet: 5th position, croisé, left foot front.	Starting position of the arms: A.

Off-beat *(4th),* *1st eighth*	ASSEMBLÉ with the right leg to the side (change), change also épaulement croisé.	A
2nd, 3rd *eighth*	ASSEMBLÉ with the left leg to the side (change), change also épaulement croisé.	A
4th, 1st *eighth*	JETÉ with the right leg to the side, left foot ends sur le cou-de-pied back, change épaulement croisé.	The arms come up to the side, then 6th (right arm bent).
2nd, 3rd *eighth*	BALLOTTÉ with the right leg front, croisé.	6th (right arm bent).
4th, 1st *eighth*	BALLOTTÉ with the left leg to the side, in écarté front (to corner No. 8)	2nd allongée (palms down).
2nd eighth	TOMBER PIED DESSOUS on the left foot.	A
3rd eighth, *4th, 1st* *eighth*	STEP - COUPÉ right foot to the side (No. 3).	3rd arabesque (left arm in front), end in A position.
2nd, 3rd *eighth*	ASSEMBLÉ with the left leg back (through 1st position), croisé (end in 5th position demi-plié). Come up from demi-plié.	A

4 bars   Repeat the exercise on the other leg.

Total accompaniment
8 bars

(*Pause*)
Repeat the exercise in the reverse direction.

Measure 2/4
Tempo
moderate   **8. SMALL JUMPS**
Introduction
(1 bar)   Preparation

Starting position of the feet: 4th   Starting position of
position, croisé, left leg extended to   the arms: 6th position
the back, pointe tendue.   (right arm bent).

Off-beat	DEMI-PLIÉ	6th (right arm bent),
(4th),	on the right leg, carry on with	then
1st eighth,	BALLOTTÉ	6th (left arm bent).
	with the right leg front, in effacé	
	(bend the body slightly backward),	
	then	
2nd eighth	lower the right leg on half toe (with a	
	passing movement), keeping the body	
	leaning slightly backward. Then	
	continue with	
3rd eighth	BALLOTTÉ	
	with the right leg front, in effacé.	
4th, 1st	BALLOTTÉ	6th (right arm bent).
eighth	with the left leg back, in effacé (bend	
	the body slightly forward).	
2nd eighth,	Lower the left leg on half toe (with a	
	passing movement), keeping the body	
	leaning slightly forward, then	
	continue with	
3rd eighth	BALLOTTÉ	
	with the left leg back, in effacé.	
4th, 1st	BALLOTTÉ	2nd (hands turned
eighth	with the right leg to side (No. 3)	out).
	(the body leans slightly to the left).	
2nd, 3rd	BALLOTTÉ	
eighth	with the left leg to side (No. 7)	
	(the body leans slightly to the right),	
	then	
· 4th eighth	Lower the left leg in demi-plié (behind	2nd (hands turned
	the right leg).	in).

1st, 2nd, 3rd eighth	STEP - COUPÉ with the right leg forward diagonally to corner No. 2.	A - 1st, end in 1st position (wide).
	JETÉ EN AVANT with the left leg forward, in croisé.	

4 bars	Repeat the exercise on the other leg.	

Total accompaniment
8 bars

(*Pause*)
Repeat the exercise.

Measure 2/4
Tempo
moderate
Introduction
(2 bars)

9. MEDIUM JUMPS

	Preparation Starting position of the feet: 4th position, croisé, left foot extended to the front, pointe tendue.	Starting position of the arms: A.

Start from corner No. 6.

Off-beat (4th), 1st, 2nd, 3rd eighth	GLISSADE with the right foot forward diagonally, corner No. 2 (do not change).	A, then the arms open slightly to the side, close again.
	JETÉ EN AVANT Forward with the right leg in effacé.	2nd arabesque through 1st position (left arm in front).
7th, 8th sixteenth	PAS DE BOURÉE EN DEHORS (changing feet).	The left arm opens to the side: 2nd position - A.
1st eighth, 2nd, 3rd eighth	JETÉ FERMÉ with the right leg to side (No. 3). The left leg ends in 5th position front.	2nd allongée (palms down), end position A.
4th, 1st eighth	SISSONNE TOMBÉE with the left leg front, in croisé (position "under the arm").	A - 1st - 5th (left arm up).

2nd, 3rd *eighth*	SISSONNE TOMBÉE with the left leg front, in croisé (the head and the body turn slightly to the right).	2nd (hands turned out).
4th, 1st *eighth*	COUPÉ-DESSOUS on the left foot. JETÉ EN TOURNANT EN DEHORS with the right leg, end in croisé front (attitude croisée).	A, then 5th position through 1st position (left arm up).
2nd, 3rd *eighth*	PETIT JETÉ with the left leg to side (No. 7), right foot ends sur le cou-de-pied back.	The left arm lowers to the side: 2nd position, then A.
4th, 1st,	GLISSADE with the right foot forward, diagonally to corner (No. 2) (do not change).	A, then the arms open slightly to the side and close again.
2nd, 3rd *eighth*	JETÉ EN AVANT with the right leg in effacé front.	2nd arabesque through 1st position (left arm in front).
7th, 8th *sixteenth*	PAS DE BOURRÉE EN DEHORS (changing feet).	The left arm opens to the side: 2nd position - A.
1st eighth, *2nd, 3rd* *eighth*	JETÉ FERMÉ with the right leg to side (No. 3), the left leg ends in 5th position front.	2nd allongée (palms down), end position A.
4th, 1st *eighth*	SISSONNE TOMBÉE with the left leg front, in effacé.	The left arm opens to the side going through 1st position, simultaneously the right arm moves to the side.
3rd, 4th *sixteenth*	PAS DE BOURRÉE EN DEHORS (changing feet), stepping to the side twice on half toe.	2nd

CONCLUDING EXERCISE FOR THE MEN'S CLASS:

3rd eighth	DEMI-PLIÉ on the right leg, the left foot sur le cou-de-pied back.	6th (right arm bent).
4th, 1st *eighth*	PETIT ASSEMBLÉ with the left leg back, in croisé.	
2nd, 3rd *eighth*	DOUBLE TOUR EN L'AIR EN DEHORS. End in 5th position, right foot back.	The right arm opens during the movement, then the arms meet between A and 1st, end in 2nd position (hands turned out).

CONCLUDING EXERCISE FOR THE WOMEN'S CLASS:

3rd eighth	End in 4th position croisé, right leg in front in plié à quart.	6th (right arm bent).
4th eighth	DÉGAGÉ with the left leg to the side (45°), on the right leg demi-plié.	The right arm opens to the side, then the arms in 3rd position, end in 2nd (hands turned out).
1st, 2nd, *3rd eighth*	PIROUETTES EN DEDANS. End in 5th position, left foot front.	

Total accompaniment
8 bars

(*Pause*)
Repeat the exercise on the other leg
(start from corner No. 4).

Jeté en tournant en dehors (from preparation: sissonne tombée backward, in croisé, with the right leg, coupé dessous with the left foot) ending in front, in attitude croisée

Nicolai Fadeyechev

Measure 3/4
Tempo
moderate
Introduction
(2 bars)

10. BIG JUMPS

Preparation
Starting position of the feet: 4th
position, croisé, left foot extended to
the front, pointe tendue.

Starting position of
the arms: A.

Start from side No. 7.

Off-beat *2nd, 3rd* *fourth,* *1 bar,* *1st, 2nd* *fourth*	GLISSADE with the right foot to side (No. 3), do not change. JETÉ PASSÉ with the right leg to side (No. 3), the left leg ends in the back, in attitude croisée.	A, then the arms open to the side and close again. 5th position through 1st position (left arm up).
3rd, 1st, 2nd *fourth*	SISSONNE TOMBÉE with the left leg back, in croisé (the body leans slightly to the left).	The left arm lowers to the side - 2nd position (hands turned out).
3rd, 1st, 2nd *fourth*	PETIT DÉVELOPPÉ (45°) with the right leg front, in croisé, simultaneously rise on half toe of the left foot.	A - 1st (wide), hands turned out.
3rd fourth	TOMBÉ on the right foot front, in croisé.	2nd (hands turned out).
1 bar, *1st, 2nd* *fourth,* *5th eighth*	PAS COURU with the left foot (traveling forward diagonally to corner No. 8). GRAND JETÉ EN AVANT with the right leg, in croisé front.	A - 1st 5th (left arm up).
6th eighth, *1 bar,* *1st, 2nd* *fourth*	PAS COURU with the left foot (traveling forward diagonally, to corner No. 8). GRAND ASSEMBLÉ with the right leg in front, croisé (lean the head slightly forward, looking to the right "under the arm").	The left arm lowers to the side, then the arms come down. A - 1st - 3rd

3rd, 1st, 2nd fourth	SISSONNE TOMBÉE with the right leg front, in effacé, then	The right arm lowers in front, simultaneously the left moves to the side (hands turned out), then
5th eighth	Lower the left leg in demi-plié behind the right foot, turn the body to the left. Simultaneously	turn the hands in, raise the right arm forward (palms facing down), 2nd arabesque.
6th eighth	bring the right leg back through 1st position to corner No. 3 and lift it to 45°, 2nd arabesque position.	
1st, 2nd fourth	TEMPS LEVÉ on the left leg, in 2nd arabesque position.	2nd arabesque arm position.
3rd, 1st, 2nd fourth	CHASSÉ with the right leg backward to corner No. 3, end position en face, then	The right arm opens to the side, then 2nd.
3rd fourth	DEMI-PLIÉ on the right leg, stepping to side No. 3. Simultaneously DÉGAGÉ with the left leg to the side (45°).	2nd allongée.
1st, 2nd fourth	SOUTENU EN TOURNANT EN DEDANS on the left foot.	A - 1st - 3rd

CONCLUDING EXERCISE FOR THE MEN'S CLASS:

3rd fourth, *3 bars,* *1st fourth*	PRÉPARATION POUR PIROUETTES EN DEHORS with the right foot in 2nd position.	2nd - 6th (right arm bent).
	PIROUETTES EN DEHORS. End in 4th position, croisé, the left leg in front in plié à quart.	The right arm opens during the movement, then the arms meet between A and 1st, end in 1st position (wide).

CONCLUDING EXERCISE FOR THE WOMEN'S CLASS:

5th eighth	PRÉPARATION POUR CHAÎNÉS-DÉBOULÉS. Step on the left foot to side No. 7, bring the right leg front, croisé, pointe tendue.	2nd - 6th (right arm bent).
6th eighth, *3 bars,* *1st fourth*	CHAÎNÉS-DÉBOULÉS. traveling straight to side No. 3, end in effacé, the left leg extended to the back, pointe tendue, the head turned to the left.	The right arm opens during the movement, then the arms meet between A and 1st, end in 5th (left arm up).

Total accompaniment
16 bars

(*Pause*)
Repeat the exercise on the other leg
(start from corner No. 3).

Measure 2/4
Tempo
moderate
Introduction
(2 bars)

11.   SMALL JUMPS WITH BEATS

Preparation
Starting position of the feet:
5th position, croisé, left foot front.

Starting position of
the arms: A.

Start from corner No. 6.

Off-beat *(4th),* *1st eighth*	BRISÉ-DESSUS with the right leg, the left foot ends sur le cou-de-pied front.	A, the arms open slightly to the side, then 6th (right arm bent).
2nd, 3rd *eighth*	BRISÉ-DESSUS with the left leg, the right foot ends sur le cou-de-pied back.	6th (left arm bent).
4th eighth, *6 bars,* *1st, 2nd, 3rd* *eighth*	Repeat the combination consecutively 7 more times, gradually traveling forward diagonally (to corner No. 2).	

Total accompaniment
8 bars

(Pause)
Repeat the exercise on the other leg
(start from corner No. 4).

Measure 3/4
Tempo
moderate
Introduction
(2 bars)

12. BIG JUMPS

Preparation
Starting position of the feet: 4th
position, effacé the left leg extended
to the back, pointe tendue.

Starting position of
the arms: 1st
arabesque (right arm
front).

Start from corner No. 2.

Off-beat
(2nd, 3rd)
fourth,
2 bars

CHASSÉ
with the left leg back, in effacé
(with a half turn to the left).
JETÉ ENTRELACÉ
(end in 1st arabesque position, in
effacé).

Position 1st arabesque,
then 2nd position
allongée.
A - 1st - 3rd, end in
first arabesque (right
arm in front).

2 bars

PAS COURU
with the left foot travel diagonally to
corner No. 6 (the body turns to the
left).
GRAND JETÉ EN AVANT
with the left leg forward to corner No.
6, in 2nd arabesque position.

2nd allongée

The right arm moves
down and forward:
2nd arabesque.

1 bar,
1st, 2nd
fourth,
5th eighth

PAS COURU
with the right foot travel to corner
No. 6 (with the subsequent half turn
to the left).
CABRIOLE
with the left leg back, in effacé.

2nd allongée
A - 1st - 2nd
arabesque (left arm
in front).

CONCLUDING EXERCISE FOR THE MEN'S CLASS:

6th eighth,
1 bar,
1st, 2nd
fourth,
5th eighth

PRÉPARATION
(Chassé back, with the left leg, in
effacé, then step on the left foot to side
No. 6, bring the right leg front, croisé,
pointe tendue.)

2nd
6th (right arm bent).

6th eighth, *3 bars,* *1st, 2nd* *fourth* *5th eighth*	4 JETÉS EN TOURNANT EN DEHORS (execute the jumps one after the other traveling forward diagonally to corner No. 2) on the right leg, the left leg held back, in effacé, and so forth, then	The right arm moves forward, 1st arabesque, then the arms meet between A and 1st, etc. End in 6th (right arm bent).
6th eighth, *2 bars,* *1st fourth*	CHAÎNÉS-DÉBOULÉS forward diagonally to corner No. 2, end in 5th position demi-plié (right foot front).	The right arm opens during the movement, then the arms meet between A and 1st. End in 6th (right arm bent).
2nd, 3rd *fourth*	DOUBLE TOUR EN L'AIR TIRE-BOUCHON EN DEHORS (end on the left leg demi-plié, right leg retiré in front).	3rd position.
1st fourth	STEP on the right foot front (to corner No. 2), extend the left leg to the back, pointe tendue (turn the head to the left).	The right arm lowers to the side, 5th (left arm up).

CONCLUDING EXERCISE FOR THE WOMEN'S CLASS:

6th eighth, *1 bar,* *1st, 2nd* *fourth*	SISSONNE TOMBÉE with the left leg back, in effacé. PAS DE BOURRÉE EN DEDANS (stepping over twice), then going through demi-plié in 4th position, step on the right leg, the left leg extended in front, croisé, pointe tendue, stand in this pose.	5th (left arm up), 2nd (hands open), A and 1st, then the right arm moves to the front, simultaneously the left moves to the side (palms down).
3rd fourth, *1 bar,* *1st, 2nd* *fourth*	GLISSADE with the right foot forward diagonally (to corner No. 2) do not change. GRAND JETÉ PAS DE CHAT with the right leg (traveling to corner No. 2).	A - 2nd allongée, then the arms come down and move in front (the right higher than the left). At the end of the movement the arms come down through the front.

Glissade-grand jeté pas de chat

Rimma Karelskaya

3rd fourth, *1 bar,* *1st, 2nd* *fourth*	GLISSADE with the right foot forward diagonally (to corner No. 2) do not change. GRAND JETÉ PAS DE CHAT with the right leg traveling to corner No. 2.	2nd allongée, then the arms come down and move in front (the right higher than the left). At the end of the movement the arms come down through the front.
3rd, 1st *fourth* *2nd, 3rd,* *1st fourth,* *2nd fourth*	SISSONNE TOMBÉE with the right leg front, in effacé. PAS DE BOURRÉE EN DEHORS (stepping to the side twice), end in 4th position croisé, the left leg in front in plié à quart, stand in the preparatory position for pirouettes en dehors.	The right arm opens in front going through the 1st position, the left to the side, then 3rd arabesque arm position (right arm in front).
3rd fourth *1 bar,* *1st fourth*	DEMI-PLIÉ in 4th position. PIROUETTES EN DEHORS (end in 4th position croisé, the left leg forward in plié à quart).	3rd arabesque arm position, then the right arm opens during the movement, the arms meet between A and 1st. End in 3rd arabesque (right arm in front).

Total accompaniment
16 bars

(*Pause*)
Repeat the exercise on the other leg
(start from corner No. 8).

Measure 2/4
Tempo
lively
Introduction
(2 bars)

13. JUMPS
(FOR THE MEN'S CLASS)

Preparation

Starting position of the feet: 5th position, croisé, right foot in front.	Starting position of the arms: A.

Start from corner No. 4.

Off-beat
(2nd, 3rd,
(4th) eighth

RISE
on half toe in 5th position.

6th (right arm bent).

1st eighth

DEMI-PLIÉ
in 5th position.

A

2nd, 3rd, 4th,
1st, 2nd, 3rd
eighth

SISSONNE TOMBÉE EN TOURNANT
EN DEHORS
with a double turn; end on the right
leg front, croisé, the left leg held
back in croisé (25°), and with the
extended leg, continue

3rd position, end
3rd arabesque arm
position (left arm in
front).

4th, 1st
eighth

PETIT ASSEMBLÉ
with the left leg back, in croisé.

6th (right arm bent).

2nd, 3rd, 4th
eighth,
9 bars

Execute five more times the
combination sissonne tombée en
tournant en dehors, petit assemblé,
traveling forward diagonally to corner
No. 8, then

Arm position as
above (end in
position A).

1 bar

PRÉPARATION POUR PIROUETTES
EN DEHORS
with the right foot (in 2nd position).

A - 1st
2nd - 6th (right arm
bent).

2 bars,
1st eighth

PIROUETTES EN DEHORS
(end in 4th position croisé, the right
leg back, the left leg in front in plié à
quart, turn the head to the left).

The right arm opens
during the movement,
then the arms meet
between A and 1st;
end in 5th (right arm
up).

---

16 bars   Repeat the exercise.

Total accompaniment
32 bars

(Pause)

Repeat the exercise on the other leg
(start from corner No. 6).

Measure 2/4
Tempo slow
Introduction
(1 bar)

14. ENTRECHATS ET CHANGEMENTS DE PIEDS
(FOR THE MEN'S CLASS)

Preparation
Starting position of the feet: Starting position of
5th position, croisé, right foot front.   the arms: A.

Off-beat
(4th)
eighth,
4 bars

ENTRECHAT-SIX[1]   A position.
8 times consecutively, then

1 bar,
1st, 2nd, 3rd
eighth

7 PETITS CHANGEMENTS DE PIEDS.

4th eighth

PRÉPARATION POUR PIROUETTES   A - 1st - 2nd - 6th
EN DEHORS   (left arm bent).
with the left foot in 2nd position.

1 bar,
1st, 2nd, 3rd
eighth

PIROUETTES EN DEHORS.   The left arm opens
End in 4th position croisé, left foot   during the movement,
back, the right leg in front in plié à   then the arms meet
quart.   between A and 1st.
                                                       End in 1st position
                                                       (wide).

Total accompaniment
8 bars

(*Pause*)
Repeat the exercise on the other leg.

[1] Change épaulement croisé on each entrechat-six.

Measure 3/4
(Waltz)
Tempo slow
Introduction
(2 bars)

15. PORT DE BRAS AND BENDING OF THE BODY

(FOR THE MEN'S CLASS)

Preparation
Starting position of the feet: 1st
position (halfway turned out).

Starting position of
the arms: 2nd
position.

This exercise corresponds to exercise
15 (exercises in the center) of the first
class (see page 108).

Total accompaniment
32 bars

Measure 2/4
Tempo lively
Introduction
(1 bar)

16. FIRST EXERCISE ON POINTES

Preparation
Starting position of the feet: 5th
position croisé, right foot front.

Starting position of
the arms: A.

Off-beat
(4th) eighth,
1 bar

ÉCHAPPÉ
in 4th position, croisé.

A, then 4th arabesque
arm position (right
arm in front), end in
A.

1 bar

ÉCHAPPÉ
in 2nd position, en face (change).

A - 1st - 2nd, end
position A.

2 bars

Repeat the enumerated steps on the
other leg.

3 bars,
1st, 2nd, 3rd
eighth

4 ÉCHAPPÉS
in 2nd position (change).

A

8 bars

Repeat the exercise.

Total accompaniment
16 bars

Measure 2/4	
Tempo	
moderate	**17. SECOND EXERCISE ON POINTES**
Introduction	
(1 bar)	

Preparation

Starting position of the feet: 4th position croisé, the left leg extended to the back, pointe tendue.

Starting position of the arms: 6th position (right arm bent).

Off-beat (4th) eighth, 1 bar

PAS DE BOURRÉE BALLOTTÉ (without changing feet) traveling forward, in effacé.

6th (right arm bent), then 6th (left arm bent).

1 bar

PAS DE BOURRÉE BALLOTTÉ traveling backward, in effacé.

6th (right arm bent).

1 bar

PAS DE BOURRÉE BALLOTTÉ traveling forward, in effacé.

6th (left arm bent).

1st, 2nd eighth

STEP - PIQUÉ SUR LA POINTE forward on the right foot in effacé.
PETIT DÉVELOPPÉ (45°) with the left leg front, in croisé.

The left arm opens in the front and continues moving to the side (hands turned out).

3rd, 4th eighth

TOMBER PIED DESSUS on the left foot, the right foot sur le cou-de-pied back.

The left arm bends in front: 6th position.

4 bars

Repeat the exercise on the other leg.

PAS DE BOURRÉE (in one spot) in 5th position, without coming down off pointes.
   Breakdown:

1st eighth
2nd eighth

Step on pointe of the left foot dessous, then on the right foot dessus.

6th (right arm bent).

3rd, 4th eighth

On the left foot dessous (bend the knee, without coming down off pointe). Simultaneously bend the right leg in front in petit retiré (bring the right shoulder slightly backward, the left shoulder in front).

6th (left arm bent).

1st eighth	On the right foot dessus.	6th (left arm bent).
2nd eighth	On the left foot dessous.	
3rd, 4th eighth	On the right foot dessus (bend the knee without coming down off pointe). Simultaneously bend the left leg in the back in petit retiré (bring the left shoulder slightly backward, the right shoulder in front).	6th (right arm bent).
1st, 2nd eighth	On the left foot dessous, simultaneously bend the right leg in front in petit retiré (turn the head slightly to the left, the left shoulder forward).	A
3rd, 4th eighth	On the right foot dessus, simultaneously bend the left leg in the back in petit retiré (turn the head slightly to the right shoulder forward).	A
1 bar	COUPÉ on the left foot.	A - 1st - 2nd, end in
	BALLONNÉ with the right leg to the side (end sur le cou-de-pied back, the left leg lowers in demi-plié).	6th (left arm bent).
	PAS DE BOURRÉE (in one spot) in 5th position, without coming down off pointes. *Breakdown:* Step on pointes.	
1st eighth	On the right foot dessous.	6th (left arm bent).
2nd eighth	On the left foot dessus.	
3rd, 4th eighth	On the right foot dessous (bend the knee), bend the left leg forward in petit retiré (bring the left shoulder slightly to the back, the right shoulder forward).	6th (right arm bent).
1st eighth	On the left foot dessus.	6th (right arm bent).
2nd eighth	On the right foot dessous.	

3rd, 4th *eighth*	On the left foot dessus (bend the knee). Bend the right leg in the back in petit retiré (bring the right shoulder slightly to the back, the left shoulder forward).	6th (left arm bent).
1st, 2nd *eighth*	On the right foot dessous, bend the left leg in front in petit retiré (turn the head slightly to the right, the right shoulder forward).	A
3rd, 4th *eighth*	On the left foot dessus, bend the right leg in the back in petit retiré (turn the head slightly to the left, the left shoulder forward).	A
1st, 2nd, 3rd *eighth*	COUPÉ on the right foot.	A - 1st - 2nd, end in
	BALLONNÉ with the left leg to the side (end with the left foot sur le cou-de-pied back, the right leg lowers in demi-plié).	6th (right arm bent).

Total accompaniment
16 bars

(*Pause*)
Repeat the exercise on the other leg.

Measure 3/4
Tempo
moderate
Introduction
(2 bars)

18. THIRD EXERCISE ON POINTES

Preparation
Starting position of the feet: 5th position croisé, right foot front.

Starting position of the arms: A.

Start from corner No. 6.

Off-beat *(6th) eighth,* *2 bars*	PAS SUIVI traveling forward diagonally to corner No. 2.	A position, then gradually raise the right arm in front during the movement. Simultaneously the left arm comes up to the side (palms facing down).
1st fourth	STEP - PIQUÉ on the right foot front, in effacé, lift the left leg in the back (45°), in effacé.	1st arabesque arm position (right arm in front), then, remaining in the same position, 3rd arabesque (right arm in front).
2nd, 3rd *fourth,* *1 bar*	Stand in 1st arabesque position, then BRING the left leg front through 1st position in croisé and come down in 4th position demi-plié.	
1 bar	PIROUETTES EN DEHORS. (End the turn on left leg demi-plié. Simultaneously move the right foot sur le cou-de-pied back, épaulement croisé.)	The right arm opens during the movement, then the arms meet between A and 1st, end in 6th (left arm bent).
1st, 2nd *fourth*	PAS DE BOURRÉE EN TOURNANT EN DEHORS (stepping under twice), then	1st
3rd fourth	TOMBÉ on the right foot to the side. DÉGAGÉ with the left leg to the side (45°).	The arms open to the side - 2nd.

1 bar,	PIROUETTES EN DEDANS	3rd, then
1st, 2nd	(end in 5th position croisé, in	2nd - A
fourth	demi-plié, the left foot in front).	
5th eighth		

8 bars	Repeat the exercise on the other leg.

Total accompaniment
16 bars   *(Pause)*
     Repeat the exercise.

Tour en dedans

Rimma Karelskaya

19. FOURTH EXERCISE ON POINTES

Measure 3/4
Tempo lively
Introduction
(2 bars)

Preparation
Starting position of the feet:
4th position croisé, right leg extended
to the front, pointe tendue.

Starting position of
the arms: 6th (right
arm bent).

Start from corner No. 6.

Off-beat
(2nd, 3rd)
fourth

DEMI-PLIÉ
on the left leg, simultaneously lift
the right leg in front (25°) and bring
it to corner No. 2.

The right arm opens
during the movement,
then the arms meet
between A and 1st.

1 bar

TOUR PIQUÉ EN DEDANS
(during the turn on the right leg, the
left foot is sur le cou-de-pied back).

The arms open to the
side, then meet
between A and 1st.

1 bar

DOUBLE TOUR PIQUÉ EN DEDANS
(turn on the right leg).

3 bars,
1st, 2nd
fourth,
5th eighth

Repeat this combination 2 more times
traveling forward diagonally to corner
No. 2. Then

As above. End in 6th
(right arm bent).

6th eighth,
1 bar
1st, 2nd
fourth

CHAÎNÉS-DÉBOULÉS
forward diagonally to corner No. 2.

The right arm opens
during the movement,
then the arms meet
between A and 1st.
End in 6th (right
arm bent).

3rd fourth,
7 bars,
1st fourth

Repeat the whole combination. End
chaînés-déboulés in 4th position
croisé, right leg back, the left leg
in front in plié à quart.

As above.

End in 1st position
(wide).

Total accompaniment
16 bars

(Pause)
Repeat the exercise on the other leg
(start from corner No. 4).

Measure 2/4
Tempo
moderate
Introduction
(2 bars)

20. FIFTH EXERCISE ON POINTES

Preparation
Starting position of the feet: 4th
position, croisé, the left leg extended
to the front, pointe tendue.

Starting position of
the arms: 5th (right
arm up).

Start from corner No. 2.

Off-beat *(4th) eighth,*	PRÉPARATION through passer la jambe (90°) a quick développé of the left leg to the back, in effacé, with a small sliding hop on the right leg backward, continue with	The right arm comes down in 1st position (with a passing movement), then moves forward, stretching in the elbow, 1st arabesque arm position.
3 bars, *1st, 2nd, 3rd* *eighth*	15 small sliding hops on the right leg backward (in demi-plié) traveling diagonally backward to corner No. 6 (the left leg is raised back, in effacé), then	
4th eighth	BRING the left leg to the side à la seconde (45°), in demi-plié on the right leg.	The right arm opens to the side, 2nd position.
3 bars	6 TOURS PIQUÉS EN DEHORS gradually traveling forward diagonally to corner No. 2 (preparation for each tour requires préparation dégagée of the left leg to the side, 45°, etc.), then	The arms meet between A and 1st, then open to the side going through 1st position, etc.
1st, 2nd *eighth*	DOUBLE TOUR PIQUÉ EN DEHORS. End in 5th position demi-plié, right foot back.	As above. End in 2nd position (hands slightly turned out).
3rd eighth	RELEVÉ SUR LES POINTES in 5th position, épaulement croisé.	3rd position.

Total accompaniment
8 bars

(Pause)
Repeat the exercise on the other leg
(start from corner No. 8).

Measure 3/4
Tempo
moderate
Introduction
(2 bars)

21. SIXTH EXERCISE ON POINTES

Preparation

Starting position of the feet: 4th position croisé, right leg extended to the back, pointe tendue.

Starting position of the arms: 5th (right arm up).

Start from corner No. 6.

PAS DE BOURRÉE
"iolotchka" executed without coming down off pointe.

The general design of the arms is built on a continuous circular movement of the hands.

Breakdown:

Off-beat
(6th) eighth
1st eighth

Demi-plié on the left leg, simultaneously bend the right leg slightly and through petit retiré bring it forward, then

step on the right pointe, in front of the left leg, bringing it slightly to the left, in order to obtain a crossing of the legs and immediately lift the left leg in petit retiré back, then

2nd eighth

Step on the left pointe (behind the right leg) and lift immediately the right leg in petit retiré front, then

3rd, 4th
eighth

a small step - piqué (on pointe) on the right foot to the side, bend the left leg in petit retiré front, then

5th eighth

step on the left pointe, both legs sur les pointes in 5th position, épaulement croisé.

6th eighth,
6 bars,
1st, 2nd
fourth,
5th eighth

Repeat the whole combination 7 more times (without coming down off pointe) gradually traveling diagonally forward to corner No. 2.
Then

The first movement starts with the right hand turned in, and when the hand outlines the half turn, the left hand joins independently in the circular movement (first turn inward). The right hand continues the movement, concluding a whole turn, and following it the left hand completes its circular movement.

6th, 1st *eighth* *2nd, 3rd* *4th, 5th* *eighth*	PAS SUIVI. Start with a small step - piqué on the left pointe forward to corner No. 8. Then step over four times (the body starts to turn slightly to the left).	The left arm opens in the front, simultaneously the right arm lowers to the side, then 6th (right arm bent).
6th, 1st *eighth* *2nd, 3rd* *4th, 5th* *eighth*	PAS SUIVI EN TOURNANT EN DEDANS. Start with a small step - piqué on pointe, on the right leg to side No. 7, then step over four times (turn to the left).	The right arm opens in the front, then the arms move to 6th (left arm bent).
6th eighth, *3 bars,* *1st, 2nd* *fourth,* *5th eighth*	Repeat this combination (pas suivi) 2 more times, then continue with	Arm movements as above.
6th, 1st, 2nd, *3rd, 4th, 5th* *eighth*	PAS SUIVI. Start with a small step - piqué on the left leg front to corner No. 8, then step over four times.	The left arm opens to the front, the right arm to the side.
6th, 1st, 2nd *eighth*	PAS DE BASQUE with the left leg to the front, end with the right leg front, in croisé, in 4th position demi-plié.	2nd - A - 1st
3rd eighth	RELEVÉ on the right leg, simultaneously lift the left leg in attitude croisée (raise the head slightly upward, looking at the raised left hand).	5th (left arm up).
4th, 5th *eighth*	STAND in attitude croisée.	5th (left arm up).

Total accompaniment
16 bars

(Pause)
Repeat the exercise on the other leg
(start from corner No. 4).

Measure 2/4
Tempo lively
Introduction
(1 bar)

22. SEVENTH EXERCISE ON POINTES

Preparation
Starting position of the feet: 5th
position, en face, right foot front.

Starting position of
arms: A.

Off-beat
(4th) eighth,
7 bars,
1st, 2nd, 3rd
eighth

16 PETITS CHANGEMENTS DE
PIEDS SUR LES POINTES.

A - 1st - 3rd - 2nd -
A

Total accompaniment
8 bars

Measure 3/4
(Waltz)
Tempo slow
Introduction
(2 bars)

23. PORT DE BRAS AND BENDING
OF THE BODY

Preparation
Starting position of the feet: 1st
position (halfway turned out).

Starting position of
arms: 2nd position.

This exercise corresponds to exercise 15
(exercises in the center) of the first
class (see page 108).

Total accompaniment
32 bars

PHOTO BY JUDY CAMERON

Fifth Class

EXERCISES AT THE BARRE

Musical-rhythmical accompaniment	DANCING EXERCISES

Measure 3/4 (Waltz) Tempo slow Introduction (2 bars)

1. GRANDS PLIÉS

Preparation
Starting position of the feet: 1st position.

Starting position of the right arm: 2nd position.

This exercise corresponds to exercise 1 (exercises at the barre) of the first class (see page 55).

Total accompaniment 32 bars

Measure 2/4
Tempo
moderate   ## 2. BATTEMENTS TENDUS
Introduction
(1 bar)
Preparation
Starting position of the feet: 5th   Starting position of
position, right foot front.   the right arm: 2nd
                                            position.

Off-beat *(4th),* *1st, 2nd, 3rd* *eighth*	2 BATTEMENTS TENDUS with the right foot front.	2nd position.
4th, 1st, *2nd, 3rd* *eighth*	2 BATTEMENTS TENDUS with the right foot to the side (change).	
4th, 1st, *2nd, 3rd* *eighth*	BATTEMENT TENDU with the right foot front in 5th position demi-plié, then come up from demi-plié.	
4th, 1st, 2nd, *3rd* *eighth*	BATTEMENT TENDU with the right foot to the side (change), in 5th position demi-plié, then come up from demi-plié.	
4 bars	Repeat the exercise in the reverse direction.	
8 bars	Repeat the whole combination.	

Total accompaniment
16 bars

Turn to the other side and repeat
the exercise on the other leg.

Measure 2/4
Tempo lively
Introduction
(1 bar)

3. BATTEMENTS TENDUS JETÉS

Preparation
Starting position of the feet: 5th position, right foot front.

Starting position of the right arm: 2nd position.

Off-beat
(4th),
1st, 2nd, 3rd
eighth

2 BATTEMENTS TENDUS JETÉS with the right foot front.

2nd position.

4th, 1st,
2nd, 3rd
eighth

2 BATTEMENTS TENDUS JETÉS with the right foot to the side (change).

4th, 1st
eighth

BATTEMENT TENDU JETÉ with the right foot front.

2nd, 3rd
eighth

BATTEMENT TENDU JETÉ with the right foot to the side (change).

BATTEMENTS TENDUS JETÉS BALANÇOIRE (25°) with the right leg.
Breakdown:

4th eighth   Kick back.
1st eighth   Kick front.
2nd eighth   Kick back.
3rd eighth   Bring the right leg to 5th position back.

4 bars   Repeat the exercise in the reverse direction.

8 bars   Repeat the whole combination.

Total accompaniment
16 bars

Turn to the other side and repeat the exercise on the other leg.

<table>
<tr><td>Measure 3/4
Tempo lively
Introduction
(2 bars)</td><td colspan="2">

4. RONDS DE JAMBE À TERRE

Preparation
Starting position of the feet[1]</td><td>Starting position of
the right arm: 2nd
position.</td></tr>
<tr><td>2 bars</td><td>2 RONDS DE JAMBE À TERRE EN
DEHORS
with the right leg.</td><td>2nd</td></tr>
<tr><td>1 bar</td><td>1 ROND DE JAMBE À TERRE IN
DEMI-PLIÉ.</td><td>A - 1st - 2nd</td></tr>
<tr><td>1 bar</td><td>1 ROND DE JAMBÉ À TERRE.</td><td></td></tr>
<tr><td>1 bar</td><td>1 GRAND ROND DE JAMBE JETÉ.</td><td></td></tr>
<tr><td>1st, 2nd
fourth</td><td>GRAND BATTEMENT JETÉ
with the right leg front (kick upward).
Then</td><td>2nd position.</td></tr>
<tr><td>3rd fourth</td><td>PASSER LA JAMBE (90°)
right leg.</td><td></td></tr>
<tr><td>1st, 2nd
fourth</td><td>DÉVELOPPÉ
with the right leg back, then lower the
right leg and through 1st position.
Continue</td><td></td></tr>
<tr><td>1 bar</td><td>ROND DE JAMBE À TERRE EN
DEHORS.</td><td></td></tr>
<tr><td>8 bars</td><td>Repeat the exercise once more en
dehors with the following change at
the end of the combination: the last
rond de jambe à terre is not done,
the right leg slides through 1st position
front, pointe tendue.</td><td></td></tr>
<tr><td>8 bars</td><td>Repeat the exercise in the reverse
direction en dedans.</td><td></td></tr>
</table>

[1] Execute the ronds de jambe à terre, immediately after preparation, continuing the movement of the preparatory rond.

8 bars

Repeat the exercise once more en dedans, with the following change at the end of the combination: the last rond de jambe à terre is not done; after développé bring the right leg to 5th position front.

Start immediately the following combination:

Tempo slow
32 bars

PORT DE BRAS ET BATTEMENTS RELEVÉS LENTS (90°).
This section of the exercise corresponds to port de bras and battements relevés lents of exercise 5 (exercises at the barre) of the first class (see page 62).

Total accompaniment
64 bars

Turn to the other side and repeat the exercise on the other leg.

Measure 2/4
Tempo slow
Introduction
(2 bars)

5.   BATTEMENTS FONDUS

Preparation
Starting position of the feet: 2nd   Starting position of
position, right foot pointe tendue.   the right arm: 2nd
                                                position.

Off-beat
(4th),   BATTEMENT FONDU   2nd position.
1st, 2nd, 3rd   with the right leg front (45°).
eighth

4th, 1st,   BATTEMENT FONDU
2nd, 3rd   with the right leg to the side.
eighth

4th, 1st   BRING
eighth   the right leg front (45°), on the left
                   leg demi-plié.

2nd, 3rd   ROND DE JAMBE EN DEHORS
eighth   with the right leg back (45°),
                   simultaneously come from demi-plié.

4th, 1st   LOWER
eighth   the right leg to the floor, on the left
                   leg demi-plié.

2nd, 3rd   LIFT
eighth   the right leg up, 45°, simultaneously
                   come up from demi-plié.

4 bars   Repeat the exercise in the reverse
                   direction.

8 bars   Repeat the whole combination on half
                   toe.

Total accompaniment
16 bars

                   Turn to the other side and repeat the
                   exercise on the other leg.

Measure 2/4
Tempo
moderate
Introduction
(1 bar)

6. BATTEMENTS FRAPPÉS ET RONDS DE JAMBE EN L'AIR

Preparation
Starting position of the feet: 2nd position, right foot pointe tendue.

Starting position of the right arm: 2nd position.

Off-beat
(4th),
1st, 2nd,
3rd, 4th,
1st, 2nd, 3rd
eighth

7 BATTEMENTS FRAPPÉS with the right foot to the side (45°), change.

2nd position.

4th, 1st,
2nd, 3rd
eighth
4th eighth

3 RONDS DE JAMBE EN L'AIR EN DEHORS with the right leg (45°), then lift the right leg slightly upward.

1st, 2nd
eighth
3rd eighth

FLIC-FLAC EN TOURNANT EN DEHORS with the right foot, then open the right leg to the side (45°).

The arms come down to A, then the right arm opens to the side (through 1st position). In 2nd position, place the left arm on the barre.

4 bars

Repeat the exercise in the reverse direction.

8 bars

Repeat the whole combination on half toe.

Total accompaniment
16 bars

Turn to the other side and repeat the exercise on the other leg.

Measure 3/4
(Waltz)   **7.   ADAGIO**
Tempo slow
Introduction   Preparation   Starting position of
(2 bars)   Starting position of the feet: 5th   the right arm: 2nd
                       position, right foot front.   position.

2 bars   DÉVELOPPÉ   A - 1st - 2nd
                       right leg front.

2 bars   LOWER   The right arm comes
                       the right leg and through 1st position   down, then moves up
                       LIFT   and front to 2nd
                       to the back (90°).   arabesque.

4 bars   GRAND ROND DE JAMBE EN DEDANS   1st - 2nd
                       with the right leg. End in front.
                       Demi-plié on the left leg.

4 bars   GRAND ROND DE JAMBE EN DEHORS   2nd - A, then the
                       with the right leg, simultaneously   right arm moves up
                       come up from the left leg demi-plié, and stretches
                       end in 2nd arabesque position.   forward; 2nd
                                                            arabesque.

2 bars   COME UP   3rd
                       on half toe of the left foot,
                       simultaneously bring the right leg in
                       attitude, then

1 bar   ALLONGÉE   3rd, then the hand
                       the right leg to the back,   turns, palm facing
                       simultaneously come down from half   front (the arm
                       toe of the left foot to a flat foot. slightly to the side).

1 bar   Bring the right leg down in 5th position   The right arm
                       back.   lowers to the side,
                                                            then down to position
                                                            A.

16 bars   Repeat the exercise in the reverse
                       direction.

Total accompaniment
32 bars

                       Turn to the other side and repeat the
                       exercise on the other leg.

Measure 2/4 *Tempo lively* *Introduction* *(1 bar)*	### 8. BATTEMENTS DOUBLES FRAPPÉS ET PETITS BATTEMENTS SUR LE COU-DE-PIED	
	Preparation Starting position of the feet: 2nd position, right foot pointe tendue.	Starting position of the right arm: 2nd position.
Off-beat *(4th),* *1st eighth*	BATTEMENT DOUBLE FRAPPÉ with the right foot ending in front, pointe tendue.	2nd position.
2nd, 3rd *eighth*	BATTEMENT DOUBLE FRAPPÉ ending to the side.	
4th, 1st *eighth*	BATTEMENT DOUBLE FRAPPÉ ending in back.	
2nd, 3rd *eighth*	BATTEMENT DOUBLE FRAPPÉ ending to the side.	
4th, 1st, 2nd *3rd,* *4th, 1st, 2nd* *eighth*	7 PETITS BATTEMENTS SUR LE COU-DE-PIED (accent front), with the right foot.	A
3rd eighth	DÉGAGÉ with the right foot to the side, pointe tendue.	Through 1st to 2nd position.
4 bars	Repeat the exercise in the reverse direction.	
8 bars	Repeat the whole combination on half toe, execute the battements doubles frappés coming up and down from half toe of the supporting foot; the working leg ends the movement on the floor (pointe tendue).	
16 bars	After this combination balance on half toe of the left foot in various poses. (Look for description in the second part of exercise 11, exercises at the barre, of the first class. See page 71.)	

Total accompaniment
32 bars
 Turn to the other side and repeat the exercise on the other leg.

Measure 2/4
Tempo
moderate
Introduction
(1 bar)

9. GRANDS BATTEMENTS JETÉS

Preparation
Starting position of the feet: 5th
position, right foot front.

Starting position of
the right leg: 2nd
position.

Off-beat
(4th)
1st, 2nd, 3rd,
4th, 1st,
2nd, 3rd,
4th, 1st,
2nd, 3rd
eighth

6 GRANDS BATTEMENTS JETÉS
with the right leg front.

The right arm in 3rd
position.

4th, 1st,
2nd, 3rd
eighth

DEMI-PLIÉ
in 5th position,
HALF TURN
on half toe to the left.
Come down from half toe in 5th
position, left foot front.

2nd, then through 1st
position.
Place the right hand
on the barre, open the
left arm to the side
in 2nd position.

4th, 1st,
2nd, 3rd,
4th, 1st,
2nd, 3rd,
4th, 1st,
2nd, 3rd
eighth

6 GRANDS BATTEMENTS JETÉS
with the left leg front.

The left arm in 3rd
position.

4th, 1st,
2nd, 3rd
eighth

DEMI-PLIÉ
in 5th position.
HALF TURN
on half toe to the right, end in
5th position, right foot front.

2nd, then through 1st
position.
Place the left hand
on the barre, open
the right arm to the
side in 2nd position.

4th, 1st,
2nd, 3rd,
4th, 1st,
2nd, 3rd,
4th, 1st,
2nd, 3rd
eighth

6 GRANDS BATTEMENTS JETÉS
with the right leg to the side
(change).

The right arm in 2nd
position.

4th, 1st, *2nd, 3rd* *eighth*	DEMI-PLIÉ in 5th position. HALF TURN on half toe to the left, end in 5th position, left foot front.	2nd, then through 1st position. Place the right hand on the barre, open the left arm to the side in 2nd position.
4th, 1st, *2nd, 3rd,* *4th, 1st,* *2nd, 3rd,* *4th, 1st,* *2nd, 3rd* *eighth*	6 GRANDS BATTEMENTS JETÉS with the left leg to the side (change).	The left arm in 2nd position.
4th, 1st, *2nd, 3rd* *eighth*	DEMI-PLIÉ in 5th position. QUARTER TURN on half toe to the right, end in 5th position, right foot front, facing the barre.	2nd - 1st - place the hands on the barre.
4th, 1st, *2nd, 3rd,* *4th, 1st,* *2nd, 3rd,* *4th, 1st,* *2nd, 3rd,* *eighth*	6 GRANDS BATTEMENTS JETÉS with the left leg to the back.	Hands on the barre.
4th, 1st, *2nd, 3rd* *eighth*	BATTEMENT TENDU with the left foot to the side (change).	
4th, 1st, *2nd, 3rd,* *4th, 1st,* *2nd, 3rd,* *4th, 1st,* *2nd, 3rd,* *eighth*	6 GRANDS BATTEMENTS JETÉS with the right leg to the back.	Hands on the barre.
4th, 1st, *2nd, 3rd* *eighth*	BATTEMENT TENDU with the right foot to the side (change).	

Total accompaniment
24 bars

Measure 3/4
(Waltz)
Tempo slow
Introduction
(2 bars)

10. PORT DE BRAS AND BENDING
OF THE BODY

Preparation
Starting position of the feet: 1st
position, facing the barre.

Starting position of
the arms: both hands
on the barre.

This exercise corresponds to exercise
13 (exercises at the barre) of the first
class (see page 75).

Total accompaniment
32 bars

Measure 3/4
(Waltz)
Tempo slow
Introduction
(2 bars)

10a. STRETCHING OF THE LEGS AND
BENDING OF THE BODY

Preparation
Starting position of the legs: the right
leg is raised and front placed on the
barre, the heel turned outward.

Starting position of
the arms: arms in 3rd
position.

STRETCHING FORWARD
Breakdown:

2 bars
The right leg slides forward on the
barre (with the heel turned outward);
simultaneously the body bends toward
the right leg.

3rd position.
The arms lower
to the front
simultaneously with
the bending of the
body (palms facing
down).

2 bars
The body returns to the starting
position; simultaneously the right leg
slides back into the starting position.

The arms return to
3rd position.

2 bars	The body bends backward.	3rd position.
2 bars	The body returns to the starting position.	
2 bars	The body turns to the right.	
2 bars	The body returns to the starting position.	
2 bars	The body turns to the left.	
2 bars	The body returns to the starting position.	

16 bars	Repeat the exercise on half toe.	
	At the end of the stretching, lift the right leg above the barre and hold a short time.	3rd position.
	Then lower the leg gently to 5th position front.	2nd - A

Total accompaniment
32 bars

Turn to the other side and repeat the exercise on the other leg.

Measure 2/4
Tempo lively
Introduction
(1 bar)

11. RELEVÉS

Preparation
Starting position of the feet: 1st
position, facing the barre.

Starting position of
the arms: both hands
on the barre.

Off-beat
(4th),
1st, 2nd, 3rd,
4th, 1st,
2nd, 3rd,
4th, 1st,
2nd, 3rd,
4th, 1st,
2nd, 3rd,
eighth

8 RELEVÉS
on the right leg, left foot sur le
cou-de-pied back (come down without
demi-plié).

Hands on the barre.

4th eighth

1st eighth

DÉGAGÉ
with the left foot to the side, step on
it on half toe, right foot sur le cou-
de-pied back, come down from half
toe on left foot (without demi-plié)
and continue

2nd, 3rd,
4th, 1st,
2nd, 3rd,
4th, 1st,
2nd, 3rd,
4th, 1st,
2nd, 3rd
eighth

7 RELEVÉS
on the left leg, right foot sur
le cou-de-pied back.

---

8 bars

Repeat the exercise (changing the
position of the foot sur le cou-de-pied
front).

Total accompaniment
16 bars

EXERCISES IN THE CENTER

Measure 3/4
(Waltz)
Tempo slow
Introduction
(2 bars)

1. SMALL ADAGIO

Preparation
Starting position of the feet: 5th position croisé, right foot front.

Starting position of the arms: 2nd position.

Off-beat
(3rd) fourth

DEMI-PLIÉ
in 5th position.

2nd - A

1 bar

TEMPS LIÉ
with the right foot forward, end in croisé, the left leg extended to the back, pointe tendue.

A - 1st - 5th (left arm up).

1 bar

ROND DE JAMBE À TERRE EN DEDANS
with the left leg in effacé front, end on the right leg demi-plié.

The right arm comes up, simultaneously the left arm lowers to the side: 5th position.

2 bars

STEP
on the left leg (simultaneously turn the body slightly to the right). Transfer the right leg in effacé front (pointe tendue), then through 1st position (with a passing movement).

LIFT
the right leg back 90°, croisé, 3rd arabesque position.

The right arm lowers in 1st position, then stretches forward: 3rd arabesque position.

3 bars,
1st, 2nd
fourth

TOUR LENT EN DEHORS
(turn to the right) in 3rd arabesque.

3rd arabesque arm position (right arm in front), then

3rd fourth

PASSER LA JAMBE 90°
right leg.

A

1 bar,
1st, 2nd
fourth

DÉVELOPPÉ
right leg front, in effacé, then

1st - 5th (left arm up).

3rd fourth,	DEMI-PLIÉ on the left leg.	The left arm lowers in 1st position,
2 bars	STEP OVER on the right leg front.	then 2nd arabesque (left arm in front).
	LIFT the left leg back (90°) in effacé, 2nd arabesque position.	
1st, 2nd, 3rd *1st, 2nd* *fourth* *3rd fourth*	BRING the left leg to the side à la seconde 90°, en face. DEMI-PLIÉ on the right leg.	The left arm opens to the side (through 1st position) to 2nd position.
1 bar	PAS DE BOURRÉE EN DEHORS (changing feet), end in 5th position croisé, left foot front.	A
1st, 2nd *fourth*	Stand in 5th position (pause).	

16 bars	Repeat the exercise on the other leg.	
32 bars	Repeat the whole combination in the reverse direction.	

Total accompaniment
64 bars

2. BATTEMENTS TENDUS

Measure 2/4
Tempo
moderate
Introduction
(1 bar)

Preparation	Starting position of
Starting position of the feet: 5th position croisé, right foot front.	the arms: 2nd position.

Off-beat (4th), 1st, 2nd, 3rd eighth

2 BATTEMENTS TENDUS
with the right foot front, croisé.

6th (right arm bent).

4th, 1st, 2nd, 3rd eighth

BATTEMENT TENDU
with the right foot to the side, en face,
in demi-plié in 2nd position, end in
5th position back.

The right arm opens
to the side to 2nd,
then 6th (right arm
bent), then 2nd.

4th, 1st, 2nd, 3rd eighth

2 BATTEMENTS TENDUS
with the right foot back, croisé.

6th (left arm bent).

4th, 1st, 2nd 3rd eighth

BATTEMENT TENDU
with the right foot to the side, en face,
in demi-plié in 2nd position, end in
5th position front.

2nd - 6th (right arm
bent), then 2nd.

4th, 1st, 2nd, 3rd, eighth

3 BATTEMENTS TENDUS JETÉS
with the right foot to the side
(change).

2nd

4th, 1st eighth

BATTEMENT TENDU JETÉ
(throw to the side) with the right
leg, end the movement with

FLIC
with the right foot front,
simultaneously come up on half toe of
the left foot.

A

CONCLUDING EXERCISE FOR THE MEN'S CLASS:

2nd, 3rd, 4th eighth

PRÉPARATION POUR PIROUETTES
EN DEHORS
with the right foot in 2nd position.

A - 1st - 2nd
6th (right arm bent).

1 bar, 1st, 2nd, 3rd eighth

PIROUETTES EN DEHORS
end in 5th position, right foot back,
épaulement croisé.

The right arm opens
during the movement,
then the arms meet
between A and 1st,
end in 2nd position.

CONCLUDING EXERCISE FOR THE WOMEN'S CLASS:

2nd, 3rd, 4th *eighth*	PRÉPARATION POUR PIROUETTES EN DEHORS with the right foot in 4th position croisé.	A - 1st - 3rd arabesque (right arm in front).
1 bar, *1st, 2nd, 3rd* *eighth*	PIROUETTES EN DEHORS end in 5th position, right foot back, épaulement croisé.	The right arm opens during the movement, then the arms meet between A and 1st, end in 2nd.

8 bars	Repeat the exercise on the other leg.
16 bars	Repeat the whole combination.

Total accompaniment
32 bars

Measure 3/4 *Tempo slow* *Introduction* *(2 bars)*	### 3. BATTEMENTS FONDUS	
	Preparation Starting position of the feet: 5th position croisé, right foot front.	Starting position of arms: 2nd position.
Off-beat *(3rd)* *fourth,* *1 bar*	RISE on half toe in 5th position (with a passing movement). Then come down from half toe of the left foot in demi-plié, simultaneously bend the right leg sur le cou-de-pied front and continue with	2nd - 6th (right arm bent).
	BATTEMENT FONDU with the right leg front, croisé, on the left leg (half toe).[1]	

[1] Repeat all the following battements fondus on half toe.

1 bar *1st fourth*	DEMI-PLIÉ on the left leg. FOUETTÉ EN TOURNANT EN DEHORS (45°) right leg. End à la seconde on the left leg demi-plié (45°).	The right arm opens during the movement, then the arms meet between A and 1st, then 1st - 2nd.
2nd, 3rd, *fourth,* *1 bar*	PAS DE BOURRÉE EN TOURNANT EN DEHORS continuing with BATTEMENT FONDU with the left leg to the side.	A - 1st - 2nd
1 bar	TOMBÉ on the left foot to the side, right foot sur le cou-de-pied back, continue with BATTEMENT FONDU with the right leg to the side.	A - 1st - 2nd
1 bar	TOMBÉ on the right foot to the side, left foot sur le cou-de-pied back, continue with BATTEMENT FONDU with the left leg to the back, in effacé.	A - 1st - 6th (left arm bent).
1st fourth	TOMBÉ on the left foot back, in effacé, continue with	The left arm comes up: 5th position.
2nd, 3rd *fourth* *1st fourth*	PAS DE BOURRÉE EN DEDANS (stepping over twice). End in 4th position, croisé, right leg back, the left leg in front in plié à quart.	Then the arms come down to position A. Move to 3rd arabesque arm position (through 1st), right arm in front.
2nd fourth	Stand in the preparatory position for pirouettes en dehors.	
3rd fourth	DEMI-PLIÉ in 4th position.	The right arm opens during the movement,
1 bar, *1st, 2nd* *fourth*	PIROUETTES EN DEHORS. (End on the left leg demi-plié.)	then the arms meet between A and 1st.

3rd fourth	RELEVÉ on the left leg (half toe).	The right arm opens in front, the left to the side (hands slightly turned out).
1st fourth	TOMBÉ on the right foot front, in effacé.	
2nd, 3rd fourth *1st, 2nd fourth*	PAS DE BOURRÉE EN DEHORS (stepping under twice). End on the right leg demi-plié, the left leg in front croisé, on the floor.	2nd - 6th (left arm bent).
3rd fourth	PRÉPARATION TEMPS RELEVÉ EN DEHORS with the left leg (right leg in demi-plié).	The left arm opens during the movement then the arms meet between A and 1st.
1 bar *1st, 2nd fourth* *3rd fourth*	PIROUETTES EN DEHORS. (During the turn on the right leg, the left foot sur le cou-de-pied back.) End développé with the left leg back, in croisé (90°). DEMI-PLIÉ on the right leg.	End position arms 4th arabesque (right arm in front).
1 bar *1st, 2nd fourth*	PAS DE BOURRÉE EN TOURNANT EN DEHORS. (End in 5th position, croisé, left foot in front.) Stand in 5th position.	The arms come down position A.

16 bars	Repeat the exercise on the other leg.

Total accompaniment
32 bars

(*Pause*)
Repeat the exercise in the reverse direction.

Measure 2/4
Tempo
moderate
Introduction
(1 bar)

4. BATTEMENTS FRAPPÉS ET RONDS DE JAMBE EN L'AIR

Preparation

Starting position of the feet: 2nd position, right foot pointe tendue.	Starting position of the arms: 2nd position.

Off-beat (4th), 1st, 2nd, 3rd eighth	3 BATTEMENTS FRAPPÉS on the floor, with the right foot front, croisé.	5th (right arm up).
4th, 1st, 2nd, 3rd eighth	3 BATTEMENTS FRAPPÉS on the floor, with the right foot front, effacé.	5th (left arm up).
4th, 1st, 2nd, 3rd, 4th eighth	BRING the right leg to the side, lifting 45°, en face, continue with	2nd
	3 RONDS DE JAMBE EN L'AIR EN DEHORS with the right leg (end the third rond in demi-plié).	2nd
1st, 2nd eighth	FLIC-FLAC EN TOURNANT EN DEHORS with the right foot, then	A
3rd eighth	step on the right foot moving slightly to the side. Simultaneously DÉGAGÉ with the left leg to the side (45°).	A - 1st - 2nd
4th, 1st, 2nd, 3rd, 4th eighth	3 RONDS DE JAMBE EN L'AIR EN DEDANS with the left leg (end the third rond in demi-plié).	2nd
1st, 2nd eighth	FLIC-FLAC EN TOURNANT EN DEDANS with the left foot, then	A
3rd eighth	lower the left leg in demi-plié, right foot sur le cou-de-pied front.	6th (right arm bent).

4th eighth, *1 bar* *1st, 2nd, 3rd* *eighth*	CHAÎNÉS-DÉBOULÉS (straight forward to side No. 3). End in 5th position right foot back, épaulement croisé.	The right arm opens during the movement, then the arms meet between A and 1st. End in 2nd position.
8 bars	Repeat the exercise on the other leg.	
16 bars	Repeat the whole combination in the reverse direction. Chaînés-déboulés remain in the same direction, straight forward to No. 3.	

Total accompaniment
32 bars

5. GRAND ADAGIO

Measure 3/4 *(Waltz)* *Tempo slow* *Introduction* *(2 bars)*	Preparation Starting position of the feet: 5th position, en face.	Starting position of the arms: 2nd position.
2 bars	GRAND PLIÉ in 5th position, moving down then from this position.	The right arm lowers and comes up in front, bending in the elbow: 6th position.
2 bars	PIROUETTES EN DEHORS (during the turn on the left leg, the right foot is sur le cou-de-pied front), end in attitude croisée, with the right leg.	The right arm opens during the movement, then the arms meet between A and 1st, end in 5th (right arm up).
1 bar, *1st, 2nd* *fourth* *3rd fourth*	STRETCH the right leg to the back, in croisé, stand in 3rd arabesque. DEMI-PLIÉ on the left leg.	3rd arabesque arm position (right arm in front).
1 bar, *1st, 2nd* *fourth*	STEP UNDER on the right leg back, in croisé. LIFT the left leg in front (90°), croisé.	5th (left arm up).

3rd fourth	PASSER LA JAMBE $(90°)$ left leg.	The right arm lowers to the side, from the
1 bar, *1st, 2nd* *fourth*	DÉVELOPPÉ with the left leg to the back, in effacé, stand in 2nd arabesque.	down position the left arm moves to the front: 2nd arabesque arm position.
3rd fourth	DEMI-PLIÉ on the right leg.	
1 bar, *1st, 2nd* *fourth*	STEP UNDER on the left leg back, in effacé. LIFT the right leg front $(90°)$ in effacé.	5th (left arm up).
3rd fourth	LOWER the right leg in demi-plié, turn facing side No. 3, bend the left foot sur le cou-de-pied back.	The left arm lowers in the front, bend in the elbow: 6th position. The left
1 bar	DÉVELOPPÉ À LA SECONDE $(90°)$ with the left leg, on the right leg (half toe), turn facing side No. 5.	arm opens to the side - 2nd allongée, then
1 bar	GRAND FOUETTÉ EN TOURNANT EN DEDANS with the left leg, end in 1st arabesque facing side No. 3.	The arms come down to A - 1st - 3rd. 1st arabesque (right arm in front).
2 bars	PAS DE BOURRÉE EN DEHORS stepping to the side twice, then	A
	TEMPS LIÉ forward, with the left leg, end croisé, the right leg extended to the back, pointe tendue.	A - 1st - 5th (right arm up).
	PORT DE BRAS *Breakdown:*	
1 bar	Lean the body forward and down (on the left leg demi-plié, the right leg is extended in the back, on the floor).	The right arm lowers in front (palms down). Then the left
1 bar	Raise the body, simultaneously turn to the other side (right) and stand in position croisé, the right foot extended to the front, on the floor.	arm moves down to meet the right arm in 1st position, and afterward the arms come in 5th position (left arm up).
1 bar	Bend backward.	5th (left arm up).

1 bar	Straighten the body and move over through demi-plié in 4th position croisé (with a passing movement). The left leg is extended to the back, on the floor.	5th (left arm up).
1 bar	Lean the body forward and down (on the right leg demi-plié, the left leg is extended to the back, on the floor), then	The left arm, bent at the elbow, comes down to the level of the 1st position.
1 bar	While raising the body, simultaneously make a rond de jambe à terre en dedans with the left leg to effacé front, come up from demi-plié.	The left arm opens to the side, simultaneously the right arm comes up to 5th position.
1 bar	Bend backward.	5th (right arm up), then
1st, 2nd fourth	Straighten the body and stand in 4th position effacé (wide), the left leg in plié à quart.	The right arm lowers in the front (palms down), 2nd arabesque position.
3rd fourth	DEMI-PLIÉ in 4th position.	2nd arabesque (right arm in front).
2 bars	TOURS EN DEHORS in 3rd arabesque, end in 4th arabesque position (right leg in back, 90°) croisé.	The arms remain in the same position— 3rd arabesque. End in 4th arabesque arm position (left arm in front).
1 bar	PAS DE BOURRÉE EN TOURNANT EN DEHORS stepping under twice (ending 4th position croisé, wide, right leg in front in plié à quart).	A - 1st - 6th (right arm bent).
1st, 2nd fourth	Stand in the preparatory position for tours en dedans.	6th (right arm bent).
3rd fourth	DEMI-PLIÉ in 4th position.	
1 bar, 1st, 2nd fourth	TOURS EN DEDANS in 1st arabesque, then (without lowering the left leg)	1st arabesque (right arm in front).

3rd fourth	DEMI-PLIÉ on the right leg, continue with	
	GRAND TEMPS RELEVÉ EN DEDANS with the left leg.	4th position (right arm up), end with the same position,
2 bars	PIROUETTES EN TIRE-BOUCHON EN DEDANS the left leg in retiré front, end in 5th position croisé, in demi-plié, the left leg in front.	turn the hands out, stretching the arms slightly forward.

32 bars	Repeat the exercise on the other leg.

Total accompaniment
64 bars

Measure 2/4 *Tempo lively* *Introduction* *(1 bar)*	## 6. GRANDS BATTEMENTS JETÉS	
	Preparation Starting position of the feet: 5th position, croisé, right foot front.	Starting position of the arms: 2nd position.
Off-beat *(4th),* *1st, 2nd, 3rd* *eighth*	GRAND BATTEMENT JETÉ PIQUÉ with the right leg front, in croisé.	5th (left arm up).
4th, 1st, *2nd, 3rd* *eighth*	GRAND BATTEMENT JETÉ PIQUÉ with the left leg to the back, in croisé.	The left arm comes down and moves to the front: 3rd arabesque.
4th, 1st, *2nd, 3rd* *eighth*	GRAND BATTEMENT JETÉ PIQUÉ with the right leg to the side (en face), end with right foot in 5th position back.	2nd
4th, 1st *2nd, 3rd* *eighth*	GRAND BATTEMENT JETÉ PIQUÉ with the right leg to the side, end with the left foot in 5th position back.	2nd

4th eighth	DEMI-PLIÉ in 5th position.	6th (right arm bent).
1 bar, *1st, 2nd, 3rd* *eighth*	PIROUETTES EN DEHORS. End in 4th position, croisé, right leg back, left leg in front in plié à quart.	The right arm opens during the movement, then the arms meet between A and 1st, end in 3rd arabesque (right arm in front).
4th eighth	DEMI-PLIÉ in 4th position.	3rd arabesque (right arm in front).
1 bar, *1st, 2nd, 3rd* *eighth*	PIROUETTES EN DEHORS. End in 5th position, right foot back, épaulement croisé.	The right arm opens during the movement, then the arms meet between A and 1st, end in 2nd position.

8 bars	Repeat the exercise on the other leg.

Total accompaniment
16 bars

(*Pause*)
Repeat the exercise in the reverse
direction (pirouettes remain en
dehors).

Measure 2/4
Tempo
moderate
Introduction
(1 bar)

7. SMALL JUMPS

Preparation
Starting position of the feet: 5th position, croisé, left foot front.

Starting position of the arms: **A.**

Off-beat (4th), 1st eighth	ASSEMBLÉ with the right leg to the side (change), changing épaulement croisé.	A
2nd, 3rd eighth	ASSEMBLÉ with the left leg to the side (change), changing épaulement croisé.	A
4th, 1st eighth	SISSONNE OUVERTE with the left leg to the side (45°), then, without dropping the leg,	2nd through 1st position (hands slightly turned out). Hands turn in, the arms come down to position A.
2nd, 3rd eighth	JETÉ with the left leg traveling slightly to side No. 7, the right foot ends sur le cou-de-pied front, épaulement croisé.	
4th, 1st, 2nd, 3rd eighth	PAS DE BASQUE with the right leg front, ending the movement with PETIT ASSEMBLÉ with the right leg back, in effacé.	A - 1st - 2nd, then the right arm goes down and moves to the front: 3rd arabesque. End position A.
4th, 1st eighth	PETIT CHANGEMENT DE PIEDS. Change épaulement croisé, end in 5th position demi-plié.	A
2nd, 3rd eighth	Come up from demi-plié in 5th position.	

4 bars	Repeat the exercise on the other leg.
8 bars	Repeat the whole combination.

Total accompaniment
16 bars

(Pause)
Repeat the exercise in the reverse direction.

Measure 2/4
Tempo
moderate
Introduction
(2 bars)

8. SMALL JUMPS WITH BEATS

Preparation
Starting position of the feet: Starting position of
5th position, croisé, right foot front.   the arms: A.

Off-beat *(4th),* *1st eighth*	ENTRECHAT-QUATRE.	A
2nd, 3rd *eighth*	ENTRECHAT-CINQ. (The right foot ends sur le cou-de-pied front, the left leg in demi-plié.)	A - 6th (right arm bent).
4th, 1st, *2nd, 3rd* *eighth*	3 EMBOÎTÉS EN TOURNANT traveling straight forward (to side No. 3) with the right leg, etc. End facing backward, left leg bent forward (45°), right leg in demi-plié.	6th (left arm bent). 6th (right arm bent). 6th (left arm bent).
4th, 1st, *2nd, 3rd* *eighth*	3 EMBOÎTÉS EN TOURNANT traveling straight forward (to side No. 3) with the left leg, etc. End facing backward, right leg bent in front (45°), in croisé, the left leg in demi-plié.	6th (right arm bent). 6th (left arm bent). 6th (right arm bent).
4th, 1st, *2nd, 3rd* *eighth*	PAS DE BASQUE BATTU with the right leg to the front, ending the movement with PETIT ASSEMBLÉ with the right leg back, in croisé.	The right arm opens in front and to the side, then, first moving down, rises and stretches to the front: 3rd arabesque. End in position A.

4 bars	Repeat the exercise on the other leg.
8 bars	Repeat the whole combination.

Total accompaniment
16 bars

Measure 2/4
Tempo
moderate
Introduction
(2 bars)

9. MEDIUM JUMPS

Preparation
Starting position of the feet: 5th position, croisé, right foot front.

Starting position of the arms: **A.**

Off-beat (4th), 1st eighth *2nd, 3rd eighth*	SISSONNE OUVERTE with the left leg in the back, in effacé (without dropping the leg). JETÉ with the left leg traveling slightly to side No. 7, the right foot ends sur le cou-de-pied front, épaulement croisé.	A - 1st - 1st arabesque (right arm in front). 2nd allongée, end position **A.**
4th, 1st, 2nd, 3rd eighth	PAS DE BASQUE with the right leg in front, ending the movement with PETIT ASSEMBLÉ with the right leg back, in croisé.	A - 1st - 2nd, then the right arm moves down, rises and stretches to the front: 3rd arabesque. End in position **A.**
4th, 1st eighth	SISSONNE OUVERTE EN ATTITUDE CROISÉE with the right leg.	1st - 5th (right arm up).
2nd, 3rd eighth	BALLOTTÉ with the left leg to side No. 7.	2nd (hands turned out).
4th eighth	TOMBER PIED DESSOUS on the left foot.	2nd
1st, 2nd, 3rd eighth	STEP - COUPÉ with the right foot to side No. 3. ASSEMBLÉ with the left leg to the front (through 1st position), in croisé.	6th (left arm bent).

4 bars   Repeat the exercise on the other leg.

Total accompaniment
8 bars

(*Pause*)
Repeat the exercise in the reverse direction.

Measure 3/4
Tempo
moderate
Introduction
(2 bars)

10. BIG JUMPS

Preparation
Starting position of the feet: 4th
position, croisé, left foot front pointe
tendue.

Starting position of
the arms: 1st position
(wide) hands slightly
turned out.

Start from corner No. 6.

Off-beat *(2nd, 3rd)* *fourth,* *1 bar,* *1st, 2nd* *fourth*	**GLISSADE** (do not change) with the right foot diagonally to corner No. 2. **GRAND PAS DE BASQUE** with the right foot forward diagonally to corner No. 2, etc., end with tombé on the left foot front, in croisé.	The arms move to the side, simultaneously the hands turn fluidly in, then A - 1st - 3rd, and 2nd (hands turned out) - A.
3rd fourth, *1 bar,* *1st, 2nd* *fourth*	**GLISSADE** (do not change) with the right foot diagonally to corner No. 2. **GRAND PAS DE BASQUE** backward, with the right foot, turn halfway to the left, end facing corner No. 6, then, with the raised left leg in the back,	A, the arms come up to the side, then down to position A. 1st arabesque through 1st position (right arm in front).
3rd fourth	**GLISSADE** (do not change) with the left foot diagonally to corner No. 2.	2nd allongée, then the arms come down to A.
1st fourth	**STEP - COUPÉ** with the left foot front, diagonally to corner No. 2.	A
2nd, 3rd *fourth,* *1 bar*	**PAS CISEAUX** with the right leg front, in effacé, end with the left leg to the back, in effacé, stand in 1st arabesque position, on the right leg demi-plié.	1st - 3rd, then 1st arabesque (right arm in front).

Glissade pas ciseaux, ending in 1st arabesque

Nicolai Fadeyechev

1 bar	COME UP on the right leg (half toe) in 1st arabesque, effacé.	1st arabesque (right arm in front).
1 bar	DEMI-PLIÉ on the right leg. CHASSÉ to the back, with the left leg, in effacé, and half a turn to the left, continue with	2nd allongée (a stroke of the hands). A
2 bars	GRAND BATTEMENT JETÉ À LA SECONDE (90°) SAUTÉ EN TOURNANT EN DEDANS with the right leg, end en face, on the left leg demi-plié. JETÉ ENTRELACÉ ending in 1st arabesque.	A - 1st - 3rd, then 2nd - A - 1st - 3rd. 1st arabesque (right arm in front).
1st, 2nd fourth	PETIT JETÉ with the left leg to the side.	A - 1st, then the left arm opens in the front, simultaneously
3rd, 1st fourth	SISSONNE TOMBÉE with the left leg front, in effacé.	the right to the side (hands slightly turned out), then A.
2nd, 3rd fourth	PAS DE BOURRÉE EN DEHORS stepping to the side twice, then	A

CONCLUDING EXERCISE FOR THE MEN'S CLASS:

1 bar	End pas de bourrée en dehors in 5th position, right foot front, croisé.	A
1 bar, 1st fourth	PRÉPARATION POUR TOUR EN L'AIR EN DEHORS. Rise on half toe in 5th position, then demi-plié.	6th (right arm bent).
2nd, 3rd fourth 1st fourth	DOUBLE TOUR EN L'AIR EN DEHORS. End in 1st arabesque (left leg demi- plié), facing side No. 7.	3rd, end 1st arabesque (left arm in front).

Chassé-grand battement jeté à la seconde (90°) sauté en tournant en dedans,
jeté entrelacé, ending in 1st arabesque

Nicolai Fadeyechev

Tour en l'air en dehors, ending in 1st arabesque

Nicolai Fadeyechev

CONCLUDING EXERCISE FOR THE WOMEN'S CLASS:

1st fourth	End pas de bourrée en dehors in 4th position croisé, right foot in front in plié à quart.	6th (right arm bent).
2nd fourth	Stand in the pose.	
3rd fourth	DÉGAGÉ with the left leg to the side (45°), simultaneously demi-plié on the right leg.	The right arm opens during the movement. Then
2 bars, *1st fourth*	PIROUETTES EN DEDANS. End in 5th position croisé, left foot in front.	3rd 2nd (hands slightly turned out).

Total accompaniment
16 bars

(*Pause*)
Repeat the exercise on the other leg.

(*Pause*)
Repeat the whole combination.

Measure 2/4
Tempo lively
Introduction
(2 bars)

11. SMALL JUMPS

Preparation
Starting position of the feet: 4th   Starting position of
position croisé, left leg extended back,   the arms: 6th (right
pointe tendue.   arm bent).

Off-beat *(4th)* *eighth*	DEMI-PLIÉ on the right leg, simultaneously the left leg bends slightly in the back.	6th (right arm bent).
1st, 2nd, 3rd *eighth*	COUPÉ-DESSOUS left foot. 2 RONDS DE JAMBE EN L'AIR EN DEHORS SAUTÉ with the right leg; end on the left leg demi-plié, the right leg open to the side 45°, then with the raised right leg.	The right arm opens to the side, 2nd (hands slightly turned out).
4th, 1st *eighth*	JETÉ BATTU with the right leg to the side, the foot ends sur le cou-de-pied back.	2nd (hands turned in), the arms come down, position A.
2nd, 3rd *eighth*	JETÉ BATTU with the left leg to the side, the right foot ends sur le cou-de-pied back, épaulement croisé.	A

2 bars   Repeat the exercise on the other leg.

4 bars   Repeat the whole combination.

Total accompaniment
8 bars

(*Pause*)
Repeat the exercise in the reverse
direction.

Measure 3/4
(*Waltz*
brillante)
Tempo lively
Introduction
(*2 bars*)

12. BIG JUMPS
(FOR THE MEN'S CLASS)

Preparation

Starting position of the feet: 4th
position, croisé, left leg extended to
the front, pointe tendue.

Starting position of
the arms: 1st position
(wide) hands slightly
turned out.

Start from corner No. 6.

Off-beat
(*2nd, 3rd*)
fourth
1 bar

PAS COURU
traveling forward diagonally to corner
No. 2.

The arms open to the
side (palms down).

1 bar

JETÉ PASSÉ (FRONT - BACK)
Breakdown:

The left leg with the movement of
grand battement jeté kicks forward
in croisé. Simultaneously the right leg
takes off and in the jump is sharply
kicked forward, coming down then
in demi-plié. During this time the
left leg (through 1st position) is moved
to the back (90°), in effacé: 2nd
arabesque position.

The right arm comes
up 5th position, then
the right arm lowers
to the side.
Simultaneously the
left arm comes down
and continues
moving forward:
2nd arabesque.

Isandr Shmelnitsky, Vladimir Nikonov
Pose in 2nd arabesque (45°)

2 bars	PAS COURU traveling forward diagonally to corner No. 2. JETÉ PASSÉ (FRONT - BACK) with the left leg (through 1st position).	Arm movement same as above.
1 bar	PAS COURU traveling forward diagonally to corner No. 2.	2nd (palms down).
1st fourth	STEP - PIQUÉ (on half toe) on the right foot front to side No. 3, lift the left leg to the back (45°).	The left arm comes down and continues the movement forward, 2nd arabesque.
2nd fourth	DEMI-PLIÉ on the right leg (and in the position of the raised left leg).	2nd arabesque.
3rd fourth, *1 bar* *1st, 2nd* *fourth*	CHASSÉ to the back, with the left leg and with a quarter turn to the left, end in position en face. DOUBLE SAUT DE BASQUE with the left leg to side No. 7.	The arms move to 2nd allongée. A - 1st - 3rd
3rd, 1st, 2nd *fourth*	SISSONNE TOMBÉE with the left leg front, in effacé.	The left arm lowers in front, simultaneously the right to the side (hands turned out).
3rd fourth *1 bar*	FAILLI with the right foot, ending front in croisé, then	2nd allongée (a slight stroke of the hands), then the right arm moves down and in front (palms facing down).

Revoltade (from préparation: failli, coupé dessous), ending in 3rd arabesque

Nicolai Fadeyechev

2 bars	COUPÉ-DESSOUS left foot.	A - 1st - 3rd; end 3rd arabesque
	REVOLTADE ending in 3rd arabesque, the left leg back in croisé, and without dropping it,	position (the left arm in front), then the arms come down to position A.
	PETIT ASSEMBLÉ with the left leg to the back, in croisé.	
1 bar	PRÉPARATION POUR PIROUETTES EN DEHORS with the right foot in 2nd position.	A - 1st - 2nd - 6th (right arm bent).
2 bars, *1st fourth*	PIROUETTES EN DEHORS. End in 4th position croisé, right leg back, the left leg in front in plié à quart.	The right arm opens during the movement, then the arms meet between A and 1st; end in 1st position (wide).

Total accompaniment
16 bars

(*Pause*)

Repeat the exercise once more.

(*Pause*)

Repeat the exercise on the other leg
starting from corner No. 4.

Revoltade (from préparation glissade), ending in 1st arabesque

Nicolai Fadeyechev

Measure 3/4
(Waltz
brillante)
Tempo lively
Introduction
(2 bars)

12a. BIG JUMPS
(FOR THE WOMEN'S CLASS)

Preparation   •
Starting position of the feet: 4th
position croisé, left leg extended to
the front, pointe tendue.

Starting position of
the arms: 1st position
(wide) hands
turned out.

Start from corner No. 6.

Off-beat *(2nd, 3rd)* *fourth,* *2 bars*	PAS COURU traveling forward diagonally to corner No. 2. JETÉ PASSÉ (FRONT - BACK) with the left leg front, in croisé, then bring the left leg through 1st position back, in effacé: 2nd arabesque position.[1]	The arms open to the side (palms down). The right arm comes up to 5th position, then 2nd arabesque arm position (left arm in front).
1 bar, *1st, 2nd* *fourth,* *5th eighth*	Repeat the combination, then	Arm movements as above.
6th eighth	STEP ON the left leg forward diagonally to corner No. 2.	The left arm opens to the side.
1st fourth *2nd, 3rd,* *1st, 2nd* *fourth*	STEP - PIQUÉ (on half toe) of the right foot front to side No. 3, lift the left leg to the back (45°). Stand in 2nd arabesque position.	The left arm moves down, rises in front: 2nd arabesque arm position. 2nd arabesque.
3rd fourth, *2 bars*	DEMI-PLIÉ on the right leg and from the position of the raised left leg. CHASSÉ to the back with the left leg and with a quarter turn to the left, end in position en face.	2nd arabesque, then the arms move into 2nd allongée.

---

[1] The breakdown of the movement is given in exercise 12 (see page 329).

	SAUT DE BASQUE with the left leg to side No. 7.	A - 1st - 3rd
1st fourth *2nd, 3rd,* *1st, 2nd* *fourth*	STEP - PIQUÉ (on half toe) of the left foot front to side No. 7, lift the right leg to the back (45°). Stand in 2nd arabesque position.	The left arm lowers to the side, simultaneously the right arm makes a circular movement to the side, down and in front: 2nd arabesque arm position.
3rd fourth, *1 bar,* *1st, 2nd* *fourth,* *5th eighth*	DEMI-PLIÉ on the left leg and from the position of the raised leg. CHASSÉ straight to the back with the right leg and a quarter turn to the right, end in position en face.	2nd arabesque, then the arms move into 2nd allongée.
	SAUT DE BASQUE with the right leg to side No. 3.	A - 1st - 3rd
6th eighth, *1st, 2nd* *fourth,* *3rd fourth,* *2 bars*	CHASSÉ with the right leg diagonally forward to corner No. 2, continue with CHAÎNÉS-DÉBOULÉS traveling straight forward to side No. 3.	3rd - 2nd, end in 6th (right arm bent). The right arm opens during the movement, then the arms meet between A and 1st.
1st fourth	End in effacé, the left leg extended back, pointe tendue.	3rd position.

Total accompaniment
16 bars

(*Pause*)
Repeat the exercise on the other leg
starting from corner No. 4.

Measure 2/4
Tempo
moderate
Introduction
(2 bars)

13. JUMPS
(FOR THE MEN'S CLASS)

Preparation
Starting position of the feet: 5th   Starting position of
position croisé, right foot front.   the arms: A.

Off-beat *(4th) eighth,* *1st eighth*	PRÉPARATION POUR TOUR EN L'AIR EN DEHORS. Rise in 5th position (half toe). Come down in demi-plié.	A - 6th (right arm bent).
2nd, 3rd eighth	DOUBLE TOUR EN L'AIR EN DEHORS. End with the right foot sur le cou-de-pied front, the left leg in demi-plié, épaulement croisé.	The arms meet between A and 1st.
4th, 1st, *2nd, 3rd* *eighth*	PAS DE BASQUE with the right leg to the front. End with the movement PETIT ASSEMBLÉ with the right leg back, in croisé.	1st - 2nd, then the right arm moves down, rises, and comes to the front: 3rd arabesque. End position A.

2 bars   Repeat the exercise on the other leg.

4 bars   Repeat the whole combination.

Total accompaniment
8 bars

(*Pause*)
Repeat the whole exercise.

14. CHANGEMENTS DE PIEDS
(FOR THE MEN'S CLASS)

Measure 2/4 *Tempo lively* *Introduction* *(1 bar)*	Preparation Starting position of the feet: 5th position, en face, right foot front.	Starting position of arms: A.
Off-beat *(4th) eighth,* *1 bar* *1st, 2nd, 3rd* *eighth*	4 PETITS CHANGEMENTS DE PIEDS.	A
4th eighth	PETIT ÉCHAPPÉ in 2nd position, and from this position	6th (right arm bent).
1 bar *1st, 2nd, 3rd* *eighth*	PIROUETTES EN DEHORS. During the turn on the left leg the right foot is sur le cou-de-pied front, end in 5th position, right foot back.	The right arm opens during the movement, then the arms meet between A and 1st position.
4th eighth, *1 bar* *1st, 2nd, 3rd* *eighth*	4 PETITS CHANGEMENTS DE PIEDS.	A
4th eighth	PETIT ÉCHAPPÉ in 2nd position, and from this position.	6th (left arm bent).
1 bar *1st, 2nd, 3rd* *eighth*	PIROUETTES EN DEHORS. During the turn on the right leg the left foot is sur le cou-de-pied front, end in 5th position, left foot back.	The left arm opens during the movement, then the arms meet between A and 1st position.
8 bars	Repeat the exercise.	

Total accompaniment
16 bars

(*Pause*)
Repeat the whole combination.

Measure 2/4
Tempo fast
Introduction
(2 bars)

15. GRANDES PIROUETTES "BLINTCHIKI"[1]
(FOR THE MEN'S CLASS)

	Preparation Starting position of the feet: 5th position croisé, right foot front.	Starting position of the arms: 2nd position.
(Pause)	PRÉPARATION POUR PIROUETTES EN DEHORS with the right foot in 2nd position. PIROUETTES EN DEHORS right leg in retiré front. The right leg ends with a quick développé à la seconde (90°), then continue after the turn	2nd, 6th (right arm bent). The right arm opens during the movement, then the arms meet between A and 1st. Then (through 1st position) open the arms in 2nd position.
2 bars	GRANDES PIROUETTES EN DEHORS "blintchiki"—(8 times), the right leg à la seconde (90°), then continue after the turn	2nd
2 bars	GRANDES PIROUETTES EN DEHORS "blintchiki"—(8 times), in 3rd arabesque, then, after the turn,	3rd arabesque.
3 bars	GRANDES PIROUETTES EN DEHORS "blintchiki"—(12 times), the right leg à la seconde (90°), then, after the turn,	2nd
1 bar	PIROUETTES EN DEHORS. During the turn on the left leg, the right foot is in front sur le cou-de-pied. End in 4th position croisé, the right leg back; the left leg in front in plié à quart.	The arms meet between A and 1st. End in 2nd position.

Total accompaniment
8 bars

---

[1] Grandes pirouettes "blintchiki" (in a number of poses) are executed in a fast tempo, on the demi-plié of the supporting leg. The turn is worked out through the displacement of the heel toward the side of the turn; each move is accented with a pressure of the heel onto the floor.

(Pause)

Repeat the exercise.

(Pause)

Repeat the whole combination on the other leg.

Measure 2/4
(Waltz)
Tempo slow
Introduction
(2 bars)

16. PORT DE BRAS AND BENDING OF THE BODY
(FOR THE MEN'S CLASS)

Preparation
Starting position of the feet: 1st position (halfway turned out).

Starting position of the arms: 2nd position.

This exercise corresponds to exercise 15 (exercises in the center) of the first class (see page 108).

Total accompaniment
32 bars

Measure 2/4
Tempo lively
Introduction
(1 bar)

17.   FIRST EXERCISE ON POINTES

Preparation
Starting position of the feet: 5th   Starting position of
position croisé, right foot front.   the arms: A.

Off-beat   3 ÉCHAPPÉS   A - 4th arabesque
(4th) eighth,   in 4th position croisé, traveling   (right arm in front),
3 bars,   forward diagonally to corner No. 8.   then A, etc.

1st, 2nd, 3rd   ÉCHAPPÉ   A - 1st - 2nd - A
eighth   in 2nd position (change), en face.

---

4 bars   Repeat the exercise on the other leg.

8 bars   Repeat the whole combination.

16 bars   Repeat the exercise in the reverse
                    direction.

Total accompaniment
32 bars

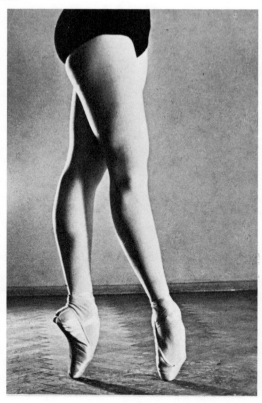

Relevé in 4th position, croisé

18. SECOND EXERCISE ON POINTES

Measure 2/4
Tempo
moderate
Introduction
(2 bars)

Preparation
Starting position of the feet: 5th
position, en face, right foot front.

Starting position of
the arms: A.

Off-beat
(4th), 1st,
2nd
eighth

DEMI-PLIÉ
in 5th position.

A

DÉGAGÉ
with the right leg to the side (45°).
Simultaneously rise on half toe (left
foot), continue with

A - 1st - 2nd

2 RONDS DE JAMBE EN L'AIR
EN DEHORS
with the right leg, then

2nd

3rd, 4th
eighth

FOUETTÉ EN TOURNANT EN
DEHORS
with the right leg, the left leg in
demi-plié, then rising up on pointe.

A - 1st - 6th (right
arm bent).

1st, 2nd
eighth

End on left pointe with the right leg
croisé front (45°).

3rd, 4th
1st, 2nd
eighth

TOMBÉ
on the right foot front croisé. Then

The right arm opens
to the side, 2nd
position.

DÉGAGÉ
with the left leg to the side (45°),
rise on the right pointe and continue

2 RONDS DE JAMBE EN L'AIR
EN DEDANS
with the left leg. Then

2nd

3rd, 4th
eighth
1st, 2nd
eighth

FOUETTÉ EN TOURNANT EN
DEDANS
with the left leg, right leg in demi-
plié, then rise on pointe and end on
right pointe with the left leg in back,
croisé (45°).

A - 1st - 3rd
arabesque (left arm
in front).

3rd eighth

TOMBÉ
on the left foot back, the right foot
sur le cou-de-pied front.

A

4th, 1st, 2nd
eighth

PETIT DÉVELOPPÉ
with the right leg front, in effacé
(45°), on the left pointe.

Through 1st position
to 6th position (right
arm bent).

3rd, 4th *eighth,*	TOMBÉ on the right foot front, in effacé. Continue with DÉGAGÉ with the left leg to the side (45°).	The right arm opens to the side.
1st, 2nd, 3rd *eighth*	DOUBLE TOUR PIQUÉ EN DEHORS. During the turn on the left leg, the right foot is sur le cou-de-pied front. End with the right leg in front, in effacé (45°).	The arms meet between A and 1st. End in the 6th (right arm bent).
4th eighth	TOMBÉ on the right foot front, in effacé.	The right arm opens to the front, then 2nd position.
1st, 2nd *eighth,* *3rd, 4th* *eighth*	PAS DE BOURRÉE EN DEHORS stepping to the side twice. End in 4th position croisé, demi-plié.	A
1st, 2nd *eighth*	RELEVÉ SUR LA POINTE on the left leg, the right leg rises in back (halfway bent), in attitude croisée (90°).	A - 1st - 5th (right arm up).
3rd eighth	Come down in 5th position demi-plié.	The arms come down, position A.

8 bars	Repeat the exercise on the other leg.

Total accompaniment
16 bars

Measure 3/4
(Waltz)
Tempo
moderate
Introduction
(2 bars)

19. THIRD EXERCISE ON POINTES

Preparation

	Starting position of the feet: 5th position, en face, right foot front.	Starting position of the arms: A.
Off-beat		
(3rd) fourth,	DEMI-PLIÉ in 5th position.	A
1st, 2nd fourth	DÉVELOPPÉ À LA SECONDE (90°) with the right leg, simultaneously spring up to left pointe.	A - 1st - 2nd
3rd fourth	DEMI-PLIÉ on the left leg, the right leg à la seconde (90°).	2nd
1st, 2nd fourth	RELEVÉ-FOUETTÉ from pose to pose, in a quarter turn to the left, end in 1st arabesque on left pointe.	1st arabesque (left arm in front).
5th eighth	DEMI-PLIÉ on the left leg.	A - 1st - 3rd, 3rd arabesque (right arm front).
6th eighth, 1st, 2nd fourth	GRAND FOUETTÉ EN TOURNANT EN DEDANS with the right leg, end in 3rd arabesque on left pointe.	
3rd fourth	DEMI-PLIÉ on the left leg.	3rd arabesque (right arm in front).
1st, 2nd fourth	RELEVÉ on the left pointe, in 3rd arabesque.	
4 bars	Repeat the exercise on the other leg.	
8 bars	Repeat the whole combination.	

Total accompaniment
16 bars

Relevé à la seconde (90°) fouetté en dehors, from pose to pose ending in 1st arabesque

Rimma Karelskaya

20. FOURTH EXERCISE ON POINTES

Measure 3/4
Tempo
moderate
Introduction
(2 bars)

Preparation
Starting position of the feet: 4th
position croisé, left leg extended to
the back, pointe tendue.

Starting position of
the arms: **A**.

Off-beat *(6th) eighth* *1 bar,*	PAS DE BOURRÉE DESSUS with the left foot.	A - 1st - 2nd (hands slightly turned out).
1st, 2nd *fourth,* *5th eighth*	PAS DE BOURRÉE DESSOUS with the right foot.	2nd - A
6th eighth, *1 bar,* *1st, 2nd*	PAS DE BOURRÉE DESSUS with the left foot.	A - 1st - 2nd (hands slightly turned out).
fourth, *5th eighth*	PAS DE BOURRÉE DESSOUS with the right foot.	2nd - A
6th eighth, *1 bar,* *1st, 2nd* *fourth,*	PAS DE BOURRÉE DESSUS EN TOURNANT EN DEDANS with the left foot.	A - 1st - 2nd (hands slightly turned out).
5th eighth	PAS DE BOURRÉE DESSOUS EN TOURNANT EN DEHORS with the right foot.	2nd - A
6th eighth, *1 bar,* *1st, 2nd* *fourth,*	PAS DE BOURRÉE DESSUS EN TOURNANT EN DEDANS with the left foot.	A - 1st - 2nd (hands slightly turned out).
5th eighth	PAS DE BOURRÉE DESSOUS EN TOURNANT EN DEHORS with the right foot.	2nd - A

8 bars   Repeat the exercise.

Total accompaniment
16 bars

(*Pause*)
Repeat the exercise on the other leg.

Measure 2/4
Tempo lively
Introduction
(2 bars)

21. FIFTH EXERCISE ON POINTES

Preparation
Starting position of the feet: 5th
position, en face, right foot front.

Starting position of
the arms: 2nd
position.

Off-beat
(4th)
eighth

DEMI-PLIÉ
in 5th position.

6th (right arm bent).

15 bars,
1st, 2nd, 3rd
eighth

TOURS EN DEHORS.
Execute 16 times in a row.
The right foot remains sur le cou-de
pied front during all the turns.
End in 4th position croisé, right leg in
the back, the left leg in front in plié
à quart.

The right arm opens
during the movement,
the arms meet
between A and 1st
position. Then the
arms open to the side
(through 1st
position), then meet
between A and 1st,
etc. End in 2nd
position (hands
slightly turned out).

Total accompaniment
16 bars

(Pause)
Repeat the exercise.

(Pause)
Repeat the exercise on the other leg.

22. SIXTH EXERCISE ON POINTES

Measure 2/4
Tempo fast
Introduction
(2 bars)

Preparation
Starting position of the feet: 4th position croisé, right leg extended to the front, pointe tendue.

Starting position of the arms: 6th (right arm bent).

Start from corner No. 8.

Off-beat (2nd, 3rd, 4th) eighth, 11 bars 1st, 2nd, 3rd eighth

TOUR PIQUÉ EN DEHORS.
Execute 12 times in a row from préparation dégagée of the left leg to the side, 45°, etc., traveling gradually in a circle clockwise. Then after the turn

The right arm opens to the side, then the arms meet between A and 1st, then the arms open to the side (through 1st position), then meet between A and 1st, etc. End in 6th position (right arm bent).

4th eighth, 2 bars, 1st, 2nd eighth

CHAÎNÉS-DÉBOULÉS
traveling forward diagonally to corner No. 2.

The right arm opens during the movement, then the arms meet between A and 1st.

3rd, 4th eighth,

STEP
on the right foot front diagonally to corner No. 2, end in demi-plié.

Through 1st position, 1st arabesque (right arm in front).

1st eighth

RELEVÉ SUR LA POINTE
on the right leg, simultaneously lift the left leg back in effacé (90°). Stand in 1st arabesque.

Total accompaniment
16 bars

(*Pause*)
Repeat the exercise.

(*Pause*)
Repeat the exercise on the other leg. Start from corner No. 2, traveling in a circle counterclockwise.

Measure 2/4
Tempo lively
Introduction
(2 bars)

23.   SEVENTH EXERCISE ON POINTES

Preparation
Starting position of the feet: 4th   Starting position of
position, en face, left leg front in plié   the arms: 2nd
à quart.   arabesque (right arm
                                             in front).

Off-beat   32 FOUETTÉS EN TOURNANT EN   The right arm opens
(2nd, 3rd,   DEHORS (45°).[1]   during the movement,
4th)   Open the right leg each time à la   then the arms meet
eighth,   seconde (45°).   between A and 1st,
31 bars,   then the arms open to
1st eighth   the side (through 1st
                                                      position) and meet
                                                      between A and 1st,
                                                      etc.

                  End the last fouetté en tournant en   End in 1st position
                  dehors in 4th position croisé, right leg   (wide), hands
                  back, the left leg in front in plié à   slightly turned out.
                  quart.

Total accompaniment
32 bars

(Pause)
Repeat the exercise on the other leg.

---

[1] One should start this combination with a tour en dehors, afterward, at the end of the turn, follow with fouettés en tournant en dehors.

Measure 2/4
Tempo lively
Introduction
(1 bar)

24.   EIGHTH EXERCISE ON POINTES

Preparation
Starting position of the feet: 5th
position, en face right foot front.

Starting position of
the arms: A.

Off-beat
(4th) eighth,
7 bars,
1st, 2nd, 3rd
eighth

16 PETITS CHANGEMENTS DE
PIEDS SUR LES POINTES.

A - 1st - 3rd - 2nd- A

Total accompaniment
8 bars

Measure 3/4
(Waltz)
Tempo slow
Introduction
(2 bars)

25.   PORT DE BRAS AND BENDING
OF THE BODY

Preparation
Starting position of the feet: 1st
position (halfway turned out).

Starting position of
the arms: 2nd
position.

This exercise corresponds to exercise
15 (exercises in the center) of the
first class (see page 108).

Total accompaniment
32 bars

PHOTO BY JUDY CAMERON

Sixth Class

EXERCISES AT THE BARRE

Musical-rhythmical accompaniment	DANCING EXERCISES

Measure 3/4
(Waltz)
Tempo slow
Introduction
(2 bars)

1. GRANDS PLIÉS

Preparation
Starting position of the feet: 1st
position.

Starting position of
the right arm: 2nd
position.

This exercise corresponds to exercise
1 (exercises at the barre) of the first
class (see page 55).

Total accompaniment
32 bars

Measure 2/4
Tempo
moderate
Introduction
(1 bar)

2. BATTEMENTS TENDUS

Preparation Starting position of the feet: 5th position, right foot front.	Starting position of the right arm: 2nd position.

Off-beat
(4th),
1st, 2nd, 3rd
eighth

2 BATTEMENTS TENDUS with the right foot front.	2nd

4th, 1st,
2nd, 3rd
eighth

BATTEMENT TENDU with the right foot front with demi-plié in 4th position.	2nd - 3rd (right arm up) - 2nd.

4th, 1st,
2nd, 3rd
eighth

2 BATTEMENTS TENDUS with the right foot to the side (change).	2nd

4th, 1st,
2nd, 3rd
eighth

BATTEMENT TENDU with the right foot to the side with demi-plié in 2nd position. End in 5th position back.	2nd - 1st - 2nd

4th, 1st,
2nd, 3rd
eighth

2 BATTEMENTS TENDUS with the right foot back.	2nd

4th, 1st,
2nd, 3rd
eighth

BATTEMENT TENDU with the right foot back, with demi-plié in 4th position.	2nd - 3rd (right arm up) - 2nd.

4th, 1st,
2nd, 3rd
eighth

2 BATTEMENTS TENDUS with the right foot to the side (change).	2nd

4th, 1st,
2nd, 3rd
eighth

BATTEMENT TENDU with the right foot to the side, with demi-plié in 2nd position. End in 5th position front.	2nd - 1st - 2nd

8 bars   Repeat the exercise.

Total accompaniment
16 bars

Turn to the other side and repeat
the exercise on the other leg.

Measure 2/4
Tempo lively
Introduction
(1 bar)

3. BATTEMENTS TENDUS JETÉS

Preparation
Starting position of the feet: 5th
position, right foot front.

Starting position of
the right arm: 2nd
position.

Off-beat
(4th), 1st,
2nd, 3rd
eighth

2 BATTEMENTS TENDUS JETÉS
with the right foot front.

2nd position.

4th, 1st,
2nd, 3rd

3 BATTEMENTS TENDUS JETÉS
with the right foot front.

4th, 1st,
2nd, 3rd
eighth

2 BATTEMENTS TENDUS JETÉS
with the right foot to the side (change).

4th, 1st,
2nd, 3rd
eighth

3 BATTEMENTS TENDUS JETÉS
with the right foot to the side (change).

4th, 1st,
2nd, 3rd
eighth

2 BATTEMENTS TENDUS JETÉS
with the right foot back.

4th, 1st,
2nd, 3rd
eighth

3 BATTEMENTS TENDUS JETÉS
with the right foot back.

4th, 1st,
2nd, 3rd
eighth

2 BATTEMENTS TENDUS JETÉS
with the right foot to the side
(change).

4th, 1st,
2nd, 3rd
eighth

3 BATTEMENTS TENDUS JETÉS
with the right foot to the side
(change).

8 bars

Repeat the exercise.

Total accompaniment
16 bars

Turn to the other side and repeat the
exercise on the other leg.

4. RONDS DE JAMBE À TERRE

	Preparation Starting position of the feet[1]	Starting position of the right arm: 2nd position.
4 bars	4 RONDS DE JAMBE À TERRE EN DEHORS with the right leg.	2nd
1 bar	1 ROND DE JAMBE À TERRE, IN DEMI-PLIÉ.	A - 1st - 2nd
2 bars	2 GRANDS RONDS DE JAMBE JETÉS.	2nd
1 bar	1 ROND DE JAMBE À TERRE.	2nd
8 bars	Repeat the exercise, en dedans (with a change at the end of the combination: do not execute the last rond de jambe à terre, bring the right foot through 1st position front pointe tendue).	
8 bars	Repeat the exercise in the reverse direction, en dedans.	
8 bars	Repeat the exercise, en dedans (with a change at the end of the combination: do not execute the last rond de jambe à terre; the right leg comes down in 5th position front).	

Immediately thereafter execute the following combination:

Tempo slow
32 bars

PORT DE BRAS ET BATTEMENTS RELEVÉS LENTS (90°).
This section of the exercise corresponds with port de bras et battements relevés lents of exercise 5 (exercises at the barre) of the first class (see page 62).

Total accompaniment
64 bars   Turn to the other side and repeat the exercise on the other leg.

[1] Execute the ronds de jambe à terre, immediately after preparation, continuing the movement of the preparatory rond.

Measure 2/4
Tempo slow
Introduction
(2 bars)

5. BATTEMENTS FONDUS

Preparation
Starting position of the feet: 2nd   Starting position of
position, right foot pointe tendue.   the right arm: 2nd
position.

Off-beat
(4th), 1st,   BATTEMENT FONDU   2nd position.
2nd, 3rd   with the right leg front (45°).
eighth

4th, 1st, 2nd,   BATTEMENT FONDU
3rd   with the right leg to the side.
eighth

4th, 1st, 2nd,   BATTEMENT FONDU
3rd   with the right leg back.
eighth

4th, 1st   DEMI-PLIÉ
eighth   on the left leg.
2nd, 3rd   ROND DE JAMBE EN DEDANS
eighth   with the right leg, simultaneously
                   come up from demi-plié, end in front
                   (45°).

4th, 1st   PETIT BATTEMENT SUR LE
eighth   COU-DE-PIED
                   with the right foot, ending in
                   demi-plié, continue with

2nd, 3rd   BATTEMENT FONDU
eighth   with the right leg to the back.

4th, 1st, 2nd,   BATTEMENT FONDU
3rd   with the right leg to the side.
eighth

4th, 1st, 2nd,   BATTEMENT FONDU
3rd   with the right leg to the front.
eighth

4th, 1st   DEMI-PLIÉ
eighth   on the left leg.
2nd, 3rd   ROND DE JAMBE EN DEHORS
eighth   with the right leg, simultaneously
                   come up from demi-plié, end in the
                   back (45°).

8 bars   Repeat the exercise on half toe.

Total accompaniment
16 bars

         Turn to the other side and repeat
         the exercise on the other leg.

Measure 2/4
Tempo slow
Introduction
(1 bar)

6. BATTEMENTS FRAPPÉS ET RONDS DE JAMBE EN L'AIR

Preparation
Starting position of the feet: 2nd
position, right foot pointe tendue.

Starting position of
the right arm: 2nd
position.

Off-beat
(4th), 1st,
2nd,
3rd, 4th
eighth

BATTEMENT FRAPPÉ
with the right leg front on the floor.

BATTEMENT FRAPPÉ
on the floor, with the right leg to the
side.

BATTEMENT FRAPPÉ
on the floor, with the right leg back.

BATTEMENT FRAPPÉ
on the floor, with the right leg to the
side. Then lift the right leg to the
side (45°), and continue with

2nd position.

1st, 2nd, 3rd
eighth

3 RONDS DE JAMBE EN L'AIR EN
DEDANS
with the right leg (45°).

4th, 1st, 2nd,
3rd
eighth

3 RONDS DE JAMBE EN L'AIR EN
DEHORS
with the right leg (45°).

4th eighth,	PRÉPARATION TEMPS RELEVÉ EN DEHORS with the right leg (45°).	A - 1st, then
1st, 2nd, 3rd eighth	FOUETTÉ EN TOURNANT EN DEHORS (45°) with the right leg, end à la seconde.	The arms meet between A and 1st, then, through 1st position, the right arm opens in 2nd position; the left arm is placed on the barre.

4 bars	Repeat the exercise in the reverse direction.
8 bars	Repeat the whole combination on half toe.

Total accompaniment
16 bars

Turn to the other side and repeat the exercise on the other leg.

Measure 3/4
(Waltz)
Tempo slow
Introduction
(2 bars)

7.   ADAGIO

Preparation
Starting position of the feet: 5th
position, right foot front.

Starting position of
the right arm: 2nd
position.

2 bars	DÉVELOPPÉ with the right leg front, then	A - 1st - 2nd
1 bar	RISE on half toe (left foot).	2nd
1 bar	PASSER LA JAMBE $(90°)$ the right leg, remaining on half toe (left foot).	A
2 bars	DÉVELOPPÉ À LA SECONDE with the right leg, on half toe (left foot).	A - 1st - 2nd
2 bars	BRING the right leg to the front $(90°)$, simultaneously come down from half toe (left foot) in demi-plié.	2nd - 1st
2 bars	STEP ON the right leg in front. LIFT the left leg in the back $(90°)$.	The right arm moves to the front (palm down).
2 bars	DEMI-PLIÉ on the right leg. STEP ON the left leg in the back. LIFT the right leg in front $(90°)$.	1st
2 bars	GRAND ROND DE JAMBE EN DEHORS with the right leg, end in the back $(90°)$, then	The right arm moves in 2nd position, then down and up, stretches forward:
1 bar	RISE on half toe (left foot).	2nd arabesque arm position.

1 bar	Bring the right leg to 5th position back. Simultaneously come down from half toe.	The right arm comes down to A.

16 bars	Repeat the exercise in the reverse direction.

Total accompaniment
32 bars

Turn to the other side and repeat the exercise on the other leg.

Measure 2/4 *Tempo lively* *Introduction* *(1 bar)*	**8. BATTEMENTS DOUBLES FRAPPÉS ET PETITS BATTEMENTS SUR LE COU-DE-PIED**	
	Preparation Starting position of the feet: 2nd position, right foot pointe tendue.	Starting position of the right arm: 2nd position.
Off-beat *(4th), 1st,* *2nd, 3rd* *eighth*	BATTEMENT DOUBLE FRAPPÉ on the floor, with the right leg ending front.	2nd position.
4th, 1st, *2nd, 3rd* *eighth*	BATTEMENT DOUBLE FRAPPÉ on the floor, with the right leg ending in back.	
4th, 1st, *2nd, 3rd,* *4th, 1st,* *2nd, 3rd* *eighth*	3 PETITS BATTEMENTS SUR LE COU-DE-PIED right foot. DÉGAGÉ with the right foot to the side, pointe tendue.	
4th, 1st, *2nd, 3rd* *eighth*	BATTEMENT DOUBLE FRAPPÉ on the floor, with the right foot ending in back.	
4th, 1st, *2nd, 3rd* *eighth*	BATTEMENT DOUBLE FRAPPÉ on the floor, with the right foot, ending in the front.	

4th, 1st, *2nd, 3rd,* *4th, 1st,* *2nd, 3rd* *eighth*	3 PETITS BATTEMENTS SUR LE COU-DE-PIED right foot, then DÉGAGÉ with the right foot to the side, pointe tendue.
8 bars	Repeat the exercise on half toe, execute the battements doubles frappés coming up on half toe and down on the supporting foot; the working leg ends each movement on the floor (pointe tendue).
16 bars	At the end of the whole combination, balance on half toe (left foot) in various poses (see the description in the second part of exercise 11, exercises at the barre, of the first class, page 71).

Total accompaniment
32 bars

Turn to the other side and repeat the
exercise on the other leg.

9. GRANDS BATTEMENTS JETÉS

Measure 2/4
Tempo moderate
Introduction (1 bar)

Preparation

Starting position of the feet: 5th position, right foot front.	Starting position of the right arm: 2nd position.

Off-beat (4th),
1st eighth

GRAND BATTEMENT JETÉ with the right leg front.

2nd position.

2nd, 3rd eighth

GRAND BATTEMENT JETÉ with the right leg to the side (change).

GRANDS BATTEMENTS JETÉS BALANÇOIRE (90°) with the right leg.
   Breakdown:

4th eighth	Kick the leg back.
1st eighth	Kick the leg front.
2nd eighth	Kick the leg back.
3rd eighth	Bring the leg to 5th position back.

4th, 1st,
2nd, 3rd
eighth

2 GRANDS BATTEMENTS JETÉS with the right leg to the side (change).

GRANDS BATTEMENTS JETÉS À LA SECONDE (90°) with the right leg, accent up.
   Breakdown:

4th eighth

Kick the leg to the side.
Lower the leg to 1st position (with a passing movement).

2nd position.

1st eighth

Kick the leg to the side (accent up).
Lower the leg to 1st position (with a passing movement).

2nd eighth
3rd eighth

Kick the leg to the side (accent up).
Lower the leg to 5th position back.

4 bars

Repeat the exercise in the reverse direction.

Total accompaniment
8 bars

Turn to the other side and repeat the exercise on the other leg.

Measure 3/4
(Waltz)   **10.   PORT DE BRAS AND BENDING**
Tempo slow   **OF THE BODY**
Introduction
(2 bars)   Preparation
                       Starting position of the feet: 1st   Starting position of
                       position, facing the barre.   the arms: both arms
                                                                   on the barre.

                       This exercise corresponds to exercise
                       13 (exercises at the barre) of the
                       first class (see page 75).

Total accompaniment
32 bars

Measure 3/4
(Waltz)
Tempo slow   **10a.   STRETCHING OF THE LEGS**
Introduction
(2 bars)   Preparation
                       Starting position of the feet: 5th   Starting position of
                       position, right foot front.   the right arm: 2nd
                                                                   position.

                       STRETCHING FORWARD
                            Breakdown:
2 bars   Bend the right leg in retiré front,   With the right hand
                       90°.   grab the heel of the
                                                                   right leg (hold in
                                                                   hand with the inward
                                                                   side of the heel).

                       Développé with the right leg front, in   Stretch the right arm
                       demi-plié (left leg).   forward, holding the
                                                                   heel.

1 bar   Bring the right leg to the side (higher   Bring the right arm
1st, 2nd   than 90°). Simultaneously come up   to the side, holding
fourth   from demi-plié (left leg), then   the heel.

3rd fourth   bend the right leg, in retiré front   Bring the right arm
                       (90°).   down, holding the
                                                                   heel.

8 bars	Repeat the combination twice, starting with développé front.	

4 bars	End the combination on half toe, the right leg à la seconde, higher than 90°, hold the leg up for a while, then slowly bring it down to 5th position back.	The right arm is in 3rd position, then comes down to position A.

Total accompaniment
16 bars

(*Pause*)

STRETCHING BACKWARD
    Breakdown:

2 bars	Lift the right leg (bent) to the back (90°) in attitude.	Grab the right knee with the right hand.
	Stretch the right leg back (90°) in arabesque, in demi-plié (left leg). Bend the body slightly backward, turn the head to the right.	The right hand holding the leg pulls it upward.
2 bars	Bring the right leg to the side (higher than 90°), simultaneously come up from demi-plié (left leg).	The right hand holds the leg from the inside, pulling it up stretching the extension.
8 bars	Repeat the combination twice.	

4 bars	End the combination on half toe, the right leg à la seconde, higher than 90°, hold the leg up for a while, then slowly bring it up to 5th position front.	The right arm in 3rd position, then it comes down to position A.

Total accompaniment
16 bars

Turn to the other side and repeat the combination (stretching of the legs forward and back) with the other leg.

Position of the raised leg in front
(the turned out heel of the right foot
is held in the hand)

Position of the raised leg to the side
(the turned out heel of the right foot
is held in the hand)

Elena Tcherkaskaya

Position of the raised leg in front, in demi-plié
(the heel of the right foot is held
by the hand outwardly to the side)

Position of the raised leg to the side
(the heel of the right foot is held
by the hand outwardly to the side)

Position of the raised leg in the back
(the left leg is grabbed by the hand)

Nina Sorokina

Measure 3/4
(Waltz)
Tempo slow   **10b.   STRETCHING OF THE LEGS**
Introduction
(2 bars)   Preparation
                            Starting position of the feet: 3rd   Starting position of
                            position, right foot front.   the arms: A.

                            STRETCHING OF THE LEGS
                            "SHPAGAT" (SPLIT)
                                Breakdown:
4 bars   Slide the right leg forward on the   The right arm
                            floor to the full extension of the split,   stretches forward,
                            then   simultaneously the
                                                                        left arm comes up to
                                                                        the side (palms
                                                                        down).

2 bars   the body leans forward toward the   The left arm comes
                            right leg.   up and lowers front
                                                                        toward the right leg.

2 bars   The body bends back toward the left   The right arm comes
                            leg.   up, simultaneously
                                                                        the left arm bends
                                                                        in front: 4th position.

_____

Total accompaniment
8 bars

                            Turn to the other side and repeat
                            the combination on the other leg.

Stretching "Shpagat" or split

Elena Tcherkaskaya

Measure 2/4
Tempo lively
Introduction
(1 bar)

11. RELEVÉS
(FOR THE WOMEN'S CLASS)

Preparation
Starting position of the feet: 1st   Starting position of
position facing the barre.   the arms: both hands
                                             on the barre.

This exercise corresponds to exercise
14 (exercises at the barre) of the
first class (see page 78).

Total accompaniment
16 bars

Measure 2/4
Tempo lively
Introduction
(1 bar)

11a. RELEVÉS
(FOR THE MEN'S CLASS)

Preparation
Starting position of the feet: 1st   Starting position of
position, facing the barre.   the arms: both hands
                                             on the barre.

This exercise corresponds to exercise
11 (exercises at the barre) of the fifth
class (see page 306).

Total accompaniment
16 bars

EXERCISES IN THE CENTER

Measure 3/4
(Waltz)
Tempo slow
Introduction
(2 bars)

1. SMALL ADAGIO

Preparation
Starting position of the feet: 5th position croisé, right foot front.

Starting position of the arms: 2nd position.

PORT DE BRAS
Breakdown:

2 bars	Lean the body forward-down. Return to the starting position. Slide the right leg front, on the floor (pointe tendue), croisé.	2nd - A A - 1st - 5th (right arm up).
2 bars	Bend the body backward, return to the starting position, right foot pointe tendue.	5th (right arm up).
1 bar	**BRUSH** the right leg to the back (through 1st position).	The right arm lowers and moves to the front: 2nd arabesque position.
1st, 2nd fourth, 5th eighth	**LIFT** the right leg in the back, in effacé (90°). Stand in 2nd arabesque position.	
6th eighth	**DEMI-PLIÉ** on the left leg.	5th (right arm up).
2 bars	**STEP ON** the right leg back. **LIFT** the left leg in front, in effacé (90°).	
1 bar, 1st, 2nd fourth, 5th eighth	**BRING** the left leg in croisé front, at 90°. Lean the head slightly to the front looking to the left "under the arm."	5th (left arm up).

6th eighth	DEMI-PLIÉ on the right leg.	5th (left arm up).
2 bars	STEP ON the left leg front. LIFT the right leg in the back, in croisé (90°). Stand in 4th arabesque position.	4th arabesque position (left arm in front).
2 bars, *1st, 2nd* *fourth*	GRAND ROND DE JAMBE EN DEDANS with the right leg to croisé front (lean the head slightly to the front, looking to the right "under the arm"), then	The left arm opens to the side (through 1st position) to 2nd position, then the right arm comes up to 5th arm position.
3rd fourth	DEMI-PLIÉ on the left leg, the right foot sur le cou-de-pied front.	The right arm opens to the side: 2nd position (hands slightly turned out).
1 bar	PAS DE BOURRÉE EN TOURNANT EN DEDANS. End with the right foot in 5th position back, épaulement croisé.	A - 1st 2nd

16 bars	Repeat the exercise on the other leg.

Total accompaniment
32 bars

(*Pause*)
Repeat the exercise in the reverse
direction.

2. BATTEMENTS TENDUS

Measure 2/4
Tempo
moderate
Introduction
(1 bar)

Preparation
Starting position of the feet: 5th position croisé, right foot front.

Starting position of the arms: 2nd position.

Off-beat (4th), 1st, 2nd, 3rd eighth	2 BATTEMENTS TENDUS with the right foot in front, croisé.	6th (left arm bent).
4th, 1st, 2nd, 3rd eighth	2 BATTEMENTS TENDUS with the left foot to the back, croisé.	6th (right arm bent).
4th, 1st, 2nd, 3rd eighth	2 BATTEMENTS TENDUS with the right foot in front, in effacé.	6th (left arm bent).
4th, 1st, 2nd, 3rd eighth	2 BATTEMENTS TENDUS with the left foot to the back, in effacé.	6th (right arm bent).
4th, 1st, 2nd, 3rd eighth	3 BATTEMENTS TENDUS JETÉS with the right foot to the side (change).	2nd
4th, 1st, 2nd, 3rd eighth	3 BATTEMENTS TENDUS JETÉS with the left foot to the side (change).	2nd

CONCLUDING EXERCISE FOR THE MEN'S CLASS:

4th eighth,	PRÉPARATION POUR PIROUETTES EN DEHORS with the right foot in 2nd position.	2nd - 6th (right arm bent).
1 bar, 1st, 2nd, 3rd eighth	PIROUETTES EN DEHORS end in 4th position croisé, the right leg back, the left leg in front in plié à quart.	The right arm opens during the movement, then the arms meet between A and 1st. End in 1st position (wide).

CONCLUDING EXERCISE FOR THE WOMEN'S CLASS:

4th eighth, *1 bar*	PRÉPARATION POUR PIROUETTES EN DEHORS with the right foot in 4th position croisé.	A - 1st - 3rd arabesque position (**right arm** in front).
1st, 2nd, 3rd eighth	PIROUETTES EN DEHORS. End in 4th position croisé, the right leg back, the left leg in front in plié à quart.	The right arm opens during the movement, then the arms meet between A and 1st. End in 1st position (wide).

8 bars	Repeat the exercise on the other leg.

Total accompaniment
16 bars   (*Pause*)
Repeat the exercise in the reverse
direction (pirouettes remain en
dehors).

Measure 3/4
Tempo slow
Introduction
(2 bars)

3.   BATTEMENTS FONDUS

	Preparation Starting position of the feet: 5th position croisé, right foot front.	Starting position of the arms: 2nd position.
Off-beat *(3rd) fourth,* *1 bar*	BATTEMENT FONDU with the right leg front, in effacé, on half toe (left leg).[1]	2nd - A - 1st - 6th (right arm bent).
1st fourth,	TOMBÉ on the right foot front, in effacé.	The right arm opens in front (hands open).
2nd, 3rd fourth	PAS DE BOURRÉE EN DEHORS (changing feet) stepping to the side twice, remain on half toe (right foot), the left foot sur le cou-de-pied front, then	2nd (hands turned in).

[1] All the following battements fondus are on half toe.

1st fourth	DEMI-PLIÉ on the right leg, continue with	A - 1st - 6th (left arm bent).
2nd, 3rd fourth	BATTEMENT FONDU with the left leg in front, in effacé.	
1st fourth	TOMBÉ on the left foot front, in effacé.	The left arm opens in front (hands turned out).
2nd, 3rd fourth	PAS DE BOURRÉE EN DEHORS (changing feet), stepping to the side twice. Remain on half toe (left foot), the right foot sur le cou-de-pied front, then	2nd (hands turned in).
1st fourth,	DEMI-PLIÉ on the left leg and continue	A
2nd, 3rd fourth	BATTEMENT FONDU with the right leg to the side.	A - 1st - 2nd
1st fourth,	TOMBER PIED DESSOUS on the right foot, the left foot sur le cou-de-pied front and continue	A
2nd, 3rd fourth	BATTEMENT FONDU with the left leg to the side.	A - 1st - 2nd
1st fourth,	DEMI-PLIÉ on the right leg.	2nd
2nd, 3rd fourth	PAS DE BOURRÉE EN DEHORS (changing feet), stepping to the side twice.	A - 1st
1st fourth	End in 4th position, croisé (wide), the left leg in front in plié à quart.	6th (left arm bent).
2nd fourth	Stand in the preparatory position for tours en dedans.	6th (left arm bent).
3rd fourth	DEMI-PLIÉ in 4th position.	
2 bars	TOURS EN DEDANS in attitude effacée, then	3rd position.
	ALLONGÉE the right leg back, in effacé, in demi-plié (left leg).	5th allongée (right arm up).
1st, 2nd fourth	PAS DE BOURRÉE EN DEHORS (changing feet), stepping to the side twice.	The arms come down to A.
3rd fourth	End in 4th position, croisé (wide), the right leg in front in plié à quart.	1st - 6th (right arm bent).

1st, 2nd fourth	Stand in the preparatory position for tours en dedans.	6th (right arm bent).
3rd fourth	DEMI-PLIÉ in 4th position.	
2 bars	TOURS EN DEDANS in attitude effacée, then	3rd position.
	ALLONGÉE the left leg back, in effacé, in demi-plié (right leg).	5th allongée (left arm up).
1st, 2nd fourth	PAS DE BOURRÉE EN DEHORS (changing feet), stepping to the side twice.	The arms come down to position A.
3rd fourth	End in 5th position croisé, the left foot front.	
1st, 2nd fourth	Stand in 5th position (pause).	A

16 bars	Repeat the exercise on the other leg.

Total accompaniment
32 bars

(Pause)
Repeat the exercise in the reverse direction. After tours en dehors in attitude croisée - allongée, repeat pas de bourrée en tournant en dehors, etc.

4. BATTEMENTS FRAPPÉS

Measure 2/4
Tempo
moderate
Introduction
(1 bar)

Preparation

	Starting position of the feet: 2nd position, right foot pointe tendue.	Starting position of arms: 2nd position.
Off-beat (4th) eighth, 1st, 2nd, 3rd eighth	3 BATTEMENTS FRAPPÉS on the floor, with the right leg front, croisé.	5th (right arm up).
4th, 1st, 2nd, 3rd eighth	2 BATTEMENTS DOUBLES FRAPPÉS with the right leg, ending to the side (change).	2nd
4th, 1st, 2nd, 3rd eighth	3 BATTEMENTS FRAPPÉS with the right leg to the back, croisé.	5th (left arm up).
4th, 1st, 2nd, 3rd eighth	2 BATTEMENTS DOUBLES FRAPPÉS with the right leg, ending to the side (change), then	2nd
4th eighth	BRING the right foot sur le cou-de-pied front, épaulement croisé.	A
1st, 2nd, 3rd, 4th, 1st, 2nd, 3rd eighth	7 PETITS BATTEMENTS SUR LE COU-DE-PIED right foot (accent front). End the last battement in demi-plié (left leg).	A 6th (right arm bent).
4th eighth, 1 bar, 1st, 2nd, 3rd eighth	CHAÎNÉS-DÉBOULÉS with the right leg diagonally forward to corner No. 2, end in 5th position croisé, right foot back.	The right arm opens during the movement, then the arms meet between A and 1st. End in 2nd position.

8 bars Repeat the exercise on the other leg.

Total accompaniment
16 bars

(*Pause*)
Repeat the exercise.

Measure 3/4
(Waltz)
Tempo slow   ## 5. GRAND ADAGIO
Introduction
(2 bars)   Preparation
                  Starting position of the feet: 5th   Starting position of
                  position croisé, right foot front.   the arms: A.

Off-beat	2 GLISSADES	Position A, then the
(2nd, 3rd)	(change) with the right foot to the	arms open slightly
fourth,	side, changing épaulement, end in	to the side and close
1 bar	demi-plié.	back, etc.
1st, 2nd	PETIT DÉVELOPPÉ	A - 1st
fourth,	right leg front, in effacé,	
3rd fourth	remain in demi-plié (left leg).	
2 bars	STEP	1st - 1st arabesque
	on the right leg.	(right arm in front).
	LIFT	
	the left leg back, in effacé (90°).	
2 bars,	LEAN	1st arabesque arm
	the body forward and down, in 1st	position (right arm
	arabesque position.	in front).
1 bar	LIFT	
1st, 2nd	the body to the starting position.	
fourth		
3rd fourth	PASSER LA JAMBE (90°)	A
	left leg.	
2 bars	DÉVELOPPÉ	A - 1st - 5th (right
	the left leg front, in croisé,	arm up).
	in demi-plié (right leg).	
2 bars	GRAND FOUETTÉ EN DEDANS	3rd - 5th (left arm
	with the left leg, turn from position	up).
	to position, end attitude croisée,	
	left leg.	
1 bar	STRETCH	3rd arabesque (left
	the left leg back, in croisé (90°),	arm in front).
	in demi-plié (right leg).	
1st, 2nd	GRAND FOUETTÉ EN DEHORS	1st - 5th (right arm
fourth	with the left leg, turn from position	up).
	to position, end front in croisé (90°)	
	on half toe (right foot).	

3rd fourth	**TOMBÉ** on the left foot front, in croisé. Simultaneously **DÉGAGÉ** with the right leg to the side (45°).	The right arm moves to the side (through 1st position), palms down.
1st, 2nd fourth	**PAS DE BOURRÉE EN DEDANS** stepping to the side twice, then	A
3rd fourth, 1 bar	**TEMPS LIÉ** with the right leg to the back, croisé, end position croisé, the left leg extended to the front, pointe tendue.	A - 1st - 5th (right arm up).
	PORT DE BRAS *Breakdown:*	
1 bar	The body leans forward and down, the right leg in demi-plié, left leg in front, pointe tendue.	The right arm comes down, the left arm moves slightly back, simultaneously turn hands palms down.
1 bar	The body rises to the starting position. Stretch the right leg, the left leg in front pointe tendue, turn the left shoulder forward, then	The right arm comes up, simultaneously the left arm comes down.
1 bar	the body bends backward, carry the right shoulder to the back, left shoulder in front.	The right arm lowers to the side; simultaneously raise the left arm, moving upward.
1 bar	The body straightens, position croisé, left foot front pointe tendue, position "under the arm," look to the left.	5th (left arm up).
1 bar	The body leans forward and down, simultaneously slide the left leg back in effacé, through 1st position (pointe tendue), the right leg in a deep demi-plié.	The left arm lowers.
1 bar	The body comes up and turns slightly to the left; simultaneously transfer the left leg front, in effacé, pointe tendue.	1st, then the left arm opens to the side, simultaneously the right arm comes up to 5th position.

1 bar	The body bends backward.	5th (right arm up).
1st, 2nd fourth, 3rd fourth	The body returns to the starting position, then lowers into 4th position effacé (wide), in demi-plié (left leg in front).	5th (right arm up). Then the right arm lowers in front, palm down: 2nd arabesque position and remaining in this position.
2 bars	TOURS EN DEHORS in 3rd arabesque (right leg raised in back).	3rd arabesque (right arm forward).
1st, 2nd fourth, 3rd fourth	PAS DE BOURRÉE EN TOURNANT EN DEHORS stepping under twice. End in 4th position croisé (wide), right leg in front in plié à quart.	2nd - A A - 1st - 6th (right arm bent).
1st, 2nd fourth	Stand in the preparatory position for tours en dedans.	
3rd fourth,	DEMI-PLIÉ in 4th position, then	6th (right arm bent).
2 bars	TOURS EN DEDANS in 2nd arabesque (left leg raised in the back).	2nd arabesque (left arm in front).
1 bar, 1st fourth	SOUTENU EN TOURNANT EN DEHORS with the left foot. End in 5th position croisé, on half toe, left foot front. Lean the body slightly backward, the head facing left.	A - 1st - 4th (left arm up, the right arm bent in front).
32 bars	Repeat the exercise on the other leg.	

Total accompaniment
64 bars

Pose in 1st arabesque (the body leans downward)

Maya Plisetskaya

6.   GRANDS BATTEMENTS JETÉS

Measure 2/4 *Tempo* *moderate*		
Introduction *(1 bar)*	Preparation Starting position of the feet: 5th position croisé, right foot front.	Starting position of the arms: 2nd position.
Off-beat *(4th),* *1st eighth*	GRAND BATTEMENT JETÉ with the right leg, in front croisé.	5th (left arm up).
2nd, 3rd *eighth*	GRAND BATTEMENT JETÉ with the left leg to the back in croisé.	The left arm moves in front: 3rd arabesque position.
4th, 1st *eighth*	GRAND BATTEMENT JETÉ to the side, kick the right leg and continue ROND DE JAMBE EN L'AIR EN DEHORS $(90°)$ with the right leg.	2nd
2nd, 3rd *eighth*	Bring the right leg down to 5th position back.	A
4th eighth, *1 bar,* *1st, 2nd, 3rd* *eighth*	Repeat this combination on the other leg, then	
4th, 1st, 2nd, *3rd, 4th* *eighth*	PRÉPARATION POUR PIROUETTES EN DEHORS with the right foot in 2nd position *(for the men's class).*	A - 1st - 2nd - 6th (right arm bent).
4th, 1st, 2nd, *3rd, 4th* *eighth*	PRÉPARATION POUR PIROUETTES EN DEHORS with the right foot in 4th position croisé *(for the women's class).*	A - 1st - 3rd arabesque (right arm in front).
1st, 2nd *eighth,*	PIROUETTES EN DEHORS. During the turn on the left leg, the right foot is sur le cou-de-pied front, end the movement with	The right arm opens during the movement, then the arms meet between A and 1st, then
3rd eighth	DÉGAGÉ with the right leg in front (45°), croisé, in demi-plié (left leg).	6th (right arm bent).

4th eighth,	PRÉPARATION TEMPS RELEVÉ EN DEHORS with the right leg, in demi-plié (left leg).	1st
1 bar, *1st, 2nd, 3rd* *eighth*	PIROUETTES EN DEHORS. During the turn on the left leg, the right foot is sur le cou-de-pied back.	3rd
	End with the right foot in 5th position back, épaulement croisé.	End in 2nd position.

---

8 bars	Repeat the exercise on the other leg.

Total accompaniment
16 bars   (*Pause*)
                    Repeat the exercise in the reverse
                    direction (pirouettes remain en
                    dehors).

Measure 2/4
Tempo
moderate

7. SMALL JUMPS

Introduction
(1 bar)

	Preparation Starting position of the feet: 5th position croisé, left foot front.	Starting position of the arms: A.
Off-beat *(4th),* *1st eighth*	ASSEMBLÉ with the right leg to the side (change) épaulement croisé.	Position A.
2nd, 3rd *eighth*	ASSEMBLÉ with the left leg to the side (change) épaulement croisé.	A
4th, 1st *eighth*	JETÉ with the right leg to the side, the left foot ends sur le cou-de-pied back, change épaulement croisé.	The arms open slightly to the side, then 6th position (right arm bent).
2nd, 3rd *eighth*	SAUTÉ on the right leg, the left foot sur le cou-de-pied back, turn the head to the right.	5th (right arm up).

4th eighth	GLISSADE (do not change), with the left foot front diagonally to corner No. 8, end with the movement	The arms open to the side (through 1st position), in 2nd allongée (palms down).
1st eighth	DÉGAGÉ (45°) with the left leg to the side, in écarté front to corner No. 8 in demi-plié (right leg).	
2nd, 3rd *eighth,*	TOMBER PIED DESSUS on the left foot, continue with	A
4th, 1st *eighth*	STEP - COUPÉ right foot to side No. 3.	A
	ASSEMBLÉ with the left leg to the back (through 1st position), in croisé, end in demi-plié in 5th position.	3rd arabesque (left arm in front) end in position A.
2nd, 3rd *eighth*	Come up from demi-plié in 5th position.	A
4 bars	Repeat the exercise on the other leg.	
8 bars	Repeat the whole combination.	

Total accompaniment
16 bars

(*Pause*)
Repeat the combination in the reverse
direction.

8. SMALL JUMPS WITH BEATS

Measure 2/4
Tempo
moderate
Introduction
(1 bar)

Preparation
Starting position of the feet: 5th position croisé, right foot front.

Starting position of the arms: A.

Off-beat (4th), 1st eighth, 2nd, 3rd eighth	ÉCHAPPÉ BATTU in 2nd position, end the échappé with a jump on the left leg, the right foot sur le cou-de-pied back, épaulement croisé, the body leans slightly to the left.	A - 1st - 2nd 6th (right arm bent).
4th, 1st eighth	SISSONNE TOMBÉE with the right leg to the back, in effacé; the body leans slightly to the back.	The right arm moves upward and continues the movement to the side (hands turned out).
2nd, 3rd eighth	COUPÉ-DESSUS left foot.	2nd allongée (palms down).
	JETÉ BATTU with the right leg to side No. 3. The left foot ends sur le cou-de-pied back, épaulement croisé. The body leans slightly to the right.	2nd allongée, end in 6th position (left arm bent).
4th, 1st eighth	SISSONNE TOMBÉE with the left leg in the back, in effacé. The body leans slightly to the back.	The left arm moves upward and continues the movement to the side (hands turned out).
2nd, 3rd eighth	COUPÉ-DESSOUS right foot.	2nd allongée (palms down).
	JETÉ BATTU with the left leg to side No. 7. The right foot ends sur le cou-de-pied back, épaulement croisé. The body leans slightly to the left.	2nd allongée, end in 6th position (right arm bent).

| 4th, 1st eighth | GLISSADE (do not change), with the right foot to side No. 3. | The right arm opens to the side, then the left arm bends in front. |
| 2nd, 3rd eighth | BRISÉ with the right foot front, diagonally to corner No. 2. The body leans slightly to the left, end in 5th position, right foot back, épaulement croisé. | 6th (left arm bent). |

| 4 bars | Repeat the exercise on the other leg. |

Total accompaniment
8 bars   (*Pause*)
Repeat the exercise in the reverse
direction.

Jeté en avant, in effacé

Measure 2/4
Tempo
moderate
Introduction
(2 bars)

9. MEDIUM JUMPS

Preparation
Starting position of the feet: 4th position croisé, left leg extended in the front, pointe tendue.

Starting position of the arms: A.

Start from corner No. 6.

Off-beat (4th), 1st eighth	GLISSADE (do not change) with the right foot forward diagonally to corner No. 2.	Position A, then the arms open to the side and then close.
2nd, 3rd eighth	JETÉ EN AVANT with the right leg front, in effacé, and continue with	A - 1st - 1st arabesque (right arm in front).
4th, 1st eighth	CABRIOLE with the left leg back, in effacé.	1st arabesque (right arm in front).
2nd, 3rd eighth	PETIT JETÉ with the left leg, traveling slightly to side No. 7. The right foot ends sur le cou-de-pied back.	2nd allongée. End in position A.
4th eighth, 1 bar, 1st, 2nd, 3rd eighth	Repeat this combination, then	
4th, 1st eighth	SISSONNE TOMBÉE with the right leg to the back, in croisé, the body leans slightly forward.	A - 1st - 5th (right arm up).
2nd, 3rd eighth	COUPÉ-DESSOUS left foot.	A - 1st
	JETÉ EN TOURNANT EN DEHORS with the right leg, end in front croisé.	5th (left arm up).
4th, 1st eighth, 2nd, 3rd eighth	COUPÉ-DESSUS left foot, JETÉ EN TOURNANT EN DEHORS with the right leg, end in front croisé, continue with	A - 1st, then 3rd arabesque arm position (left arm in front).
	CABRIOLE with the left leg in the back, in croisé.	

CONCLUDING EXERCISE FOR THE MEN'S CLASS:

4th, 1st, 2nd *eighth*	CHASSÉ with the right leg front, in croisé.	A - 1st - 3rd
3rd eighth	SISSONNE TOMBÉE with the right leg in front, croisé, end with the movement	2nd - 6th (right arm bent).
4th, 1st *eighth*	PETIT ASSEMBLÉ with the left leg to the back, in croisé.	6th (right arm bent).
2nd, 3rd *eighth*	DOUBLE TOUR EN L'AIR EN DEHORS. End in 5th position croisé, right foot back.	3rd, end in 2nd position (hands slightly turned out).

CONCLUDING EXERCISE FOR THE WOMEN'S CLASS:

4th, 1st, 2nd *eighth,* *3rd eighth*	CHASSÉ with the right leg front, in croisé. End in 4th position croisé, the right leg in front in plié à quart (preparatory position for pirouettes en dedans).	A - 1st - 3rd 2nd - 6th (right arm bent).
4th eighth	DÉGAGÉ with the left leg to the side (45°), in demi-plié (right leg).	The right arm opens to the side, then
1st, 2nd, 3rd *eighth*	PIROUETTES EN DEDANS. End in 5th position croisé, left foot front.	3rd position, end in 2nd (hands slightly turned out).

Total accompaniment
8 bars

(*Pause*)
Repeat the exercise.

(*Pause*)
Repeat the whole combination on the
other leg.

Measure 3/4
(Waltz)
Tempo
moderate
Introduction
(2 bars)

10. BIG JUMPS

Preparation
Starting position of the feet: 4th   Starting position of
position, croisé, left leg extended in   the arms: A.
the front, pointe tendue.

Start from corner No. 6.

Off-beat *(2nd, 3rd)* *fourth*	GLISSADE (do not change), with the right foot forward diagonally to corner No. 2.	Position A, then the arms open to the side and close.
1 bar, *1st, 2nd* *fourth*	CABRIOLE TOMBÉE with the right leg front, in effacé.	A - 1st - 5th (left arm up), end in 2nd (hands slightly turned out).
3rd, 1st, 2nd *fourth*	FAILLI with the left foot, ending in front croisé.	2nd allongée, then the arms come down.
3rd, 1st, 2nd *fourth*	STEP - COUPÉ with the right foot front diagonally to corner No. 2.	A - 1st
	JETÉ EN AVANT on the left leg, in croisé front.	1st (wide)
3rd fourth, *1 bar,* *1st, 2nd* *fourth*	PAS COURU traveling forward diagonally to corner No. 2.	2nd allongée.
	GRAND JETÉ EN AVANT with the left leg, in croisé front.	A - 1st - 5th (right arm up).
3rd fourth	GLISSADE (do not change), with the right foot forward diagonally to corner No. 2.	The right arm lowers to the side, then position A.
1st fourth, *2nd, 3rd,* *1st, 2nd* *fourth*	STEP - PIQUÉ on the right foot front diagonally (half toe), lift the left leg back in effacé (45°). Stand in 1st arabesque, then	A - 1st - 1st arabesque (right arm forward).

3rd, 1st, 2nd *fourth*	CHASSÉ with the left leg back, in effacé, turning halfway to the left.	2nd, then 2nd allongée.
	STEP - COUPÉ with the left foot front, to corner No. 6.	A - 1st - 4th arabesque (left arm forward).
3rd, 1st, 2nd *fourth*	GRANDE CABRIOLE FOUETTÉE with the right leg, end in 4th arabesque facing corner No. 2.	
3rd, 1st *fourth,*	SISSONNE TOMBÉE with the left leg in front, in effacé to corner No. 8, and continue with	The left arm opens in front, the hands turned fluidly out.
2nd, 3rd *fourth*	PAS DE BOURRÉE EN DEHORS (changing feet), stepping twice.	2nd (the hands turned in).

CONCLUDING EXERCISE FOR THE MEN'S CLASS:

1st, 2nd *fourth*	End (pas de bourrée en dehors) in 5th position demi-plié, the right leg front, then come up from demi-plié.	A
1 bar,	PRÉPARATION POUR PIROUETTES EN DEHORS with the right foot in 2nd position.	A - 1st - 2nd - 6th (right arm bent).
2 bars *1st fourth*	PIROUETTES EN DEHORS. End with the right foot in croisé back (90°), in demi-plié (left leg). Stand in 3rd arabesque (in demi-plié).	The right arm opens during the movement, then the arms meet between A and 1st, end in 3rd arabesque (right arm in front).

CONCLUDING EXERCISE FOR THE WOMEN'S CLASS:

	End (pas de bourrée en dehors) with the movement	
1st, 2nd *fourth*	DÉGAGÉ with the right foot front, pointe tendue, in croisé, simultaneously come down from half toe (left foot) on the flat foot, position croisé.	The right arm comes down, then - 6th position (right arm bent).

3rd fourth,
2 bars,
1st, 2nd
fourth,

CHAÎNÉS-DÉBOULÉS
forward diagonally to corner No. 2,
then, toward the same direction,

The right arm opens
during the movement,
then the arms meet
between A and 1st.
End in 1st arabesque
(right arm in front).

3rd, 1st
fourth

STEP
on the right leg front, lower in demi-
plié, lift the left leg to the back (90°),
in effacé, 1st arabesque position.

Total accompaniment
16 bars

(Pause)
Repeat the exercise.

(Pause)
Repeat the exercise on the other leg.

Vladimir Nikonov

Grand jeté en avant, croisé

Measure 2/4
Tempo lively
Introduction
(2 bars)

11. ENTRECHATS

Preparation
Starting position of the feet: 5th
position croisé, right foot front.

Starting position of
the arms: A.

Off-beat
(4th) eighth,
1 bar,
1st, 2nd, 3rd
eighth

3 ENTRECHAT-QUATRE.
ENTRECHAT-SIX
(change épaulement croisé).

Position A.

4th eighth,
5 bars,
1st, 2nd, 3rd
eighth

Repeat the combination 3 more
times.

Total accompaniment
8 bars

Measure 2/4
Tempo lively
Introduction
(2 bars)

12. JUMPS

Preparation
Starting position of the feet: 4th
position croisé, right leg extended to
the front, pointe tendue.

Starting position of
the arms: 6th position
(right arm bent).

Start from corner No. 8.

Off-beat
(2nd, 3rd,
4th
eighth)
11 bars
1st, 2nd, 3rd
eighth

12 JETÉS EN TOURNANT EN
DEHORS[1]
with the right leg to the front
traveling in a circle clockwise.
Then

The right arm
moves forward,
simultaneously the
left arm moves
slightly to the back
(palms down), then
the arms meet
between A and 1st,
etc.

4th eighth,
3 bars,
1st eighth

CHAÎNÉS-DÉBOULÉS
traveling forward diagonally to
corner No. 2. End in effacé, the
left leg extended in the back,
pointe tendue.

The arms open to
the side (through
1st position), then
meet between A and
1st. End in 5th
position (left arm
up).

Total accompaniment
16 bars

(Pause)
Repeat the exercise.

(Pause)
Repeat the whole combination on the
other leg.

[1] The given form of jeté en tournant has a horizontal action.

Measure 3/4
Tempo lively
Introduction
(2 bars)

13. JUMPS
(FOR THE MEN'S CLASS)

Preparation

Starting position of the feet: 5th position croisé, right foot front.	Starting position of the arms: 2nd position.

Off-beat *(2nd, 3rd)* *fourth*	PRÉPARATION POUR TOUR EN L'AIR EN DEHORS. Come up on half toes in 5th position. Come down in demi-plié.	6th (right arm bent).
1st fourth *2nd, 3rd* *1st, 2nd* *fourth*	DOUBLE TOUR EN L'AIR EN DEHORS. During the turn in the air, the right leg bends in a petit retiré front, land in demi-plié (left leg).	The arms meet between A and 1st.
3rd, 1st *fourth* *2nd, 3rd,* *1st, 2nd* *fourth*	SISSONNE RENVERSÉE EN DEHORS with the right leg in attitude. PAS DE BOURRÉE EN TOURNANT EN DEHORS.	1st - 3rd - 2nd, the hands are turned out, then they turn in, then 6th position (right arm bent).
3rd, 1st *fourth*	PETIT ASSEMBLÉ with the left leg to the back, in croisé.	6th (right arm bent), then the arms meet between A and 1st.
2nd, 3rd, *1st, 2nd* *fourth*	DOUBLE TOUR EN L'AIR EN DEHORS.	
3rd, 1st *fourth* *2nd, 3rd,* *1st, 2nd* *fourth*	SISSONNE RENVERSÉE EN DEHORS with the right leg in attitude. PAS DE BOURRÉE EN TOURNANT EN DEHORS.	1st - 3rd 2nd (hands turned out), then the hands turn in, then 6th position (right arm bent).
3rd, 1st *fourth* *2nd, 3rd* *1st, 2nd* *fourth*	PETIT ASSEMBLÉ with the left leg to the back, in croisé. DOUBLE TOUR EN L'AIR EN DEHORS.	6th (right arm bent). Then the arms meet between A and 1st.

3rd, 1st *fourth*	SISSONNE RENVERSÉE EN DEHORS with the right leg in attitude.	1st - 3rd 2nd (hands turned out) then
2nd, 3rd, *1st, 2nd* *fourth*	PAS DE BOURRÉE EN TOURNANT EN DEHORS. End in 5th position, right foot front.	the hands turn in position A.
3rd fourth *2 bars*	PRÉPARATION POUR PIROUETTES EN DEHORS with the right foot in 2nd position.	A- 1st - 2nd - 6th (right arm bent).
1 bar, *1st fourth*	PIROUETTES EN DEHORS. End in 4th position croisé, right leg back, the left leg in front in plié à quart.	The right arm opens during the movement, then the arms meet between A and 1st. End in 1st position (wide).

Total accompaniment
16 bars

(*Pause*)

Repeat the exercise.

(*Pause*)

Repeat the exercise on the other leg.

Double tour en l'air en dehors, sissonne renversée en dehors (in attitude), soutenu en tournant en dehors, tombé in front croisé (right foot), petit assemblé back, in croisé (left leg)

Nicolai Fadeyechev

Measure 2/4
Tempo
moderate   **14.   JUMPS**
Introduction   (FOR THE MEN'S CLASS)
(1 bar)

	Preparation Starting position of the feet: 5th position croisé, right foot front.	Starting position of the arms: A.
Off-beat *(4th)* *eighth,* *1st, 2nd, 3rd* *eighth*	GRAND ÉCHAPPÉ in 2nd position, end in 5th position right foot back.	A - 1st - 2nd (hands slightly turned out). Then (hands turned in) the arms come down to position A.
4th, 1st, *2nd, 3rd* *eighth*	GRAND ÉCHAPPÉ in 2nd position, end in 5th position right foot front.	Arms as above.
4th eighth, *1 bar,* *1st, 2nd, 3rd* *eighth*	7 PETITS CHANGEMENTS DE PIEDS. A	

4 bars   Repeat the exercise on the other leg.

Total accompaniment
8 bars

Measure 2/4
Tempo fast
Introduction
(2 bars)

15. GRANDES PIROUETTES À LA SECONDE (90°)
(FOR THE MEN'S CLASS)

Preparation

Starting position of the feet: 5th position, en face, right foot front.		Starting position of the arms: 2nd position.

Off-beat *(4th) eighth,*	PRÉPARATION POUR PIROUETTE EN DEHORS PETIT ÉCHAPPÉ in 2nd position, then from 2nd position continue	2nd, 6th (right arm bent).
6 bars	12 GRANDES PIROUETTES À LA SECONDE (90°) with the right leg, ending with	2nd position.
1 bar, *1st, 2nd, 3rd* *eighth*	PIROUETTES EN DEHORS. End in 4th position, right leg back, the left leg in front in plié à quart.	The arms meet between A and 1st. End in 1st position (wide), hands slightly turned out.

Total accompaniment
8 bars

(*Pause*)
Repeat the exercise, adding the
number of grandes pirouettes to 28.
Repeat the exercise to 16 bars.

(*Pause*)
Repeat the whole combination on the
other leg.

Measure 3/4
(Waltz)
Tempo slow
Introduction
(2 bars)

16. PORT DE BRAS AND BENDING
OF THE BODY
(FOR THE MEN'S CLASS)

Preparation
Starting position of the feet: 1st
position (halfway turned out).

Starting position of
the arms: 2nd
position.

This exercise corresponds to exercise
15 (exercises in the center) of the
first class (see page 108).

Total accompaniment
32 bars

Measure 2/4
Tempo lively
Introduction
(1 bar)

17. FIRST EXERCISE ON POINTES

Preparation
Starting position of the feet: 5th
position croisé, right foot front.

Starting position of
the arms: A.

Off-beat
(4th),
1st eighth,

ENTRECHAT-QUATRE.

A

2nd, 3rd
eighth

RELEVÉ SUR LA POINTE
on the left leg, simultaneously bring
the right leg, through petit retiré, to
5th position back, come down in
demi-plié (change épaulement
croisé).

The right arm opens
in the front (through
1st position).
Simultaneously the
left arm moves to
the side (hands
slightly turned out),
then to position A.

4th, 1st eighth	ENTRECHAT-QUATRE.	A
2nd, 3rd eighth	RELEVÉ SUR LA POINTE on the right leg, simultaneously bring the left leg, through petit retiré, in 5th position back, come down in demi-plié (change épaulement croisé).	The left arm opens in the front (through 1st position). Simultaneously the right arm moves to the side (hands slightly turned out), then to position A.
4th, 1st, 2nd, 3rd eighth	2 RELEVÉS SUR LA POINTE on the left leg. Simultaneously bring the right leg through petit retiré, first in 5th position back, then in 5th position front, lean the head and the body slightly to the right, looking down, over the right shoulder.	6th (right arm bent).
4th, 1st, 2nd eighth	DÉGAGÉ with the right leg to the side (45°), the left leg sur la pointe (en face), and continue with	Open the right arm to the side: 2nd position.
	2 RONDS DE JAMBE EN L'AIR EN DEHORS with the right leg, the left leg sur la pointe.	2nd
3rd eighth	End with the right foot in 5th position back, come down in demi-plié épaulement croisé.	A

4 bars	Repeat the exercise on the other leg.
8 bars	Repeat the whole combination.

Total accompaniment
16 bars

(*Pause*)
Repeat the exercise in the reverse
direction.

Measure 2/4
Tempo lively
Introduction
(2 bars)

18. SECOND EXERCISE ON POINTES

Preparation
Starting position of the feet: 5th
position croisé, right foot front.

Starting position of
the arms: 6th
position (right arm
bent).

Start from corner No. 6.

Off-beat
(4th) eighth,
1 bar

STEP - PIQUÉ (SUR LA POINTE)
on the right leg forward diagonally
to corner No. 2.
Continue with a half turn to the right
on pointe, simultaneously

BATTEMENT DOUBLE FRAPPÉ
with the left leg ending to the side
(45°), in écarté front, to corner No. 2,
then come down from toe in demi-plié
(right leg).

6th (right arm bent).
Then the right arm
opens in front and
moves to the side,
the left arm bends in
front, 6th position.

1 bar

PIQUÉ (SUR LA POINTE) EN
TOURNANT EN DEHORS
on the left foot, continue with

BATTEMENT DOUBLE FRAPPÉ
with the right leg ending to the side in
écarté front to corner No. 2, then
come down from toe in demi-plié
(left leg).

1st - 6th (right arm
bent).

1 bar,
1st, 2nd, 3rd
eighth

Repeat the combination, then

4th eighth,
1 bar,
1st, 2nd, 3rd
eighth

4 EMBOÎTÉS EN TOURNANT
(SUR LES POINTES)
traveling forward diagonally to
corner No. 2, start with the right leg
(with a half turn to the right), then
the left leg (with a half turn to the
left), etc.

6th (left arm bent).
6th (right arm bent).
6th (left arm bent).
6th (right arm bent).

4th eighth, 1 bar, 1st, 2nd, 3rd eighth	CHAÎNÉS-DÉBOULÉS (SUR LES POINTES) traveling forward to corner No. 2, end in 5th position, right foot back épaulement croisé.	The right arm opens during the movement, then the arms meet between A and 1st. End in 2nd position (hands slightly turned out).

8 bars	Repeat the exercise on the other leg.

Total accompaniment
16 bars   (*Pause*)

Repeat the exercise.

Measure 3/4
Tempo
moderate

19. THIRD EXERCISE ON POINTES

Introduction (*2 bars*)	Preparation Starting position of the feet: 4th position croisé, left leg extended in front, pointe tendue.	Starting position of the arms: A.
Off-beat (*2nd, 3rd*) *fourth*	DEMI-PLIÉ on the right leg, simultaneously lift the left leg in front croisé (25°).	Position A.
1st fourth	PIQUÉ SUR LA POINTE on the left foot, turn a quarter turn to left, simultaneously DÉGAGÉ with the right leg to the side (90°), in écarté front, to corner No. 2, continue with	The arms from A position move to the side (palms down). 2nd allongée.
2nd, 3rd *fourth*	2 RONDS DE JAMBE EN L'AIR EN DEDANS (90°) with the right leg, in écarté front to corner No. 2, then	2nd allongée.
1st, 2nd *fourth*	TOMBER PIED DESSUS on the right foot, the left leg bent in back.	A
3rd fourth	TOMBER PIED DESSOUS on the left foot, simultaneously DÉGAGÉ with the right leg front (25°), in croisé.	A, then the arms between A and 1st position.

1st fourth	PIQUÉ SUR LA POINTE on the right foot, turn a quarter turn to the right, simultaneously DÉGAGÉ with the left leg to the side (90°), in écarté, front to corner No. 8, continue with	The arms from A position move to the side (palms down). 2nd allongée.
2nd, 3rd fourth	2 RONDS DE JAMBE EN L'AIR EN DEDANS (90°) with the left leg, in écarté front to corner No. 8, then	2nd allongée.
1st, 2nd fourth	TOMBER PIED DESSUS on the left foot, the right leg bent in the back.	A
3rd fourth	TOMBER PIED DESSOUS on the right foot, the left leg bent in the front.	A
1st fourth	RENVERSÉ EN DEHORS on toe (right leg). Continue with	1st - 5th (right arm up). 2nd - 6th (left arm bent).
2nd, 3rd, 1st, 2nd fourth	PAS DE BOURRÉE EN TOURNANT EN DEHORS end in 4th position croisé, the left leg in front in plié à quart.	
3rd fourth	DÉGAGÉ with the right leg to the side (45°), simultaneously demi-plié on the left leg.	The left arm opens during the movement then
1st, 2nd, 3rd fourth	PIROUETTES EN DEDANS ending with the movement.	3rd position.
1st, 2nd fourth	TOMBER PIED DESSUS on the right foot, épaulement croisé.	2nd (hands turned out).
3rd fourth	TOMBER PIED DESSOUS on the left foot, simultaneously DÉGAGÉ with the right leg front, in croisé (45°).	The arms come down to position A.
7 bars, 1st fourth	Repeat the exercise on the other leg starting with piqué sur la pointe on the right leg, etc.	

Total accompaniment
16 bars   *(Pause)*
Repeat the exercise.

20. FOURTH EXERCISE ON POINTES

Measure 2/4
Tempo fast
Introduction
(2 bars)

Preparation
Starting position of the feet: 4th
position croisé, the right leg
extended in front, pointe tendue.

Starting position of
the arms: 6th
position (right arm
bent).

Start from corner No. 8
traveling in a circle clockwise; end facing corner No. 2.

Off-beat
(4th) eighth

DEMI-PLIÉ
on the left leg, simultaneously the
right leg rises in front (25°) and is
brought during the movement to

The right arm opens
during the movement,
then the arms meet
between A and 1st.

1 bar

TOUR PIQUÉ EN DEDANS.
During the turn on the right leg the
left foot is sur le cou-de-pied back.

1st, 2nd, 3rd
eighth

TOUR PIQUÉ EN DEDANS.

The arms open to the
side, through 1st
position, then meet
between A and 1st.

4th eighth,
1 bar,
1st, 2nd, 3rd
eighth

CHAÎNÉS-DÉBOULÉS SUR LES
POINTES
traveling in a circle, end on the
left leg (demi-plié), the right foot
sur le cou-de-pied front.

The arms open to the
side through 1st
position, then meet
between A and 1st.

4th eighth,
27 bars,
1st, 2nd, 3rd
eighth

Repeat the combination 7 more times
traveling in a circle. End the final
chaînés-déboulés in effacé, the left
leg extended in the back, pointe
tendue.

Arms same as above.
End in 5th allongée
(right arm up).

Total accompaniment
32 bars

(Pause)
Repeat the exercise on the other leg
starting from corner No. 2, traveling in
a circle counterclockwise. End facing
corner No. 8.

Measure 2/4
Tempo fast
Introduction
(2 bars)

21. FIFTH EXERCISE ON POINTES

Preparation
Starting position of the feet: 5th   Starting position of
position croisé, right foot front.   the arms: A.

Start from corner No. 6.

Off-beat   DEMI-PLIÉ   A
(4th)   in 5th position, then
eighth   DÉGAGÉ
2 bars   with the right leg in effacé front
                    (45°).
                    8 PETITS RONDS DE JAMBE EN   The arms gradually
                    L'AIR EN DEHORS, SAUTÉS   come up, through 1st
                    with the right leg in effacé front (after   position in 5th
                    each jump come down on the left leg,   position (right arm
                    on toe), traveling forward diagonally   up).
                    to corner No. 2, continue with

1 bar   6 PETITS RONDS DE JAMBE EN   The left arm from A
1st, 2nd   L'AIR EN DEHORS, SAUTÉS   position moves in
eighth   with the right leg, in effacé front,   front and continues
                    landing on toe (left leg), end the last   upward: 5th
                    rond in demi-plié (left leg).   position.

3rd eighth   RELEVÉ SUR LA POINTE
                    on the left leg, the right leg extended
                    in the front, in effacé (45°).

4 bars   Repeat the exercise on the other leg.

Total accompaniment
8 bars

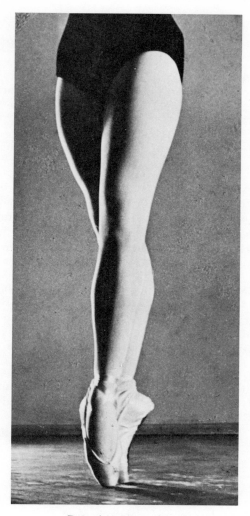

Relevé in 5th position

Measure 3/4
Tempo fast
Introduction
(2 bars)

22. SIXTH EXERCISE ON POINTES

Preparation
Starting position of the feet: 5th
position croisé, right foot front.

Starting position of
the arms: A.

Start from corner No. 8
traveling in a circle clockwise; end diagonally forward
to corner No. 2.

Off-beat *(2nd, 3rd)* *fourth,* *14 bars,*	DEMI-PLIÉ in 5th position. PAS SUIVI the right foot in front traveling in a circle, lean the head slightly forward, looking right "under the arm," then	A, then the arms gradually come up, through 1st position, to 5th position (right arm up).
1 bar	DEMI-PLIÉ on the left leg, simultaneously DÉGAGÉ with the right leg front, in effacé (45°).	Lower the right arm to the side.
1st fourth	PIQUÉ SUR LA POINTE on the right leg. Lift the left leg in the back, in effacé (90°), 2nd arabesque position.	The left arm from A position moves up and front (palms down), 2nd arabesque position.

Total accompaniment
16 bars

(Pause)
Repeat the exercise on the other leg.
Start from corner No. 2, traveling in
circle counterclockwise, end facing
corner No. 8.

23.   SEVENTH EXERCISE ON POINTES

Measure 2/4
Tempo fast
Introduction
(2 bars)

Preparation
Starting position of the feet: 4th
position, en face, the left leg in front
in plié à quart.

Starting position of
the arms: 2nd
arabesque (right arm
in front).

Off-beat
(2nd, 3rd,
4th)
eighth,
31 bars,
1st eighth

32 FOUETTÉS EN TOURNANT
EN DEHORS (45°).[1]
Open the right leg each time à la
seconde (45°). End the last fouetté
en tournant en dehors in 4th position
croisé, the right leg in the back, the left
leg in front in plié à quart.

The right arm opens
during the movement,
then the arms meet
between A and 1st.
Then the arms open
through 1st position
to the side, meet
between A and 1st,
etc.
End in 1st position
(wide), hands slightly
turned out.

Total accompaniment
32 bars

(*Pause*)
Repeat the exercise.

[1] Start the combination with tour en dehors, thereafter at the end of the turn carry on with
fouettés en tournant en dehors.

Tour en dehors, fouetté en tournant en dehors (the leg opens à la seconde, 45°)

Nina Sorokina

Measure 3/4
(Waltz)
Tempo slow
Introduction
(2 bars)

24. PORT DE BRAS AND BENDING
OF THE BODY

Preparation
Starting position of the feet: 1st
position (halfway turned out).

Starting position of
the arms: 2nd
position.

This exercise corresponds to exercise 15
(exercises in the center) of the first
class (see page 108).

Total accompaniment
32 bars

Bolshoi Theatre Artists
in Performance

Galina Ulanova, Nicolai Fadeyechev, *Chopiniana*
PHOTO BY ROGER WOOD, FROM THE DANCE COLLECTION, N.Y.P.L. AT LINCOLN CENTER,
ASTOR, LENOX AND TILDEN FOUNDATIONS

Raissa Struchkova, *Giselle*
PHOTO BY EUGENE UMNOV, MOSCOW,
COURTESY HUROK CONCERTS

Raissa Struchkova, Vladimir Romanenko, *Moszkowski Waltz*
PHOTO BY W. J. REILLY

Maya Plisetskaya, Alexander Godunov, *La Rose Malade*

PHOTO BY BEVERLEY GALLEGOS

Maya Plisetskaya, *The Dying Swan*
PHOTOS BY DAVID DANIEL AND LOUIS PÉRES (LOWER LEFT)

Ekaterina Maximova, Vladimir Vasiliev, *Don Quixote*

Maya Plisetskaya, Sergei Radchenko, *Carmen Suite*
PHOTO BY EDWARD GRIFFITHS

Ekaterina Maximova, Vladimir Vasiliev, *The Nutcracker*
PHOTO BY EDWARD GRIFFITHS

Marina Kondratieva, Vladimir Tikhonov, *Chopiniana*
PHOTO BY JUDY CAMERON

Ekaterina Maximova, Vladimir Vasiliev, *Spartacus*
PHOTO BY EDWARD GRIFFITHS

Nina Timofeyeva, Boris Akimov, *Spartacus*
PHOTO BY MIKE HUMPHREY

Maris Liepa, Marina Leonova, *Spartacus*
PHOTO BY LOUIS PÉRES

Ekaterina Maximova, Vladimir Vasiliev, *Spartacus*
PHOTO BY JUDY CAMERON

Boris Akimov, *Spartacus*
PHOTO BY MIKE HUMPHREY

Maris Liepa, *Spartacus*

Natalia Bessmertnova, Mikhail Lavrovsky, *Giselle*
PHOTO BY MIRA, COURTESY HUROK CONCERTS

Natalia Bessmertnova, Mikhail Lavrovsky, *Legend of Love*
PHOTO BY DINA MAKAROVA

Nina Sorokina, Yuri Vladimirov, *Diana and Acteon pas de deux*
PHOTO BY MIRA, COURTESY HUROK CONCERTS

Nina Sorokina, *Diana and Acteon*

Ludmilla Semenyaka, Alexander Godunov, *Swan Lake*
PHOTO BY MIRA, COURTESY HUROK CONCERTS

Ludmilla Semenyaka, *Swan Lake*
PHOTO BY JUDY CAMERON

Tatiana Golikova, Alexander Bogatryev, *Swan Lake*

Tatiana Gavrilova, Nicolai Federov, Marina Leonova, *Swan Lake*

Tatiana Bessmertnova, *Swan Lake*
PHOTO BY MIKE HUMPHREY

Tatiana Golikova, *Chopiniana*
PHOTO COURTESY COLUMBIA ARTISTS

Maya Samokhvalova, *Gayne*
PHOTO COURTESY HUROK CONCERTS

Asaf Messerer

ELLA BOCHARNIKOVA

*Every talent is not a miracle descended
from the sky but the fruit of man's
development of forces in him and his
attention to the forces that seethe in the
sea of human lives around him.*

Konstantin Stanislavsky

TALENT IS a calling, a persistent and selfless labor of the throes and joys of creation. Talent is an all-absorbing passion to fulfill one's social duty and to express to the people the ideas, thoughts, and feelings that stir in the artist. Young Mozart was once asked: "Why do you compose?" "I cannot not compose," he replied. All great masters of the arts are right in repeating these words for they also could not not create.

Konstantin Stanislavsky's entire life was an eternal search for the truth of art. He passed on all that he had discovered in his inspired works to contemporaries and the following generations. Anna Pavlova danced for the people of all the continents of the world to the last days of her great artistic life. Beethoven and Moussorgsky, although mortally ill, were in a hurry to express all that abounded in their rich souls. Obsessed is the word one can apply to the great artists of the past whose magnificent works continue to delight grateful generations.

To evaluate talents of the present generation is much harder. Perhaps appraisal of their talents is to a certain degree impeded because we see our contemporaries too closely and meet them in daily life. However, it is our duty to tell the next generation about our prominent contemporaries and to crystallize their creative experience. If we do not give recognition today to those artists who over many decades enhanced the Soviet stage and created significant artistic treasures, then who will do it for us?

This chapter is dedicated to one of our most prominent contemporaries, Asaf Mikhaïlovich Messerer, artist, ballet master, and teacher, whose name has already been known for a long time among our people as well as among admirers of the Soviet ballet in many countries of the world.

The realistic traditions of the Russian ballet as developed in the Soviet system have clearly revealed themselves in the activities of its great masters. Asaf

Messerer's creative course started in the years of the struggle to preserve the classical ballet and to enrich the Soviet ballet stage with themes and images of classical and modern world literature and works of national importance. Messerer, together with the prominent dancers of his time, Marina Semenova, Galina Ulanova, Olga Lepeshinskaya, Tatiana Vecheslova, Natalia Dudinskaya, Konstantin Sergeyev, Mikhail Gabovich, Alexei Yermalayev, Vakhtang Chabukiani, and others, assisted in the development of the young ballet theatre in every possible way.

Together with these dancers, Messerer was an active participant in the important creative processes occurring in the Soviet ballet theatre: rethinking the traditional forms of the old, classical repertoire, shaping a new performing style, and originating new, realistic ballet spectacles. He strove for high professional standards in the ballet, the development of a picturesque and interesting dance, and the refinement of the stage art.

The beginning of Messerer's creative life was unusual. He broke all the established rules and regulations existing until then in the preparation of ballet dancers. He started to study dancing as a sixteen-year-old youth. In two years he passed the entire nine-year course of studies of the ballet school and was accepted in the Bolshoi Theatre. From the first season, he successfully carried out solo roles.

"Henceforth, my life," said the young dancer, "was mainly filled with work: daily exercises, striving for maximum clarity and purity of the dance, elaborating existing steps, and searching for new ones. All this was based on the classical dance. I don't think that I shall ever cease the struggle for improvement. I picture my future as an unceasing work on myself." (*See note 1.*)

The outstanding natural gifts—originality, magnificent dancing technique, and persistence in achieving mastership—were a rich foundation for the development of Messerer's talent. In the wide-ranging repertoire of the old, classical ballets, *Swan Lake, Sleeping Beauty, Nutcracker, La Fille Mal Gardée, Coppélia, Don Quixote,* and in particular Tchaikovsky's ballets, the young dancer immediately felt free, integral, and at ease. The classical male dance was distinguished in its interpretation by the beauty, purity, and finish of design; the charm of flight, jumps, and turns, the plastic poses, and the harmonious and melodious union of all these movements. Watching Messerer, who had rapidly achieved virtuosity, everyone could say: the ballet art has acquired a talented, dedicated dancer who knows what he wants to accomplish on the stage.

Before joining the Bolshoi Theatre, Asaf Messerer was part of a young experimental group, "Drama-Ballet," and became one of its most active participants. In this group debates raged on the ways to develop the choreographic art and on the possibility of dramatizing the ballet. Studies were similar to laboratory research; daring experiments helped reveal new thoughts in the creative process.

Complacency and vanity were never Asaf Messerer's characteristics. He became an artist under the guidance of two remarkable teachers, Alexander Gorsky and Vasily Tikhomirov. He examined life with determination and absorbed the creative achievements of the older generation of ballet dancers and the living traditions of the Russian choreographic art.

The highly developed art of the Bolshoi Theatre had a wholesome effect on the young dancer's creative consciousness. Messerer's taste was influenced by the best forms of the classical opera and ballet heritage. Mastering the secrets of professional skill, he became one of the greatest representatives of the Soviet ballet, and one of the most cultivated and interesting dancers. The most characteristic features of the Soviet choreographic art received picturesque and vivid expression in his interpretation.

The artistic life of the Russian ballet took a distinctive and difficult course in the first postrevolutionary decade. There was a search for new dance forms. Under the shield of innovation, modernists became active. They openly fought against the classical dance. Various studios appeared, such as the plastic, rhythmic, and acrobatic schools. Modern influence didn't affect Messerer. The erotic and languid effeminacy of the male dancer, affected manners, signs of decadence characteristic of the Western ballet of that time, had also penetrated into the Russian classical dance. But all this was foreign to Messerer's style. His performing style was always distinguished by its masculinity and nobility. Heroic and joyous intonations corresponding to modern times prevailed in the roles he created. The breadth of the artist's creative range defined the variety of his repertoire.

Inquisitive and enamored of the dance, Messerer was tireless in creative research. "One cannot limit oneself to only one role," he said. "One has to try various types in different artistic directions. The classical dancer must develop himself in all ways, constantly enrich his professional education with new knowledge, thoroughly absorb everything, and carefully observe surrounding life in all its manifestations."

Messerer carried out his convictions in practice, showing a lively interest in various dance genres. An excellent classical dancer, he performed equally well in character and "grotesque" roles and in plastic and acrobatic dances. He created roles contrasting in character and style: romantic Prince Siegfried in *Swan Lake;* gay and mischievous Colas and Franz in the classical-comic ballets *La Fille Mal Gardée* and *Coppélia;* tragic Petrouchka; a frenzied fanatic in *Salammbô;* extremely plastic Joseph in *Joseph the Beautiful;* wild and passionate Nurali in *The Fountain of Bakhchisarai;* the elegant skater in *The Prisoner of the Caucasus;* heroic and masculine Marseillais Philippe in *The Flames of Paris;* the idol, juggler, and Japanese sailor in *Red Poppy;* jovial Letika in *Red Sails;* a willful prince in *Cinderella*. This is a far from complete list of solo parts performed by Asaf Messerer. In his repertoire there were about fifty parts in addition to a large and varied concert list.

His skill improved through the years, becoming more accomplished as the dancer's stage experience developed. As is usual for beginners, Messerer started with minor roles and classical variations. Even at the beginning of his stage activity his critics maintained that the young dancer was excellent in the solo variations he performed. "As if his entire body were saturated with flight," wrote one of his critics, "he throws his body so lightly through the air, thrusts it freely upward in the jump, neatly and rapidly changing feet in entrechat or bringing one of them to the side after cabrioles with an unusually free and graceful movement, then assuredly spins double turns. One feels that it is precisely in the flight, the separation from the earth, that his strength lies. He has nothing to fear in separating from the soil." (*See note 2.*)

From the beginning Messerer was fond of invention in the performing arts. His dancing technique developed so rapidly that he felt constrained in the standard variations. He worked hard to improve his natural elevation and his technique in turns. His leaps formed an entire symphony of movements: a daring flight, then soaring turns and glides in the air. They were so light and graceful it seemed as if flight was his natural element. His turns were astonishing for their swiftness, beauty of pattern, and precision of form. It seemed that no technical difficulties existed for Messerer. But this was the result of tremendous work, daily training, and determined concentration. Renovation of the language of the dance became characteristic of Messerer from the first years of his activity. He enriched the vocabulary of the dance with new movements and intricate technical methods. He introduced double turns in the air executed several times in succession; double jetés entrelacés and double sauts de basque, jeté entrelacé with fouetté executed in one motion, double assemblé en tournant; he increased the number of pirouettes to ten and more, led the number of beats in entrechat to eight and ten (entrechat-huit, entrechat-dix), and introduced double turns in the air ending in the first arabesque on the right and left side. Characteristic of Messerer's technique was his ability to execute all virtuoso-technical movements and whole combinations equally well whether to the right or left, that is on the right leg or the left leg. All this continually developed his movements and coordination and gave more and more freedom and brilliance to his dance. But above all, he constantly aimed at achieving a greater expression in the character of a role or in an individual episode.

An artistic, scenic image is a combination of thought, feeling, and skill. Creation of an artistic role depends on the harmony between the internal content and the external form. The means of expressing a classical dance is plastic language. The greater the performing technique, the clearer, more expressive the language. The thoughts and feelings of a dancer evoked by musical dramatic composition and the thematic content of a ballet become fuller and freer in stage roles, when they are enriched by the beauty of plastic composition and movement.

Messerer's performances were distinguished by an unusual harmony between his fine acting and his highly professional skill. From the first steps of his stage

Asaf Messerer, 1921

life Messerer aspired to natural and realistic simplicity in one of the most traditional forms of art, the classical ballet. He persistently searched for a way leading to a "true artistic experience and feeling" (*K. S. Stanislavsky*).

Revolting against the traditional archaic gestures of the ballet, Messerer has persistently striven to introduce to the stage dancers who act with effective gestures and without mannerism, who give a logical and natural interpretation of the ballet and express true feelings. He replaced the standard ballet smiles with intelligent mimicry, and the sweet pose and pseudo-beauty with a strictly natural manner of stage behavior. In searching for the role's character, he was not afraid to sharpen the plastic character of the dance steps at times, or to exaggerate them to stress the most important and essential features of the characters played in a dramatic situation of a certain scene.

The prince in *Swan Lake* was one of the earlier roles created by Messerer. Close attention to the dramatic conflict expressed in Tchaikovsky's music prompted him to choose an independent way to interpret this role. Contrary to the established interpretation of the prince as a dreaming and passive youth, Messerer, preserving the romantic, imparted his hero with a decisive and impetuous masculinity, creating a direct and noble character. The awakening love for Odette, the suffering and repentance because of the involuntary deception, the breaking of his fidelity oath, and the courage shown in his struggle against shrewd Rothbart, all these feelings Messerer expressed convincingly, simply, and truthfully. It is in *Swan Lake* that Messerer first definitely revolted against the old established mimicry and replaced incomprehensible gestures with laconic, active ones.

Lyrical-romantic roles took a prominent place in Messerer's repertoire. In these roles he demonstrated the beauty of his style and the purity and perfection of his classical dance technique. At the same time, the artist's creative individuality developed in the strongly defined character and comic roles.

In his first theatrical season and for many years after that Messerer performed the role of Colas in the ballet *La Fille Mal Gardée* (music by Peter Hertel and stage production by Alexander Gorsky). In this role he proved himself to be an actor of great comic talent. Although peasantlike imitations

Graduating class of Alexander Gorsky,
Moscow Choreographic Institute, Bolshoi Theatre, 1921

were common in the ballet theatre of that time, Messerer categorically rejected them. In his acting there was no sweetness of mannerism, and not a shade of sentimentality. His Colas was a simple, cheerful youth. He stood firmly for his right to happiness and struggled to reach it by playing clever tricks on shrewish Marcelline and on his clumsy rival, Nicaise. At the same time he sincerely and purely expressed his candid feelings for Lisa. Messerer, rightly feeling the ballet's style in its musical and choreographic significance, was able to give content to his dancing language and to penetrate it with light and joyous intonations inherent in the hero's character.

During almost his entire life, Messerer danced the role of Franz in *Coppélia*, Delibes's lyrical-dramatic ballet, which was first staged at the Bolshoi Theatre by Alexander Gorsky and then restaged by Eugenia Dolinskaya and Alexander Radunsky. In Messerer's interpretation the characterless "pale" hero of the old ballet lived a new life, acquired character, and shone with new colors. An eager and brave young man sparkling with mirth and a joy for life and passionately in love with Swanilda—this was Asaf Messerer's Franz. He danced the part of Franz excellently, as he did Colas in *La Fille Mal Gardée*, imparting to it the same charm and naturalism, and enriching it with the emotion and moods brought upon him by the enticing music of the ballet.

This was clearly demonstrated in the scenes of the second act when Franz, slightly tipsy from a drug given to him by Coppélius, mistakes Swanilda for a doll and as a result gets into absurd and comic situations. Messerer acted so integrally and with such brilliant humor that these scenes always aroused a unanimous merry reaction from the audience.

In the ballet *The Flames of Paris* (Bolshoi Theatre, 1933), Messerer danced the role of Philippe, the revolutionary fighter from Marseille. The heroic-revolutionary theme of ballet composer Boris Asafiev and ballet master Vasily Vainonen was staged with great realistic force in the images of the heroes, the temperamental dances, and the widely displayed, dynamic popular scenes. In this role Messerer revealed new sides to his artistic talent and created a heroic, strong-willed image. From his first appearance on the stage, and throughout the ballet, he was inflamed with a passionate, angry call to revolt. In his dances, sculpturally cutting the figure, impetuous and swift, an image of the courageous soldier of revolution was born. *The Flames of Paris*, as danced by Messerer in the role of Philippe, is inseparably linked with the Soviet ballet's development of a heroic style in the masculine classical dance. This style became dominant among Soviet dancers; it was the product of stormy life and turbulent times.

In 1940 the Bolshoi Theatre restaged an Alexander Gorsky production of *Don Quixote* under the ballet master Rostislav Zakharov. The democratic content and images of the ballet, a lively and colorful spontaneity, and the temperamental, dynamic rhythms of the stage action always gave this ballet an

In class, 1927

optimistic resonance. The role of Basil was one of the best in Messerer's repertoire. The life-asserting aggressiveness and realism characteristic of his talent were demonstrated particularly clearly here. His Basil was very close to Figaro. Like Figaro, a deft and merry street barber loved by crowds, he attracted everybody with his sparkling energy, direct manner, and resourcefulness. He lavishly showered witty jokes upon the people around him, fervently shared his experiences with them, or engaged them in merry dances. Messerer enacted the scene of fake suicide in the tavern with fine humor: before falling "dead" after stabbing himself with the dagger, he spread out a cape, and each time the innkeeper refused to give Kitri to him in marriage Messerer-Basil quivered in a comic way. This witty scene, invented by Messerer, became a standard production of the Bolshoi Theatre. In the broad dancing vocabulary of Basil, Messerer found many colors to enrich the plastic expression of the role. Basil's meetings with Kitri turned into temperamental dancing dialogues with vivid and rich changes in mood, and the final duet acquired a major heroic significance. In Messerer's skilled dances, the perfection of classical forms was combined with the masculine manner of execution and with sparkling optimism. In the Kirov Theatre in Leningrad, as well as at Moscow's Bolshoi Theatre, *Don Quixote* featuring Moscow soloists Olga Lepeshinskaya and Messerer was widely acclaimed. "The two dancers complement each other ideally," wrote the Leningrad press, "forming a remarkable, sculpturally finished ensemble. Lepeshinskaya provides the means of clearly understanding the part of the ever-gay Kitri through the total command of her distinctive technique rather than through a selection of head-turning pirouettes customary to the ballet. Her partner shone in the performance with a faultless technique and with an assured and noble manner in the supporting role. Messerer's swift and distinct turns and his elastic jumps as if frozen in the air were met with loud applause from the audience." (*See note 3.*)

During his artistic maturity Messerer created the fine, elegant image of a very unusual prince in Sergei Prokofiev's ballet *Cinderella.* An excellent musical description of the prince and the skilled staging of Rostislav Zakharov helped the artist create a vivid and original role. With his manner of acting and skilled dancing he created a mischievous, impetuous, and dynamic character. Disregarding the etiquette and conventions of the court his enamored hero bravely toppled the barriers standing in the way of his desired purpose.

Messerer's creativity can serve as a brilliant confirmation of the famous thesis of Stanislavsky: "There are no small roles, only small actors." (*See note 4.*)

Asaf Messerer, prominent classical dancer, was also master of the episodic dance. He choreographed many short pieces and solo numbers. In the classical ballets produced by Alexander Gorsky he danced the parts of Ocean and Slave (*The Little Humpbacked Horse*) ; the pas de trois in *Swan Lake;* the Saracen dance in *Raymonda;* the Bluebird dance in Marius Petipa's production of *Sleeping Beauty;* the horseman in "Polovtsian dances" from K. Goleizovsky's production of the opera *Prince Igor;* and Nurali in *The Fountain of Bakhchisarai* staged by Rostislav Zakharov. Each episode and dance in his interpretation, without disrupting the harmony of the entire ballet, became more important and aroused lively interest.

Glière's *Red Poppy,* staged in 1927 by Vasily Tikhomirov and Lev Lastchilin, determined the development of the national choreographic art in many ways. Messerer also took part in it. It is precisely in this first stage of the Soviet ballet, designated by M. I. Kalinin as an "excellent Soviet creation" (*see note 5*), that the dancer's many-sided talent was revealed with outstanding brilliance. Asaf Messerer created three different images in this ballet: that of the Japanese sailor, the Chinese idol, and the juggler. In each role he was transformed, not only in his external appearance but also in his subtle feeling for the style and art of internal transformation. This was particularly apparent in the dances of the idol and the juggler.

The dance of the idol was truly a technical miracle. "Jumps with the arms and legs stretched forward; jumps with the body arched like a bow and the

Alexander Gorsky

heels barely missing the back of the head; and the most difficult leap of all with the legs bent horizontally toward the sides, all pointed to the fact that the ballet had in Messerer a dancer of international reputation." (*See note 6.*) Similar reviews of his dances occurred frequently in the press. In the dance of the juggler, an intricate pattern of classical variations and many turns, Messerer skillfully manipulated a long, yellow ribbon on a short handle. It seemed as if he surrounded himself with fire rings, entwined his body with a fantastic serpent, or transformed the ribbon into a huge live hoop through which he leaped. With distinctive elasticity Messerer skillfully and precisely cut intricate dance patterns.

At the dawn of Messerer's stage activity, certain balletomanes attempted to attribute his creative achievements solely to his skillful technique. They were mistaken. From the beginning of his artistic career Messerer attempted to create a living stage image and to search for characterization. It is not in vain that he was considered to be the best performer of Petrouchka in Igor Stravinsky's ballet of that name. It would be difficult to appear more touching and pitiful. His toy clown had tragic eyes, a comic hobbling walk, and sudden clumsy movements. With these touches, and by giving a plastic expression to the entire body, Messerer solved an intricate artistic problem and unveiled the tragedy of human feelings under the guise of a comic puppet, bound by the mechanism of a doll's movements.

In *The Little Humpbacked Horse,* with the participation of Ekaterina Geltzer, Vladimir Riabtsev, Maria Reisen, Ivan Smoltsov, Nina Podgoretskaya, Valentina Kudriavtseva, Lyubov Bank, and Anastasia Abramova, experienced, famous, and talented dancers, Messerer danced the part of Ocean. His youthful figure did not have the physical power that could be artistically associated with the fantastic image of Ocean. Nevertheless, he was able to portray the image with his dynamic dancing and to impart to it distinctive beauty and majesty by the sculpture of gestures and poses and in the breadth of his movements. The role of army leader Khan Girei Nurali in *The Fountain of Bakhchisarai,* a ballet of Boris Asafiev and Rostislav Zakharov, Messerer interpreted characteristically by using laconic devices and contrasting moods. It is not a great role, but when it was interpreted by Messerer the spectacle was always enriched and the role appeared to "grow." From two or three short appearances on the stage, even from the one Tartar dance, a living, sharply drawn image of a savage warrior was born. In him servile devotion to his master was combined with craftiness, cruelty, and wild temperament. He created this image by means of a stealthy cat walk, a quick run, and sharp, dynamic movements.

In *Sleeping Beauty,* Tchaikovsky and Petipa's ballet, Messerer created a poetic image of a soaring bluebird, which bewitched Princess Florine with its

Vasily Tikhomirov and Asaf Messerer

magic singing. He danced the choreographic text of this part (big, intricate jumps and fine beats) in a strictly classical style.

Messerer created a very different tragic and grotesque fanatic in *Salammbô*, produced by Andrei Arends and Igor Moiseyev. Overwhelmed by the folly of religious ecstasy, he drives the surrounding crowd into frenzy and entices it to sanguine sacrifices with his frightening shaman dancing, while he himself leaps into the fire. Here Messerer was transformed beyond recognition. He reached a high dramatic climax with his grotesque forms of technically expert dance, expression of movements, and passionate fire of feeling.

One of Messerer's most valuable qualities was his ability to impart national color to the dances he performed. On the stage a gay festival of young people takes place: the Komsomols are celebrating an important event, the completion of construction of a youth town. The young girls and men compete in a lively dance. A dashing Ukrainian gopak is replaced by a free Russian dance. A youth enters the circle of dancers: he is a slender, black-haired, dark, slightly squinting Cossack. The orchestra stops playing. Accompanied by the syncopated rhythm of a tambourine he starts dancing slowly and rather insinuatingly; the dance becomes more rapid and intricate. The harmony of movements is extraordinary, the rhythm and the dynamic tempo of the dance are

Petrouchka

Colas, *La Fille Mal Gardée*

fantastic. The youth holds everybody's attention. He dances in an astonishing way with all his being—his arms and legs, his shoulders, his supple body, his burning eyes, his charming smile. After turns combined with leaps, swift as lightning in a circle, he comes to an instant, final stop. The entire theatre breaks into wild applause. This role of the Cossack in the ballet *Svetlana* (Dmitri Klebanov, Nikolai Popko, Lev Pospekhin, Alexander Radunsky), dedicated to Soviet youth, was created by Asaf Messerer. The attractive, living image of our contemporary, a builder of the new life, created by the master of Soviet choreography, is a remarkable event. The search for the realization of image in modern subjects in the ballet theatre of the thirties was combined with the growing interest in understanding the characteristics of national dance cultures. Asaf Messerer's outstanding success in the ballet *Svetlana* marked the great master's first step in this direction. The dances of the idol and the juggler in *Red Poppy* as performed by Messerer were reflected traditions of Chinese national choreography. His concert number *Gopak* always delighted the audience. Messerer enriched this number not only with his brilliant technique and astonishingly high leaps but also with his unchecked gaiety, dashing valor, and the purely national popular traits. Combining academic traditions with the character dance and the elements of authentic nationality made each of his numbers original and gave an impression of being unique and distinct.

Messerer always felt keenly the genre nature of the ballets he performed. To each part, episodic role, and dance he imparted the character and style corresponding to the general artistic meaning of the work. For instance, what a remarkable feeling of style the artist demonstrated in the role of "The Caucasian Prisoner" (Boris Asafiev and Rostislav Zakharov). In the scene of "The Skating Rink" the skater suddenly appears and disappears. In the difficult, rapid tempo of the variation, Messerer, in an excellent imitation of the skater's movements, drew an accurate portrait of a graceful fop; by exaggerating the manner of movements and dancing with an ironic intonation, he stressed the dandy's flippancy.

During the years of the Second World War, the Bolshoi Theatre created many new ballets. Among them was V. Yurovsky's ballet *Red Sails*. In it Asaf Messerer danced the part of Boatswain Letik. With his inherent skill, the artist embodied this small, secondary role with light humor and contagious gaiety. "A. Messerer performed his role with talent," wrote composer Shostakovich in his review of the ballet. "Being a faultless technician, he has, at the same time, a great talent for acting. The role of the gay Boatswain Letik performed by him left one of the most vivid impressions." (*See note 7.*)

In 1929 Asaf Messerer composed and performed for the first time in a concert number, *Football Player's Dance* (music by Alexander Tsfasman). The typical, well-known figure of the inveterate football player appears on the stage—the football shirt, shorts, and socks, and a tiny beret on the shaggy hair. The football player is keenly involved in the game. Nothing except the ball exists for him. He fiercely fights his unseen adversaries, takes hard his misses, and is proud of his successes. He suffers defeat, falls down, and breaks his leg. But when the ball is returned to him, the player forgets everything in the world. He gives one last decisive kick . . . and that with his broken leg! Hurrah! He scores a goal! The delighted player freezes in the triumphant pose of the victor. The dance abounds with many technical intricacies but the artist has carried them out with fine humor and magnificent plastic eloquence. Asaf Messerer created the psychologically accurate image of the sportsman full of lively modern intonations, passionately enamored of football. This was done by means of slight, warm irony and a friendly smile, which strengthened the charm of this original concert number. Faced with the task of a clearly expressed staging, Messerer skillfully combined the elements of the classical dance with acrobatic and sportive movements. He showed a keen feeling for modern dance and enriched staging by creating choreographic miniatures of a new type. The success of *The Football Player* was phenomenal. Wherever Messerer performed, at home in the USSR or as a guest abroad, he was rewarded with ovations from the audience, enthusiastic press reviews, and the admiration of his colleagues in art.

Anastasia Abramova—Lisa, Asaf Messerer—Colas,
La Fille Mal Gardée

Prince Siegfried, *Swan Lake*

Football Player, concert number

Sulamif Messerer–Kitri, Asaf Messerer–Basil, *Don Quixote*

Asaf Messerer—Basil, *Don Quixote*

Prince Siegfried, *Swan Lake*

Asaf Messerer keeps a map of the Soviet Union on which he has marked the places visited during his engagements. There are over fifty: Siberia, Crimea, Central Asia, the Baltic Sea areas, the Donets Basin, the Urals, the Ukraine, etc. Together with his partners Victorina Krieger, Margarita Kandaurova, Anastasia Abramova, Tatiana Vasilieva, Sulamif Messerer, Olga Lepeshinskaya, Natalia Dudinskaya, and Irina Tikhomirnova, he appeared in a great many varied concert numbers and ballets. Travels in his native country alternated with those abroad. At first, as a dancer, Messerer passed through almost all of Europe, then he visited many countries of the world as ballet master and teacher. In 1929 Messerer toured Latvia with Victorina Krieger. The Soviet dancers, representatives of the Bolshoi Theatre, appeared on the stage of the Riga National Theatre, unanimously winning the hearts of the Latvians. Even the hostile newspapers said that the young dancer was "quite an exceptional phenomenon in the ballet world." "I never had the occasion to observe such lightness and such departure from the earth's gravity," wrote the critic. "He accomplished impossible feats and yet remained a 'classical dancer.' In spite of the acrobatics of his lunges, they are not acrobatic, but from the first movement to the last they remain the highest display of dancing genius. Messerer's variations are a cascade of the most intricate steps, for example 'jeté with cabrioles' is astonishing, his leaps are not leaps but a flight across the stage, his gracefulness borders on witchcraft . . . Everything is imprinted with true art." (*See note 8.*)

It is to be noted that the press in its many enthusiastic reviews stressed the great continuity of professional traditions by the Soviet dancers. "Victorina Krieger and Asaf Messerer have demonstrated that the new Russian generation is not inferior in any way to the past, and in many ways it even surpasses it." (*See note 9.*) And their trip did not pass without humor. At the same time B. G. Tchukhnovsky (famous Soviet flyer) was in Riga with the ballet dancers. The newspapers published a friendly cartoon, "Two Russian flyers in Riga." While Asaf Messerer soared in the air against the background of the National Opera, Tchukhnovsky, watching him, said: "Here in Riga, Messerer is breaking air records without a motor." Asaf Messerer returned to Riga several times. He appeared there with young ballet dancer Tatiana Vasilieva

Irina Tikhomirnova–Odette, Asaf Messerer–Prince Siegfried, *Swan Lake*

and with his sister Sulamif Messerer. Each time he received more and more recognition. He was called "Chaliapin of the ballet." This designation showed high appraisal of his artistic skill.

Asaf and Sulamif were the first of the Soviet Union's dancers to tour in Western Europe and Scandinavia. The year was 1933. The Soviet dancers were met with great interest and sent off with ovations. Their tours drew the attention of the press in many capitalist countries. The French, German, English, American, Dutch, and Norwegian papers carried reviews of the thirty concerts the brother and sister gave abroad.

A Swedish critic wrote: "The bare and straight stage, black curtains, white floor, no decoration, and no special costumes—in this case all this would be superfluous as everything presented to the spectators was of such high caliber that it spoke for itself . . . Asaf Messerer—a real phenomenon of suppleness, speed, and elasticity . . . The pirouettes and entrechats of Sulamif Messerer were performed with exceptional gracefulness. Her strength lies in the perfect technique and delicacy of the classical ballet. The strict schooling in the classical

Fanatic, *Salammbô*

Dance of the Juggler, *The Red Poppy*

dance performed by the Soviet artists shows its complete discipline." (*See note 10.*)

"Since the time of Fokine and Fokina," maintained another critic, "we have seen nothing equal to this performance in Stockholm. Even Fokine was unable to show anything corresponding to the fabulous technique of Messerer's dancing. The classical style has been surpassed in the modern Russian ballet." (*See note 11.*) The Swedes said, "Asaf Messerer astonished the public. His art is varied, it combines pathos and drama. He succeeded in maintaining line in phenomenal leaps, which has hardly been seen since the time of Nijinsky, and with logically and clearly constructed choreography." (*See note 12.*) The tour of the Messerers in Sweden aroused such great interest in ballet circles that theatre directors and representatives of ballet companies of Norway, Denmark, Holland, Germany, and Finland arrived in Stockholm.

In the same year, 1933, Asaf and Sulamif performed in Paris at the Thé-âtre des Champs-Élysées. Among the spectators and critics were friends of the Soviet Union as well as enemies. Their political views determined their feelings for the Soviet art. But even those with hostile sentiments were forced to recognize the technical perfection of Messerer's dancing and his extraordinary musicality, rhythm, expression, and acting skill. It was noted that Messerer was undoubtedly an "outstanding phenomenon." Parisians called Asaf Messerer "Nijinsky's rival," yet for the French Nijinsky for many years remained the unsurpassed summit of classical dance.

In 1941, after twenty years of Messerer's work in the Bolshoi Theatre, when according to ballet tradition dancers must retire, the State Prize Laureate was conferred upon him and several other choreographic artists of the Soviet art. In this connection, it was noted in *Pravda:* "Usually a classical dancer loses with age some physical capabilities characteristic of youth. Messerer breaks this law in the same way as he 'breaks' the law of gravity in his unusually light leaps on the stage of the Bolshoi Theatre of the USSR. The lightness, airiness, and incomparable purity of the dance's classical form becomes more perfect in him with each year. The astonishing coordination of movements in the air and on the earth, the mastering of any technical difficulties, virtuosity, as well as the manifestation of academic skill are characteristic of this brilliant dancer." (*See note 13.*) The famous formula of Stanislavsky applied to actor's work also applies to actors of the ballet theatre. In the creativity of great masters it receives a par-ticularly vivid realization. Yes, the beauty of Asaf Messerer's inspired dance is a remarkable union of enormously concentrated intelligent work with creative thought and artistic research. This union where "everything difficult becomes a habit, a habit becomes easy, and easy becomes excellent . . ." (*See note 14.*)

Asaf Messerer has left the stage, but he continues to teach the art of classical dance to the new generations of dancers and to improve the performing skill

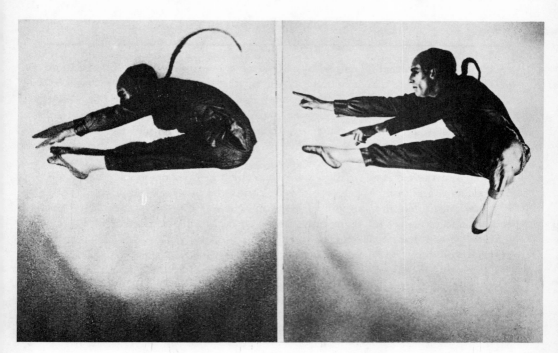

Dance of the Idol, *The Red Poppy*

of artists of the Bolshoi Theatre. Asaf Messerer knows well that the interrelation of the dancers' generations is determined by the continuity of traditions and the living relationship of experience and dancing culture. It was often said about the creativity of Asaf Messerer and Vakhtang Chaboukiani that "they breathed new life into the masculine dance of the Soviet ballet." Vakhtang Chaboukiani's admission is noteworthy. He once said: "I decided to become a dancer after I saw Messerer." (*See note 15.*) The similarity of their performing manner and their creative design were subsequently often observed. "Vakhtang Chaboukiani and Asaf Messerer could be called the kings of jumps and turns, if these constituted the purpose of their masculine, forceful dance. These inspired dancers first of all present themselves to us as an embodiment of various features of the male character," wrote Nicolai Volkov, well-known ballet critic and stage producer. (*See note 16.*)

Each new generation enters into the choreographic art absorbing the traditions, skill, and culture of their predecessors. The young people go further and set themselves higher aims. Asaf Messerer was a pupil of the famous reformer of the Moscow ballet, Alexander Gorsky, a great ballet master and

Philippe, *The Flames of Paris*

teacher. Entering the Bolshoi Theatre the young dancer worked with Vasily Tikhomirov, a prominent master of the classical dance. Messerer had the good fortune of observing the creative laboratory of the remarkable dancer Ekaterina Geltser, her methods of preparation for the ballet, and of working at the barre and in the middle of the classroom, in one word, the system of classical training. His partners in the classroom rehearsals and ballets were the well-known masters of the older generation, who assigned a special significance to the academic culture of the dance. These ballet masters were: Vladimir Ryabtsev, Leonid Zhukov, Maria Reisen, Margarita Kandaurova, Victorina Krieger, Nina Podgoretskaya, Lyubov Bank, Anastasia Abramova, Valentina Kudriavtseva, Victor Smoltsov, and N. Tarasov. Among his age group there were Igor Moiseyev, Marina Semenova, Mikhail Gabovich, and Alexei Yermolayev. Then a new generation arose headed by Galina Ulanova, Olga Lepeshinskaya, Sulamif Messerer, Irina Tikhomirnova, and Yelena Chikvaidze. In the postwar years the following appeared: Maya Plisetskaya, Raissa Struchkova, then Rimma Karelskaya, Liudmilla Bogomolova, and Marina Kondratieva. Now the playbills display the new names of talented dancers: Nina Timofeyeva, Ekaterina

Olga Lepeshinskaya—Nymph, Asaf Messerer—Faun,
Ivan Susanin, 1939

Maximova, Yelena Riabinkina, Nina Sorokina, Natalia Bessmertnova, Nicolai Fadeyechev, Vladimir Vasiliev, Maris Liepa, Boris Khokhlov, Vladimir Nikonov, Vladimir Tikhonov, Mikhail Lavrovsky, and others. In this way the choreographic art is passed from generation to generation.

In the early twenties an article, "New Forces in the Ballet," appeared in one of the Soviet papers. It described the dance evenings in which young dancers took part. Among them was Messerer, who produced a one-act ballet, *The Fairy Doll*. All the roles of the ballet, except the mimic ones, were performed by the pupils of the choreographic school of the Bolshoi Theatre; M. Shmelkina (the Fairy Doll), Alexander Tsarman (Harlequin), Sulamif Messerer (Columbine), Tatiana Vasilieva (Chinese Doll), Vera Vasilieva (Tyrol Doll), and others. In the toy store the shoppers are offered various dolls; night falls; the dolls come to life. The young producer has created interesting dances that do not present difficulties to the young dancers beyond their physical strength but, at the same time, give maximum opportunity for displaying creative individuality.

In 1927 the A. V. Lunacharsky Theatre Technical School arranged for periodic reviews of progress of the ballet students. Messerer's work stood out again among the ballets of individual teachers. They disproved the assertion that the classical dance was outmoded and incapable of expressing a modern mood. The young ballet master chose gymnasts for the heroes of his ballets and staged all the numbers using a broad range of elements from the classical dance. In the new program, he created short and unusual subjects: "Football," "Tennis," "Boxing," "Iceskaters," "Horseback Riders." Of course, in these numbers it would have been easy to be attracted by pure pantomime or the direct copying of sportive movements. However, the ballet master was able to draw these miniatures by means of dance. Messerer had demonstrated in his work independent creative thoughts, original creative views, and the ability to transform events of reality into the classical dance forms. This was, of course, daring on his part, if one remembers that at the time there was an open attack on the ballet's classical foundation, declared by some to be a survival of the old bourgeois and ruling classes culture.

Messerer's attention was always attracted to dances of the national character and those of "grotesque" genre, as this area in the ballet allowed experimentation. It made it possible to complete the usual choreographic images and to use classical dance methods in combination with national and "grotesque" forms. The appearance on stage of *Russian Prints, Turkish Dance,* and the grotesque *Pas de Trois,* a scene from *Football,* were the result of a search for an independent way in the choreographic art by a ballet master who knew the rules of classical dance, was able to invent original compositions, and had an artistic taste and feeling for modern times. These qualities later found a more complete expression in *Football Player Dance.*

Yekaterina Geltser congratulates Asaf Messerer on his twentieth anniversary.

Messerer was entrusted with increasingly more important productions. In 1930 the Bolshoi Theatre was preparing to produce A. Spendiarov's opera *Almast*. The dance directors were Messerer and Victor Tsaplin. Messerer also staged dances in several new plays of the dramatic theatres, such as the Moscow Art Academy Theatre—2; Evgeny Vakhtangov's Theatre, and Vs. Meyerhold's Theatre. He worked together with Meyerhold to produce Sergei Prokofiev's ballet *Pas d'Acier*. He revived, with Igor Moiseyev, the ballet *La Fille Mal Gardée* in the Experimental Theatre, a branch of the State Academy of the Bolshoi Theatre. All these productions contributed to the enrichment of his skill as ballet master and director. Everything incidental, temporary, and inexpressive was "sifted out" through experience. The golden sand of true discoveries was stored in his heart and memory. With experience there was an understanding that it was not easy to find the best form for expressing a thought or an idea. The clearer the thought, the clearer the form; thus the work affects the viewer more powerfully and emotionally.

The accumulation process of creative forces lasted for many years. Fifteen years had elapsed before Asaf Messerer, together with Alexander Chekrygin, Honored Art Worker, and Boris Mordvinov, Honored Artist of the RSFSR, undertook the production of *Sleeping Beauty,* an important ballet with several acts, on the stage of the Bolshoi Theatre. One of the pearls of Russian ballet music, Tchaikovsky's great work *Sleeping Beauty,* was born in 1890 on the Marinsky Theatre stage in St. Petersburg. The ballet in Marius Petipa's production is one of the best achievements of Russian classical choreography. Even in present times, it enhances many stages of the musical theatres of the world. The rebirth of *Sleeping Beauty* on the stage of the Bolshoi Theatre in the thirties was quite

natural. Creative revision of the Russian classical ballet heritage for the enrichment of the ballet repertoire of our theatres characterizes one of the important
sides of the activities of Soviet ballet masters. Messerer, Chekrygin, and Mordvinov created a new stage realization of Tchaikovsky's immortal music, having
carefully kept many of the best pieces of Petipa's classical work in the choreography. Having kept the ballet's fairy story untouched, the producers strived to
create a choreographic and musical spectacle "built according to the drama
with the subject developed without interruption and permeated with a determined idea and action, and with a logical justification of the events and behavior of the actors." (*See note 17.*) The chief means for expressing the dramatic
situations and for creating images on stage was the classical dance. A desire to
more vividly express the main theme of the fairy tale, magnificently realized in
the ballet's music, led the directors to a new decision concerning the roles of
the Fairy Carabosse and the Lilac Fairy. These roles became significantly more

Nurali, *The Fountain of Bakhchisarai*

Figure Skater, *The Prisoner of the Caucasus*

important; Fairy Carabosse acquired a developed dancing character for the first time. The fight between them and the triumph of the Lilac Fairy, personifying the idea of victory of life over death, of good over evil, were given an original and interesting interpretation in the production. Marina Semenova and Olga Lepeshinskaya, prominent Soviet dancers, were the first to perform Aurora's part. Semenova's Aurora captivated one with the beauty of plastic line and the perfection of dancing form. She transmitted the poetry of her blossoming feelings with inherent charm and spirituality. Olga Lepeshinskaya created a fascinating, lively, and timid image of Aurora. She danced with masterly brilliance, transmitting in each movement the sincere rapture of youth and the joy of being. The two dancers, different in their creative individuality, revealed with fine artistic taste the poetic content of Tchaikovsky's great music.

After the Second World War, Messerer revived *Sleeping Beauty* on two occasions. The second time he produced the ballet with Mikhail Gabovich, People's Artist of the RSFSR, who acted as the director. It is very difficult to bring to light the originality of the ballet master's design in *Sleeping Beauty*. The ballet was produced by him in cooperation with Gabovich. Undoubtedly, in the process of this work the artistic conception and choreographic decisions of each ballet master were united. *Sleeping Beauty,* a spectacle of monumental classical form, played a significant role in acquiring artistic skills and in the development and improvement of the professional culture of the dancers of the Bolshoi Theatre.

Messerer never strove for false innovations, he did not concern himself with revival for the sake of revival. In 1937 he created a new edition of the fourth act of Tchaikovsky's ballet *Swan Lake,* which has been presented on the stage of the Bolshoi Theatre in Gorsky's production since 1901. He painted an interesting image of the evil genius, changing the mimic part into a dancing image; in this way he made the acting significance of the role more important. He replaced the conventional pantomime with a dynamic, expressive dance. The director gave much drama to all the dancing compositions of the swan scenes (Odette's story, her encounter with the Prince, single combat with the evil genius), strengthened their internal expression, and completed the ballet with a poetically illuminated finale. In this refined creative work, Messerer was able not only to preserve but also to deepen the principles of the symphonic character of the music and choreography of *Swan Lake*. This ballet, in the production of Gorsky and his pupil Asaf Messerer, is one of the most popular; it has existed for many years in the repertoire of the Bolshoi Theatre.

In 1935 Messerer and the Lithuanian ballet master V. Grivitskas produced on the stage of the Vilnaius Opera Theatre a modern ballet, *At the Seaside,* with music by Yu. Yuzeliunas. This ballet, shown in Moscow during the celebration of the Decade of the Lithuanian Art and Literature, was warmly received. The authors brought national Lithuanian color into the choreography and ably used the folkloric elements of the music. They created an interesting ballet spectacle filled with action and charged with the mood of modern times.

Asaf Messerer composed many varied concert numbers. Among them were *Spring Waters* to Rachmaninoff's music; *Melody,* to Gluck's music; *Etude* by Chopin; *Pierrot and Pierette* by Drigo; *Bashkir Dance* and many other dances. These dances have existed on stage for many years; they are loved by performers and are popular with audiences.

Messerer's style is expressed most fully in *Spring Waters,* which he created to the music of Rachmaninoff's famous song. This dance enchants with its sculptured clearness of composition, unusual spectacular lifts, dynamic jumps, and whirlwind turns. Everything in it is subjected to the thoughts and moods expressed in the sparkling optimism of Rachmaninoff's music.

A young boy and girl rejoice at the spring of life. Their dance, beautiful and impetuously daring, is a symbol of the swiftly running spring waters. It is the triumph of the awakening of powerful forces in nature; it is the eternal beauty of youth. Arnold Haskell, important English researcher, scholar, and ballet critic, includes *Spring Waters* among the best typical examples of Soviet choreography. In his book *The Russian Genius in Ballet*, devoted to the historical and esthetic problems of our ballet art, he writes: "Messerer combines in *Spring Waters* an extraordinarily intricate 'acrobatic' technique with remarkable musicality in transmitting deeply lyric experience." (*See note 18.*)

Messerer also produced on the stage of the Bolshoi Theatre the dances of a number of operas (*Les Huguenots, Sadko, Lakmé*). In Budapest he staged

Letika, *Red Sails*

Swan Lake and the one-act ballet *Spring Festival;* in Peking, *Ballet Class;* and in Brussels, a concert consisting of divertissement numbers.

There is one other page in the biography of ballet master Messerer. It is his work in the Ensemble of Song and Dance of the NKVD, USSR (1939– 46). In charge of the choreographic section of the Ensemble, Messerer had the task of merging the dance and the song materials. The first program *Along the Native Land* included works of the Soviet composers and Russian, Ukrainian, and Georgian national songs and dances. They alternated in a definite thematic sequence and consisted of one subject. In the programs of *Motherland* and *Russian River* there were singing and dancing scenes and cossack dances, the famous *Apple,* and the dances of Soviet youth. Among them was *Football,* with music composed by Dmitri Shostakovich. In the fourth program *Victorious Spring,* shown on the Victory Day in 1946, Messerer staged *Great Waltz.* The press noted "the mature skill and originality of dance language" of the ballet master.

Raissa Struchkova–Cinderella, Asaf Messerer–Prince, *Cinderella*

Ekaterina Maximova, Stanislav Vlasov, *Spring Waters*

Asaf Messerer appears every morning in the rehearsal rooms of the ballet company of the Bolshoi Theatre to start his dancing class. Lessons every day of the week have their unique character. At first the dancers work at the barre, then they start their exercises in the middle of the floor. They work daily throughout their creative lives. Among the pupils of Messerer's class one can find Galina Ulanova and Maya Plisetskaya, People's Artists of the USSR and Lenin Prize Laureates, as well as many other famous solo dancers all mingling with the young beginners. No one is forced to attend classes; they come by themselves because it is very important, useful, and interesting. The fame of these lessons has spread far and wide. Those coming from near and distant towns, dancers, ballet masters, and teachers from different republics (many of them students of Messerer in the past) wish to attend Messerer's classes to enrich their experience and knowledge.

When the Royal Ballet of Great Britain was on tour in Moscow, Messerer conducted their ballet classes at their request. Famous dancers such as Margot Fonteyn, Beryl Grey, Nadia Nerina, David Blair, Michael Somes, and the entire company worked with great interest under the guidance of the prominent Soviet teacher. Alicia Alonso, Mikiko Matsuyama, and many other foreign masters of classical dance who have come to the USSR invariably desire to attend his classes.

In 1960 Messerer, People's Artist of the RSFSR and Irina Tikhomirnova, Honored Artist of the RSFSR were sent to Brussels to organize a ballet school. They taught young Belgian dancers and, at the same time, at the request of the Belgian Opera Theatre, conducted classes for actors. Their instruction, based on the Russian system, was so well implanted in the ballet company that the management asked the Soviet teachers to accompany the group on a tour to Paris, Vienna, and Monte Carlo. Classes continued without interruption and were also attended by teachers and dancers from England, Italy, and Switzerland. They came specifically to the towns where the Belgian company was performing in order to attend classes of the Soviet ballet master.

Messerer's work as a teacher became more involved when the Soviet ballet was touring the United States and Canada in 1962. Messerer gave daily lessons to the dancers of the Bolshoi Theatre. Many dancers, teachers, art workers, and theatre critics also wished to attend these classes as on the company's previous tours abroad to London, Paris, Belgium, and the Federated Republic of Germany. There arose a need for conducting special demonstration classes of the Soviet ballet artists. In addition, Messerer gave many special classes for dancers of American and Canadian ballet schools. He conducted discussions on creativity and theory with teachers of various private ballet studios, combining them with special demonstration lessons. All this helped to familiarize dancers and teachers abroad with the Soviet ballet school and gave them a visual demonstration of the method of teaching classical dance in our country.

Forty years of Messerer's work in the teaching field received an interesting artistic and creative interpretation. For a long time Asaf Messerer considered choreographing a ballet demonstrating the foundations of the Russian Soviet school of classical dance. In 1960 he produced a one-act ballet, *Ballet Class,* with students of the Bolshoi Theatre's Choreographic School. The process of teaching children ballet was demonstrated in well-defined sequence in an elegant theatrical form. On a proscenium stage small children run quickly to the ballet school. One child finds his shoe lace untied, another stands aping, a third is anxious to share news with his friend. Lively and merry scenes alternate from one end of the proscenium to the other. The children run away.

The curtain rises. An ordinary ballet classroom is shown on the stage. A dancing lesson is in progress. Small boys and girls appear in groups from the alternate wings and do beginning exercises at the barre. They are replaced by older children. In turn, first the boys then the girls perform more difficult classical exercises.

Again we see the proscenium. It is a recess not unlike other recesses. In one the boys romp, in the other the girls try on ballet slippers and attempt to stand on their toes.

Now we are back in the classroom. The exercises take place in the middle of the room. Adagio is replaced by jumps, turns, and exercises on the toes. Gradually the dance combinations become quicker and more difficult and the tempo and character of the dancing changes. The entire composition comes to an end with a march that symbolizes friendship, children's unity, their joyful attitude toward work, and their desire to learn the rules of the art of dance.

When the ballet company of the Bolshoi Theatre went on tour to the United States and Canada in 1962 this ballet was included in the program. Messerer

Yuri Faier, Dmitri Shostakovitch, and Asaf Messerer at a rehearsal of *Ballet School*

created its new edition, *Ballet Class*. The ballet master enlarged many sections, enriched them considerably technically, introduced additional sections, and composed a new finale. Only the genre scenes and the dance exercises for the children were left. The children had to be selected in each town of the USA and Canada where the Soviet ballet appeared. To select sixteen girls and eight boys, Messerer had to audition up to five hundred children each time. Actual competitions consisting of three rounds took place, arousing great interest among representatives of television and the press. Messerer had to train the chosen children to perform anew each time. Essentially he worked with them again and again in rehearsing and staging.

The ballet, renamed *Ballet School* by the Americans, demonstrated the achievements of Soviet choreographic culture and became a showpiece of the performing skill of our dancers. Messerer was able to express in compositions of the "lesson" the characteristics of the Russian style of classical dance, to

After the New York premiere of *Ballet School*

demonstrate the originality of technical methods and the skill of the dancers, and to point out their performing inspiration. He created an artistic picture of creative work filled with the joy of living and beauty and showed an understanding of the rules of the choreographic art. The press in the United States and Canada enthusiastically responded to *Ballet School*. The New York *Herald Tribune* critic stressed: "The Soviet school vividly and clearly lays emphasis on the classical dance in all its magnificence." "All the artists are magnificent," wrote the New York *Post,* "Maya Plisetskaya, and Ekaterina Maximova, Vladimir Vasiliev, Nicolai Fadeyechev, everyone." "People of persistent and strenuous effort, it is like this that we see the dancers in *Ballet School,*" stated the reviewer in the New York *Times*. "If you wish to see an exciting demonstration of the most dazzling ballet technique in the world—hurry to the Metropolitan Opera House to see *Ballet School* performed by the ballet company of the Bolshoi Theatre," wrote the New York *Times*. It was noted in the New York *Journal American:* "All the magnificence and magic of the Bolshoi Theatre ballet manifested itself in the premiere of *Ballet School*. The Soviet dancers presented to the American audience a marvelous gift in showing their premiere performance on the American soil."

Boris Lvov-Anokhin, prominent Soviet director and fine scholar of the Soviet ballet, characterized *Ballet Class* in a very interesting and accurate way: "The dancing harmony of the Russian School is convincingly asserted in the ballet: the school's high plastic interpretation, which the ballet master sees in the melodious combination, the union of separate movements, the faultlessly logical development of each dancing sentence, and the graceful harmony of dancing forms. In this work," continues Lvov-Anokhin, "Messerer not only shines with rare choreographic erudition but he also reveals the inspiration of the ballet master, able to create an unbroken integrity and unity of the dance." (*See note 19.*)

Throughout his entire stage career Asaf Messerer unceasingly searched for his own artistic dance language. He continuously refined his performing skill and deepened his professional culture. Messerer started to teach almost at the same time as he started to dance. In 1921 he was already teaching ballet in the evening courses at the Bolshoi Theatre, then in A. V. Lunacharsky's Theatre Technical School. Two years later, Messerer taught in the Choreographic School of the Bolshoi Theatre where he gave dancing classes to boys and girls for several decades and participated in the examinations at the admittance and graduation. He prepared periodic progress and graduation ballets and concerts of the school and was responsible for their production and rehearsals. He also took an active part in elaborating the method of logical foundations for choreographic education and in the artistic reviewing of the ballet school. At the beginning of his teaching career Messerer imitated his teachers, copying their methods. Possessing an excellent memory he could fully reproduce lessons of Gorsky and Tikhomirov. He did this and with lively curiosity shared his knowledge with his friends. But eventually his independent work led him to an analysis and to general conclusions. Gradually his own teaching style started to form.

The creative method, which Messerer elaborated, organically re-created the foundations of the Russian school of the classical dance. It was formed by borrowing from the experiences of teachers and older colleagues in the art and from Asaf Messerer's artistic and teaching experience.

Messerer, a man of rich talent who loved young people, did not keep a list of his pupils. And it is difficult to say how many dancers consider themselves to be his pupils. He was always happy when his pupils' creative work entered the repertoire of different ballet schools of the country, and proud when their labor and skill won a place in the art of choreography.

Messerer had always closely combined his long creative life with social work. He took an active, productive part in creating new ballets, teaching young artists, organizing numerous artistic reviews of professional artists and amateurs, and conducting seminars for teachers of musical theatres in the country.

It is not important to mention here all of the young dancers trained under Messerer's careful guidance: it is more important to say that Messerer was always concerned and interested in the creative life of all young people, independent of who had taught them ballet. "The talented young company of the Bolshoi Theatre showed themselves admirably in this important tour," Messerer wrote once after the ballet's return from abroad. "Will this turn their heads? Let us hope that their talent, industry, and high standards will serve us as a reliable protection. The true artist is always aware of his shortcomings and remembers them even if the public had missed or forgiven them. And he continues to work. Always."

This sums up Messerer—artist and teacher.

To become a teacher of classical dance is not simple. This profession is no less difficult than that of a dancer, and, in some ways, even more difficult. A dancer answers only for himself, whereas a teacher is responsible for the direction of his pupils.

Carlo Blasis, one of the greatest choreography teachers of the past, said: "Before one can aspire to the name of teacher one has to become a first-class performer of dance. Otherwise his teaching will be poor, there will be no conviction or precision in lessons. A teacher must impart to his students a sense of fascination in his art . . . Most important in the art of dance is continued practice." (*See note 20.*) These statements were the nucleus of many of Carlo Blasis' thoughts. They sound convincing even today. They are confirmed in practice of our ballet theatres beginning with the Bolshoi Theatre of the USSR and S. M. Kirov's Opera and Ballet Theatre of Leningrad, our oldest academic theatres. For many decades lessons for the advanced training of ballet

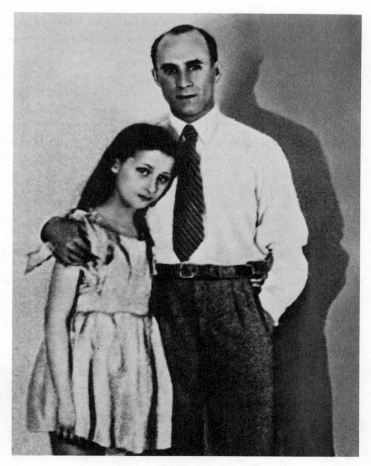

Asaf Messerer with Maya Plisetskaya

dancers in these theatres have been conducted by famous dancers with long, creative careers. Constant training with them imparts high professional skills to dancers. Among the renowned group of older teachers were Alexander Gorsky, Vasily Tikhomirov, Agrippina Vaganova, Vladimir Ponomarev, and Victor Semenov. It also includes such masters as Yelizaveta Gerdt, N. I. Tarasov, Marina Semenova, and Asaf Messerer. Each of them account for dozens of artists who completed ballet school under their guidance, as well as for many others trained by them directly on the theatre stage.

Classes for advanced training, otherwise known as artistic classes, exist now in every Soviet ballet theatre. The level of professional skill of ballet dancers depends on the organization of these classes. Their dancing technique is polished and improved there and their art of performing and their artistic tastes are refined. This is achieved through a process of continued training and relentless repetition of the strict academic forms of the classical exercises.

Addressing students of the Ballet Teachers Department of the Leningrad Conservatory, Vaganova spoke well on the importance of exercises: "The complexity of knowledge of classical exercises as well as of the classical dance is infinite, for the essence of knowledge does not lie solely in the exercises. The details and nuances which are so necessary for the stage performance are acquired through long experience." Developing her thought, she said: "The classical dance serves as a foundation for every stage performance whether it be a character, grotesque, or social dance." (*See note 21.*)

Much has been said about the teaching methods of ballet art but almost nothing about the advanced training of professional dancers. This interesting division in the choreographic teaching has not been studied or analyzed to a necessary degree. A difference exists, and not a slight one. Even in the graduating classes of the ballet schools, teachers strictly adhere to the school program. Whereas classes for the advanced training of dancers give an opportunity for a freer development of the forms and methods of teaching classical dance. But a theoretical and methodological basis for the advanced qualification of dancers does not exist, although the importance of this significant work related to cultivating the artistic skill of dancers cannot be underestimated.

Asaf Messerer conducts a class with his assistant, Irina Tikhomirnova

Irina Tikhomirnova—Kitri, Asaf Messerer—Basil,
at the dress rehearsal of *Don Quixote*

In this book the lessons that Messerer created for the artistic classes have been printed for the first time. The detailed description of six classes by Elena Golubkova, artist of the Bolshoi Theatre Ballet, and the article by Asaf Messerer preceding it reflect the creative principles and methods of his academic work. We are publishing only a small part of the records to give a sample of the methodological system of classical training of Asaf Messerer.

Each lesson is preceded by strenuous preparatory work. Messerer never repeats himself in his lessons. Each time he creates a new composition for the lesson, proceeding from the general principle of the structure of six consecutive lessons a week. He prepares his lessons beforehand in all details from the first movement to the last, and from the first dancing combination to the last. This alone shows to what degree his sense of responsibility is developed toward fulfilling his academic task. At the base of the teaching method lies the principle of developing choreographic themes, related to musical symphony. Messerer carries out this principle without breaking the academic rules in the structure of classical exercises. Each lesson has a main theme, that is a basic movement, which is developed thoroughly and in succession in a number of various dance combinations. The barre exercises vary little. Slow in tempo, his barre exercises are simple and logical, and essentially follow the conventional routine. The exercises that follow these and take place in the center of the room contain many compositional variations. It is true that even here he maintains the conventional sequence of basic movements, but their composition is distinguished by his wide variations and methodological knowledge.

The exercises in the middle of the room give ballet dancers rich opportunities for perfecting their professional skills and for polishing all aspects of their dancing technique. Cultivating the high levels of ballet performance and of artistic skill is the chief aim and task of Messerer's academic work. It is precisely because of this that creativity determines the substance of Messerer's lessons and they are not a scholastic and dry repetition of conventional methods, positions, movements, and mechanical learning.

His lessons stimulate the dancer's creative conscience and become an interesting stage in the creative process, during which the artist is made a creator of a certain role, part, or artistic image. In this, above all, Messerer is a follower and creative adopter of the methods for conducting ballet classes developed by his older prominent co-workers in art—Alexander Gorsky, Agrippina Vaganova, Vasily Tikhomirov, Yelizaveta Gerdt, and Victor Semenov.

Not pretending to give an exhaustive analysis of such an intricate and rich process that constitutes Messerer's lessons, nevertheless it is necessary to point out the following typical characteristics. First of all, a logical order and a sense of measure prevail in his lessons. There is a sequence in the increase of technical and physical intricacies and in the proportion of all dance instruction. This is manifested everywhere—in the adagio movements and in the turns and leaps combinations. There is nothing accidental or unnecessary in the lesson. There are no pseudo-sweet poses, affected breaking of strict lines, or unnecessary movements. His combinations are distinguished by inventiveness and variation. And the harmonious and logically completed structure of each composition is based on profound knowledge of the rules of classical dance and of its steps and positions.

Asaf Messerer firmly maintains two rules. The first one says: "One should not strain the dancer's strength in class; after lessons he has rehearsals, then evening performances." This principle is essentially confirmed by the position of Carlo Blasis, who considers that "too many exercises are as reprehensible as too few. An extreme is always an error." (*See note 22.*) An extreme is indeed dangerous; it tends to overwork a dancer and he will collapse on his feet.

The teacher must thoroughly know his pupils' potentials and qualities. In knowing their strong and weak sides he must strive to develop the first ones and to eradicate the latter. He also has to take into account exactly what a dancer has to do on the stage today, tomorrow, or the day after tomorrow; how difficult and intricate the rehearsals he faces are; and how much physical and emotional strength they will require from him. The teacher is closely allied to the condition in which the dancer appears on the stage.

Messerer's second, equally important rule is: "One should never prepare particularly uncomfortable, deliberately intricate compositions of steps for lessons." He does not agree with teachers who maintain that training the dancer in ultracomplicated combinations contributes to the development of freer and better coordination of movements. Messerer is convinced that coordination should be developed on the basis of a harmonious sequence of dance steps in each combination, and a logical order of their structure. At the same time, the teacher must strive for every new movement and turn to flow naturally and gracefully from the preceding ones. True coordination is developed precisely under these conditions. It gives the ballet master the future opportunity to create movements, turns, and positions of the body in any technical intricacy and in composition patterns of any precision. All this becomes accessible and easy for the dancer. Messerer frequently repeats that the level of professional culture of the dancer is determined by his versatile dance technique and the purity of his performing style.

Galina Ulanova, Maya Plisetskaya, in Asaf Messerer's class

Galina Ulanova and Irina Tikhomirnova in class

Messerer gives particularly serious attention to the harmonious interrelation between movements of the body and those of the arms, legs, and head. The development of the body is of the first importance in the general coordination of movements as well as in the training of ballet and plastic expression. A correct position of the body is no less important for the dancer than the position of the hands of a pianist. It is the fundamental basis of the ballet art. "Therefore in my combinations in class," said Messerer, "I always strive for every possible melodious and logical combination of movements and turns of the body with those of the arms, neck, head, and legs. In leaps and turns, it is necessary to strictly observe a pure, clear form of the movements' pattern and, at the same time, to achieve a feeling of rest and freedom of the body and arms. Then an impression is created that the dance is beautiful and light and the dancer's body movements and poses appear natural, plastic, flexible, and expressive."

In choreographic education of the ballet art, visual methods of teaching, a demonstration by the ballet teacher of movements and poses, play an important role. It is useful even for the mature dancers, not to mention the young ones, to test in class the accuracy of dance form, the correctness of movements of the body, arms, head, and legs, the purity of lines and poses, and the clearness of the pattern of various "épaulements" on the ideal model, which the teacher should be. Messerer not only explains but also demonstrates each movement and pose, various technical methods and dance combinations; this he does excellently with utmost clarity, precision, lightness, and beauty.

In Messerer's opinion, musical accompaniment in classes for the advanced training of dancers must always be artistically varied, rich in melody, and interesting. The music should not simply assist the dancer to move rhythmically while dancing, but it should also infect him emotionally, arouse his aspiration for intonation color in dancing combinations, and help in learning plastic expression. In Messerer's classes changes in rhythm and tempo play a big role.

Asaf Messerer and Vladimir Vasiliev at a rehearsal, London
PHOTO BY JENNIE WALTON

He expects rhythmic precision in musical accompaniment. Messerer categorically rejects a primitive, monotonous musical accompaniment, where only rhythm is dominant. His teaching combinations are very musical.

At lessons for the advanced classes Asaf Messerer is always the most disciplined, the most self-exigent, and the most creatively concentrated. Due to his daily training, he has reached the highest level in choreographic skills, maintaining it throughout his artistic life. Even now, when Messerer, elegant and neat as always, enters the classroom with light, graceful steps and starts to demonstrate movements to dancers, it seems to everyone that he is on the point of starting to dance as brilliantly as before. Messerer's advanced classes are characterized by the scope, freedom, and beauty of compositions and the elegant finish of all details. They are distinguished by the large number of dance steps, strict, logical order, noble taste, and high professional culture.

The teaching principles of Asaf Messerer are based on his own experience and have been confirmed by his thirty years of artistic practice and forty-seven years of teaching.

The art of choreography undergoes incessant movement and development. It cannot stand stagnation and mental inactivity. Artistic talent passes through many stages of trial before it becomes a reliable instrument of artistic work. It is formed by teachers, ballet masters, and directors; the dancer brings it to perfection. Of course, much depends on the nature and fantasy of the artist, his intelligence and persistence in reaching high standards, and his creative self-criticism. If a talented person has the will, character, and desire to search and innovate he will reach the highest levels.

Asaf Messerer has remained true throughout his entire life to his views on art, and he continues to work and search relentlessly. Like the horizon, which moves away as one approaches it, true art never reaches its objective. The more the artist succeeds in accomplishing, the more clearly he sees how much there remains to be done for future generations to reach genuine heights in the art of choreography. Messerer reached great heights after climbing many steps on the endless ladder of art.

"One of the principal signs of talent is industry," said Galina Ulanova. "Only a pure and honest attitude to his work can lead the artist to success." (*See note 23.*) These words of the remarkable ballerina correspond to the life and activities of Asaf Messerer, prominent Soviet artist, teacher, and ballet master. The productive work of Asaf Messerer has received wide public recognition. He was awarded the title of People's Artist of the RSFSR and the State Prize Laureate. In addition, two orders of the Red Banner were conferred upon him for his creative activity. The life, work, and creativity of Asaf Messerer are permeated with great love for art and his relentless and faithful service to it.

NOTES

1. I. E. "Asaf Messerer About Himself," newspaper *This Evening (Segodnya Vecherom)*, Riga, April 6, 1929.

2. V. Iving. "Swan Lake," journal *New Footlights (Novaya Rampa)*, 1924, number 13, page 10.

3. "Performance of O. Lepeshinskaya and A. Messerer, Laureates of the State Prize," newspaper *For Soviet Art (Za sovetskoye iskustvo)*, Leningrad, May 24, 1941.

4. K. S. Stanislavsky, "My Life in Art" (Moya zhizn v iskusstve"), Moscow, *Art,* 1962.

5. M. I. Kalinin, "On Communist Education," Moscow, *Young Guard (Molodaya gvardiya)*, 1958, page 89.

6. I. Iving. "Red Poppy, Turning Point in the Ballet," journal *Program of State Academic Theatres (Programma gosudarstvennykh akademicheskikh teatrov)*, July 21–27, 1927, number 25, pages 2–3.

7. D. Shostakovich "Red Sails," *Pravda,* February 8, 1943.

8. S. Alamzov, "Triumph of A. Messerer and V. Krieger," newspaper *This Evening (Segodnya Vecherom)*, Riga, April 4, 1929.

9. Ibid.

10. "The Messerers in Opera," newspaper *Svenska Dagbladet,* Stockholm, January 26, 1933.

11. Ibid.

12. "Third Victory of the Messerers," newspaper *Aftonbladet,* Stockholm, January 30, 1933.

13. M. Gabovich. "Pride of Soviet Choreography," *Pravda,* March 16, 1941.

14. "Conversations of K. S. Stanislavsky in the Studio of the Bolshoi Theatre in 1918–1922," Moscow, *Art,* 1952, page 46.

15. G. Gruzd. "Kings of the Dance," Moscow, *Daily News,* March 13, 1941.

16. Nicolai Volkov. "The Art of Dance," *News (Izvestiya)*, March 16, 1941.

17. A. Messerer, B. Mordvinov, and A. Chekrygin. "Sleeping Beauty," *Soviet Artist,* 1936, number 46.

18. Arnold L. Haskell. *The Russian Genius in Ballet,* Pergamon Press, London, 1963, page 36.

19. Boris Lvov-Anokhin. "New one-act ballets," *Musical Life (Muzykalnaya Zhizn)*, 1964, number 16.

20. Carlo Blasis. *Manuel Complet de la Danse,* Paris, 1830.

21. Collected articles, "A. Ya. Vaganova. Articles, Memoirs, Materials," Leningrad—Moscow, *Art,* 1958, page 113.

22. Carlo Blasis. *Manuel Complet de la Danse,"* Paris, 1830.

23. V. M. Bogdanov-Berezovsky. "G. S. Ulanova," Moscow, *Art,* 1961, page 164.

Roles and Concert Pieces Danced by Asaf Messerer at the Bolshoi Theatre

1920

As a student of the Ballet School danced in *Carmen* by Georges Bizet, choreography by A. Gorsky. Bolero.
The Magic Mirror by A. Korestchenko, choreography by A. Gorsky. Friend of the Prince.

1921

Swan Lake P. Tchaikovsky, choreography by A. Gorsky. Pas de trois, Hungarian dance.
The Magic Mirror by A. Korestchenko, choreography by A. Gorsky. Tyrolian dance pas de trois. Zephyr.
La Fille Mal Gardée by P. Hertel, choreography by A. Gorsky. Colas.

1922

Swan Lake by P. Tchaikovsky, choreography by A. Gorsky. Prince Siegfried.
The Nutcracker by P. Tchaikovsky, choreography by A. Gorsky. The Prince.
Raymonda by A. Glazounov, choreography by A. Gorsky. Saracen dance. Dance of the four cavaliers. Bernard.

1923

Petrouchka by I. Stravinsky, choreography by V. Riabtsev. Petrouchka. Arab.
Le Corsaire by A. Adam, choreography by A. Gorsky. Slave. Pirate.
La Bayadère by L. Minkus, choreography by A. Gorsky, and V. Tikhomirov. Hindu dance.

1924

The Millions of Arlequin by R. Drigo, choreography by V. Riabtsev. Arlequin.
The Little Humpbacked Horse by C. Pugni, choreographed by A. Gorsky. Slave. Ocean.
Coppélia by L. Delibes, choreography by A. Gorsky. Franz.
Prince Igor by A. Borodin, choreography by A. Gorsky. Tartar youth.

1925

Joseph the Beautiful by C. Vasilenko, choreography by K. Goleizovsky. Slave. Joseph.
Teolinda by F. Schubert, choreography by K. Goleizovsky. Zephyr.

1926

Esmeralda by C. Pugni, choreography by V. Tikhomirov. Zephyr.
The Sleeping Beauty by P. Tchaikovsky, choreography by M. Petipa. Bluebird.

1927

The Red Poppy by R. Glière, choreography by L. Lastchilin, V. Tikhomirov. Idol. Juggler. Japanese sailor.

1928

Don Quixote by L. Minkus, choreography by A. Gorsky. Basil.

1930

The Football Player by V. Oransky, choreography L. Lastshilin and I. Moiseyev. The Cascade.
The Sleeping Beauty by P. Tchaikovsky, choreography by M. Petipa. The Cat.

1932

Salammbô by A. Arends, choreography by I. Moiseyev. The fanatic. Chief signal officer.
The Flames of Paris by B. Asafiev, choreography by V. Vainonen. Philippe.

1934

Prince Igor by A. Borodin, choreography by K. Goleizovsky. Horseman.

1935

The Three Fat Boys by V. Oransky, choreography by I. Moiseyev. The Balloon Seller.

The Bright Stream by D. Shostakovitch, choreography by F. Lopoukhov. Actor.

1936

The Fountain of Bakhchisarai by B. Asafiev, choreography by R. Zakharov. Nurali.

1938

The Nutcracker by P. Tchaikovsky, choreography by V. Vainonen. The Prince.
The Prisoner of the Caucasus by B. Asafiev, choreography by R. Zakharov. The Figure Skater.

1939

Svetlana by D. Klebanov, choreography by A. Radunsky, N. Popko, L. Pospekhin. Cossack.
Ivan Susanin by M. Glinka, choreography R. Zakharov. Waltz. Faun.

1940

Don Quixote by L. Minkus, choreography A. Gorsky restaged by R. Zakharov. Basil.

1943

The Red Sails by V. Yourovsky, choreography A. Radunsky, N. Popko, L. Pospekhin. Letica.

1945

Cinderella by S. Prokofiev, choreography R. Zakharov. Prince. Jester.

1947

The Flames of Paris by B. Asafiev, choreography by V. Vainonen (new version). Philippe.

1949

Coppélia by L. Delibes, choreography by A. Gorsky. New version by Ye. Dolinsky, A. Radunsky. Franz.

Concert pieces

Gopak by M. Nicolaevsky, choreography A. Messerer.

Waltz by M. Moskovsky, choreography A. Messerer.

The Italian Beggar by C. Saint-Saens, choreography A. Messerer.

Pierrot et Pierette by R. Drigo, choreography A. Messerer.

Saint Sebastian by A. Scriabin (Etude No. 12), choreography K. Goleizovsky.

The Football Player by A. Tsfasman, choreography A. Messerer.

Spanish Dance by C. Vasilenko, choreography A. Messerer.

Russian Dance, traditional music, choreography A. Messerer.

Melody by C. Gluck, choreography A. Messerer.

Waltz by A. Khatchaturian, choreography K. Goleizovsky.

Spring Waters by S. Rachmaninoff, choreography A. Messerer.

In the concert repertoire of Asaf Messerer were performed classical pas de deux from the ballets *Swan Lake, Don Quixote, La Fille Mal Gardée,* and *Coppélia,* and *The Idol* and the *Ribbon Dance* (Chinese juggler) from the ballet *The Red Poppy, The Fanatic* from the ballet *Salammbô,* the Caucasian dance from the ballet *Svetlana,* and others.

Ballets Choreographed by Asaf Messerer

1922

The Ever Living Flowers by P. Tchaikovsky, B. Asafiev, choreography by A. Gorsky, assistant to the ballet master, A. Messerer. Novi Theatre.

1923

Concert pieces: *Czardas* by Monti, *Waltz* by V. Kreisler, and others. Ballet School of the Bolshoi Theatre.

1924

The War of Toys by F. Schumann. Lunacharsky Theatre School.

1926

The Fairy Doll by I. Bayer. Ballet School of the Bolshoi Theatre.
Le Corsaire by A. Adam. Opera Theatre of Kharkhov.

1927

Sports Suite. Russian Suite. Lunacharsky Theatre School.

1930

La Fille Mal Gardée by P. Hertel jointly with I. Moiseyev. Branch of the Bolshoi Theatre.

1936

The Sleeping Beauty by P. Tchaikovsky jointly with A. Chekrygin and B. Mordvinov (with excerpts from M. Petipa). Bolshoi Theatre.

1937

Swan Lake (Act IV) by P. Tchaikovsky. Bolshoi Theatre.

1944

The Sleeping Beauty by P. Tchaikovsky (with excerpts from M. Petipa). Bolshoi Theatre.

1945

La Fille Mal Gardée by P. Hertel (revived choreography by A. Gorsky). Branch of the Bolshoi Theatre.

1951

Swan Lake by P. Tchaikovsky. Budapest Opera House.

1952

The Sleeping Beauty by P. Tchaikovsky jointly with M. Gabovich (with excerpts from M. Petipa). Bolshoi Theatre.

The Nutcracker (Act III) by P. Tchaikovsky. "Divertissement." Choreographic Institute of the Bolshoi Theatre.

Spring Holiday. Peking. Central Song and Dance Ensemble.

1953

Sea Shore by Yu. Yuselounaz, jointly with V. Grivitzkaz. Vilna Opera House.

1960

Ballet Class by A. Liadov, A. Glazounov, D. Shostakovich. Bolshoi Theatre (Performance of the Choreographic Institute).

1961

Ballet Class by A. Liadov, A. Glazounov, D. Shostakovich. "Divertissement." Brussels. Royal Opera House and Ballet School.

1962

Ballet School by D. Shostakovich, A. Glazounov. Bolshoi Theatre.

1967

Swan Lake by P. Tchaikovsky, Minsk Opera House.

Besides, A. M. Messerer choreographed ballets and dances in the operas of the Bolshoi Theatre: *Almast, Les Huguenots, Sadko, Lakmé*.